D0871760

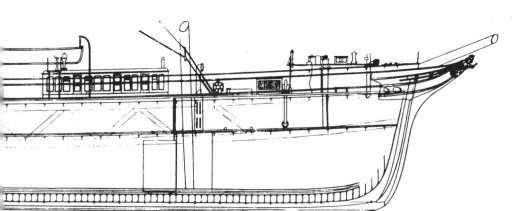

Cut-away view of the CSS *Shenandoah*.

FIRE

AND

THUNDER

EXPLOITS OF THE CONFEDERATE STATES NAVY

By

R. Thomas Campbell

 Burd Street Press

Copyright © 1997 by R. Thomas Campbell

ALL RIGHTS RESERVED—No part of this book may be reproduced in any form without permission in writing from the publisher, except by a reviewer who wishes to quote brief passages in connection with a review.

This Burd Street Press publication
was printed by
Beidel Printing House, Inc.
63 West Burd Street
Shippensburg, PA 17257-0152 USA

In respect for the scholarship contained herein, the acid-free paper used in this book meets the guidelines for permanence and durability of the Committee on Production Guidelines for Book Longevity of the Council on Library Resources.

For a complete list of available publications
please write
Burd Street Press
Division of White Mane Publishing Company, Inc.
P.O. Box 152
Shippensburg, PA 17257-0152 USA

Library of Congress Cataloging-in-Publication Data

Campbell, R. Thomas, 1937-
    Fire and thunder : exploits of the Confederate States Navy / by R. Thomas Campbell.
        p.   cm.
    Includes bibliographical references (p.   ) and index.
    ISBN 1-57249-067-5 (alk. paper)
    1. Confederate States of America. Navy--History. 2. United States--History--Civil War, 1861-1865--Naval operations, Confederate. 3. Confederate States of America--History, Naval.
I. Title.
E596.C35 1997
973.7'57--dc21   97-38176
                                                                      CIP

PRINTED IN THE UNITED STATES OF AMERICA

DEDICATED TO

THOSE WHO WORE THE NAVY GRAY,

AND THE LOVED ONES THEY LEFT BEHIND.

Table Of Contents

ILLUSTRATIONS vii

PREFACE x

ACKNOWLEDGMENTS.. xiii

CHAPTER 1 - THE PRIVATEERS STRIKE THE FIRST BLOW 1

CHAPTER 2 - THE STARS AND BARS IN THE
              ENGLISH CHANNEL 20

CHAPTER 3 - THE MOSQUITO FLEET 42

CHAPTER 4 - THE BEHEMOTHS OF NEW ORLEANS............... 66

CHAPTER 5 - VICTORY AT GALVESTON 91

CHAPTER 6 - HAVOC OFF THE EAST COAST–PART I 110

CHAPTER 7 - HAVOC OFF THE EAST COAST–PART II 133

Table of Contents

CHAPTER   8 - THE LAST BLOCKADE RUNNERS 148

CHAPTER   9 - THE RENDEZVOUS 166

CHAPTER 10 - AN ARDUOUS BEGINNING 182

CHAPTER 11 - AUSTRALIAN INTERLUDE 200

CHAPTER 12 - THE LONG VOYAGE HOME 215

EPILOGUE 246

APPENDICES 248

NOTES 273

BIBLIOGRAPHY 282

INDEX 287

Illustrations

Jefferson Davis, President of the Confederate States 3
The *Calhoun*, the first Confederate privateer 4
Lieutenant Commander Thomas M. Crossan 7
Captain Thomas J. Lockwood 8
Map of the Outer Banks of North Carolina 10
A commission blank for authorizing privateers 19
The CSS *Nashville* 21
Stephen R. Mallory, Secretary of the Confederate States Navy 22
Lieutenant Robert P. Pegram 23
The CSS *Nashville* burning the *Harvey Birch* 26
John Slidell and John M. Mason 28
First Lieutenant Charles M. Fauntleroy 32
Lieutenant Robert P. Pegram in civilian attire 32
Midshipman William H. Sinclair 32
First Lieutenant John W. Bennett 32
Midshipman James W. Pegram 33
Master John H. Ingraham 33
The CSS *Nashville* running into Beaufort, North Carolina 35
Lieutenant William C. Whittle 37
The *Rattlesnake* burns in the Ogeechee River 40
The USS *Montauk* firing on the *Rattlesnake* 41

vii

Federal troops land to attack Fort Hatteras 43
Captain William F. Lynch 44
The USS *Fanny* being attacked by the CSS *Curlew* 48
Map of the Battle for Roanoke Island 53
First Lieutenant William H. Parker 54
Commander James W. Cooke 55
The *Seabird* goes down 65
Captain George N. Hollins 68
Gun deck of the CSS *Louisiana* 71
Boiler arrangement of the CSS *Mississippi* 72
Commander Charles F. McIntosh 73
Commander John K. Mitchell 75
Midshipman William W. Wilkinson 76
Major General Mansfield Lovell 77
First Lieutenant John Wilkinson 79
Map of the lower delta region of the Mississippi 80
The CSS *Louisiana* on the way to Fort St. Philip 81
Mortar boats attacking the water battery at Fort Jackson 82
Bird's-eye view of passage of the forts by the Federal fleet 83
First Lieutenant Arthur Sinclair 85
Lieutenant James I. Waddell 86
Brigadier General Johnson K. Duncan 88
The destruction of the CSS *Louisiana* 90
Major General John B. Magruder 94
Major Leon Smith 97
Map of the Galveston waterfront 100
The *Bayou City* crashes into the *Harriet Lane* 103
Texas troops fight their way aboard the *Harriet Lane* 104
Map of Galveston Bay 106
The explosion of the USS *Westfield* 108
Lieutenant Michael P. Usina 111
Commander John Taylor Wood 112
The CSS *Tallahassee* escaping from Wilmington 116
The *Tallahassee* chasing the pilot boat, *William Bell* 119
The burning of the *Adriatic* 121
The sinking of the *Glenarvon* 122
The CSS *Tallahassee* in the harbor at Halifax 125
The approaches to the Cape Fear River 129
First Lieutenant John Wilkinson 134
Midshipman Daniel Murray Lee 135
The CSS *Chickamauga* 141
General plan of Fort Fisher 142
Colonel William Lamb 143

Map of the naval bombardment of Fort Fisher 144
The bombardment of Fort Fisher 146
The remains of a blockade runner 150
The blockade runner *Banshee II* 151
The *Banshee II* under fire as she runs into Galveston 155
First Lieutenant John W. Dunnington 157
Commander John Newland Maffitt 158
Lieutenant E. Maffitt Anderson 159
Chart depicting the approaches to Charleston 161
The blockade runner *Owl* 165
Commander James D. Bulloch 168
First Lieutenant James I. Waddell 171
First Lieutenant William C. Whittle 172
Lieutenant John F. Ramsay 174
Cut-away view of the CSS *Shenandoah* 181
Acting Master Irvine S. Bulloch 186
Acting Master Cornelius E. Hunt 188
Lieutenant Sidney Smith Lee, Jr. 189
First Lieutenant John Grimball 192
The CSS *Shenandoah* anchored in Hobson's Bay 201
Visitors crowd the deck of the *Shenandoah* 203
The CSS *Shenandoah* on the slip at Williamstown 205
Chief Engineer Matthew O'Brien 206
The *Shenandoah* eases her way through patches of ice 220
A pencil drawing of the *Shenandoah* 223
The *Shenandoah* towing whaleboats 226
The *Shenandoah's* path to the Arctic Ocean 232
Captains of the whaleships 234
Map of the cruise of the *Shenandoah* 240
The *Shenandoah* anchored at Liverpool 242
Sidney S. Lee, John T. Mason, Orris A. Browne,
    and William C. Whittle 244
Group of officers from the CSS *Shenandoah* 245

*P*reface

The story of the Confederate States Navy—their men and their ships—is one of the most inspiring accounts of courage, devotion to duty, and perseverance against insurmountable obstacles, to emerge from the War Between the States. And yet, until recently, the account of the South's innovative navy, their vessels, their officers and seamen, their victories and defeats, was little known aside from a few devoted historians. This is, however, beginning to change. Many, including this author, have been amazed at just how much the Confederate Navy was able to accomplish in the short span of its existence. So much, in fact, was achieved that it is a most difficult task to present the entire history of the Confederate Navy in a concise and logical manner.

Only two authors have accepted this challenge. J. Thomas Scharf, a midshipman in Confederate service, published his *History of the Confederate States Navy* in 1877, long before the naval official records were completed. His work, while commendable for the time, is limited in scope. Raimondo Luraghi's *A History of the Confederate Navy*, which was recently released, is a masterpiece, and may well become the defining word in a general overall study of the accomplishments of the South's naval forces. Both works, however, because of the enormity and scope of the naval conflict, suffer from a lack of detail concerning a particular action or an intriguing personality. *Fire and Thunder*, as well as the preceding works in this series, *Gray Thunder, Southern Thunder,* and *Southern Fire*, is an attempt to begin to fill this void.

Similar to the three previous works, the participants themselves are sought and quoted extensively. It was they, after all—these men in navy gray—who faced the flaming shot and shell of an overpowering enemy. Their words and their expressions convey a sense of "being there" that this author, more than 130 years later, could never hope to match. When their correspondence, reports, and diary entries are studied, one comes to a realization that these men were not ordinary men. True, they lived, they loved, they laughed, and, yes, they cried, but one important factor sets them apart—they lived their lives amid the most momentous and tumultuous era in American history. They were, in fact, the makers of that history.

Fire and Thunder introduces the reader to the many and varied facets of what can be properly termed, "Confederate Forces Afloat." Not all exploits recounted here were the product of the Confederate Navy. Early in the conflict, private citizens applied for and were granted, letters of "Marque and Reprisal" from the government in Montgomery. These privateers, as they were styled, carried the war to Northern commerce while the regular navy was being organized by the Confederate government. Branded as "pirates" by the North, these vessels with names such as *Calhoun, Dixie,* and *Jefferson Davis*, made newspaper headlines for a few short months, until Union warships appeared off the Southern ports.

Also found here is the account of the Texas Marine Department which accomplished the recapture of Galveston, Texas with the aid of two steamboats protected by cotton bales. One boat was commanded by a master in the Confederate Navy, the other by an army captain, and both vessels were manned by Texas cavalrymen. From this force, after surrendering several ships and destroying another, the remaining Federal forces abandoned the blockade and fled all the way to New Orleans.

The central theme of *Fire and Thunder* is the exhilarating successes— and sometimes the stinging defeats—of the Confederate Navy. For like the country whose flag it bore, the South's navy was ultimately consigned to destruction. While it lived, however, its courageous leaders, and their thundering guns, became known in every corner of the world. From the CSS *Nashville*, the first Confederate warship to carry the new nation's banner to England, to the CSS *Shenandoah* which lowered the Confederacy's last flag almost seven months after the surrender of Robert E. Lee and the Army of Northern Virginia, the South's navy fought a valiant and courageous fight, and contributed greatly to the defense of the Southern nation.

Excelling in the development of the casemated ironclad, the South's navy was the first in the world to use an armored vessel in an offensive action. With the success of the CSS *Virginia* on that memorable day in March of 1862, (recounted in *Gray Thunder*) the warships of almost every navy in the world became instantly obsolete. The Confederate Navy also developed, perfected, and deployed the underwater mine, or torpedo, as it was known at the time. In addition, steam-driven torpedo boats, forerunners of the famous German E-boats and American PT-boats of almost a century later, were a product of the resourceful minds of the South. Likewise, when the world's first successful submarine, the CSS *H. L. Hunley*, entered immortality off Charleston, South Carolina, on that cold February night in 1864, she added another chapter to the amazing list of innovations and successes achieved by the South's naval forces.

And then, there were the blockade runners. Some of the most exciting and inspiring accounts of courage and seamanship emerges from the tales of those fast lead-colored steamers that braved the stormy seas, the rocky shoals, and the guns of the Union Navy to deliver their supplies to the struggling Confederate armies. A tremendous incentive, of course, was profit, particularly for the civilian runners. It has been estimated that 25 percent of the steamers which braved the Federal cordon of warships that surrounded the Southern coast were government owned, in whole or in part, and were officered and crewed by Confederate Navy personnel. It is interesting to note that not a single blockade runner was ever captured while under the command of a regular Confederate naval officer.

It seems fitting, therefore, after sifting through the many and varied sources, reading the hundreds of letters, official reports and reminiscences, that this author humbly dedicates these pages to the inspiring Southern men who wore the navy gray—for this is, after all, *their* story.

Acknowledgments

Fire and Thunder is the last of a four-book series on the Confederate Navy. Previous works were: *Gray Thunder, Southern Thunder,* and *Southern Fire.* I would be remiss if I did not thank the many persons and institutions who have aided me in the compilation of these various exploits on the Southern naval forces.

Foremost, and most important among these, is my lovely wife Carole. Without her encouragement, her patience, and especially her editing expertise, these books would not have been possible. In addition, the kind folks at The Museum of the Confederacy, especially John M. Coski, have been most helpful. Thanks also to the staff of the Civil War Library and Museum in Philadelphia, and to the staff of the U.S. Army History Institute at Carlisle, Pennsylvania. A special thank you, also, for Anna B. Pebbler of the Rosenberg Library in Galveston, Texas.

The professional staff at White Mane Publishing Company, Inc., have been most helpful. I wish to especially thank Harold Collier for his encouragement, his faith in me, and his willingness to venture into the fascinating field of the Confederate Navy.

All photos, unless otherwise noted, are courtesy of the Naval Historical Foundation at the Washington Navy Yard, Washington, D.C.

Chapter One

The Privateers Strike the First Blow

Whereas Abraham Lincoln, the President of the United States, has by proclamation announced the intention of invading this Confederacy with an armed force for the purpose of capturing its fortresses and thereby subverting its independence and subjecting the free people thereof to the dominion of a foreign power; and

Whereas it has thus become the duty of this Government to repel the threatened invasion and to defend the rights and liberties of the people by all the means which the laws of nations and the usages of civilized warfare place at its disposal:

Now, therefore, I, Jefferson Davis, President of the Confederate States of America, do issue this my proclamation inviting all those who desire, by service in private armed vessels on the high seas, to aid this Government in resisting so wanton and wicked an aggression, to make application for commissions or letters of marque and reprisal to be issued under the seal of the Confederate States.   *Jefferson Davis, April 17, 1861.*[1]

***

The idea of using privately owned and armed vessels to wage war on the commerce of one's enemy is as old as naval war itself. The French were the first to send out these private raiders of the sea on a large scale. During the Seven Years War, French privateers made several

1

thousand prizes. Private vessels, sanctioned by the government of King Louis XV, destroyed more than eight hundred British trading vessels when there was scarcely a French ship-of-the-line left to fight the British. During the American Revolution and the War of 1812, American attacks on British commerce were carried on almost exclusively by these privately armed raiders.

Privateering provided a means for a weaker nation to strike a blow at an enemy's commerce, without having to build its own strong naval force. The incentive for private citizens to arm their vessels and attempt to capture the vessels of their country's enemy, of course, was profit—hopefully, patriotism and profit. Rules established in the granting of a letter of marque and reprisal, required that vessels captured by a privateer be sailed to the nearest port of the privateer's origin, where the prize was to be adjudicated by a court of law. If the prize was condemned, meaning the vessel and its cargo were found to be the property of the enemy, the ship and its cargo were sold to the highest bidder with the owners, officers, and crew of the privateer dividing the proceeds.[2]

J. Thomas Scharf, who was a Confederate midshipman during the war, described very accurately the nature of a privateer: *A privateer, as the name implies, is a private armed ship, fitted out at the owner's expense, but commissioned by a belligerent government to capture the ships and goods of the enemy at sea, or the ships of neutrals when conveying to the enemy goods (that are) contraband of war. A privateer differs from a pirate in this, that one has a commission and the other has none. A privateer is entitled to the same rights of war as the public vessels of the belligerent. A pirate ship has no rights, and her crew are liable to be captured and put to death by all nations as robbers and murderers on the high seas. The policy of neutrals recognizing privateers as legitimate belligerent ships is founded on the interest of humanity and the common desire to prevent piracy. If privateers were not recognized by neutral nations they would become pirates, and instead of making prisoners of the crews of the prize vessels, they would massacre them, appropriate the cargoes and sink the ships. But, being recognized, they are under the surveillance of the government commissioning them as well as the governments of neutral nations, and they are responsible for their acts to both.*[3]

The Lincoln government never publicly recognized Southern privateers as anything but pirates, for to do so would have conveyed the connotation that the United States recognized the Confederacy as a belligerent nation. Throughout the war, the Northern government maintained this position, denying any legitimacy to the existence of the Confederate States. To have done otherwise would have revealed that the invasion and subjugation of the Southern states were nothing

Jefferson Davis, President of the Confederate States of America, and commander and chief of the army and navy.

more than open aggression. In Europe the Confederacy was recognized as a belligerent and was granted all the rights and privileges that international law provided. Although Great Britain, France, Austria, Prussia, Russia, Sardinia, and Turkey had taken steps to abolish privateering at the Treaty of Paris in 1856, the United States had never become a signatory to the treaty. In no way then, were the former states of the Union, which now formed the Confederacy, bound by the Treaty of Paris. While Lincoln and Secretary of State William Seward fumed about the Southern "pirates," every nation of the world recognized the legitimate right of the "de facto" government in Montgomery to issue letters of marque and reprisal.

Although President Davis had issued his proclamation, he refrained from issuing any letters of marque until his decision could be approved by the House of Representatives and the Senate. On May 6, 1861, the Confederate Congress passed an act recognizing the existence of a state of war between the Confederate States and the United States. Section one of this act stated:—*The Congress of the Confederate States of America do enact, that the President of the Confederate States is hereby authorized to use the whole land and naval force of the Confederate States to meet the war thus commenced, and to issue to private-armed vessels commissions, or letters of marque and general reprisal, in such form as he shall think proper....*[4]

Just ten days after this pronouncement, on May 16, the steamer *Calhoun* chugged down the Mississippi River from New Orleans. This in itself was not unusual, as the *Calhoun* was a powerful towboat that

The *Calhoun*, the first Confederate privateer.

plied the muddy "Father of Waters" often, towing the large merchant vessels against the strong current up river to the Crescent City. Steaming out through Pass à L'Outre this time, however, the *Calhoun* was no longer a towboat. She was now armed with one 18-pounder, two 12-pounders, and two 6-pounder cannon, and her captain, John Wilson, had tucked safely away in his coat pocket, a letter of marque and reprisal. Issued only the day before by the government in Montgomery, it transformed the little steamer into the C.S. Privateer *Calhoun*. As the 508-ton vessel bumped over the bar at the mouth of the pass, she became the first privately armed warship of the Confederacy to go in search of Northern merchantmen.[5]

On April 19, Lincoln had declared a blockade of the Southern coast from South Carolina to Texas, and on the 27th of April, it was extended to include the shores of Virginia and North Carolina. Declaring a blockade was one thing; enforcing it was another. The strength of the Union Navy at this time was woefully inadequate to close all of the Southern ports, and as the *Calhoun* steamed out into the blue waters of the Gulf, not a single enemy warship was in sight. It was not long, therefore, before the New Orleans *Daily Crescent* had some exciting news to print. A columnist on the May 17 wrote that: *Yes, after some days of quietness on the flags, there was something sprung on the stret yesterday ... at about meridian the flags were all on the quid vie about the dispatch from the Pass à L'Outre, announcing the arrival of a vessel, a prize to the private-armed vessel Calhoun.*[6]

The vessel that the *Calhoun* had captured, the first private-armed prize of the war, was the 290-ton bark *Ocean Eagle* out of Rockland, Maine. Her cargo consisted of 3,144 barrels of Thomaston lime which was consigned to Creevy and Farwell in New Orleans. Turning his prize over to a towboat, which pulled the *Ocean Eagle* up river to New Orleans for adjudication, Captain Wilson steamed the *Calhoun* farther out to sea in search of more prizes. Two days later he was rewarded by the capture of two fine vessels. The first was the 699-ton *Milan*, eighty-one days out of Liverpool, with 1,500 bags of salt consigned to Meeker, Know and Company of New Orleans. The second vessel was the *Ella*, a small schooner of 92 tons carrying tropical fruits from Tampico, Mexico, to Pensacola, Florida. Taking the two prizes in tow, Wilson steamed triumphantly back to New Orleans, arriving after sundown on May 19.[7]

The *Calhoun's* owners were jubilant, and New Orleans treated the officers and crew as first rate heroes. Within a few days the Confederate privateer was once again steaming across the bar and heading for the open sea. The alarm had spread, however, and prizes were not as plentiful; but on May 21, a chase was begun only to see the prize captured by another privateer. The *Calhoun* soon had her own prizes, however, for on May 24, she came upon three New England whalers which had been cruising in the Caribbean. They were the *John Adams*, a schooner of 200 tons out of Boston; the 145-ton schooner *Mermaid* and the 158-ton brig *Panama*, both out of Provincetown, Massachusetts. Together the three vessels carried 65 crewmen and 160 barrels of oil. Placing a small prize crew on each whaler, Wilson went searching for more game. Several days later, an ominous shout came from the lookout. Just visible on the horizon was the telltale silhouette of an American warship.

The vessel which the *Calhoun's* lookout had spotted was the steam sloop, USS *Brooklyn*, with 21 heavy guns. Knowing that the little privateer was no match for the big American warship, Wilson gathered up his three prizes and ran for New Orleans. One of that city's newspapers reported rather humorously: *One of the privateers, the Calhoun, it is said, was chased for two hours off the Balize by the lumbering old war steamer Brooklyn. The men of the little vessel saw her afar off, and her guns grew awfully large. They looked grim and thunderous, but for all that the privateer fired a defiant gun or so, keeping in mind that "distance lends enchantment to the view." The little sea-rider was not to be caught by the big one, her heels being as swift as Burns' gray mare Meg, when Tam O'Shanter ran away from the witches.*[8]

With the arrival of the *Brooklyn*, the blockade was officially established off New Orleans, and while it was a simple matter for blockade runners to avoid her, because she could guard only one of the three channels, her presence effectively put an end to privateering in the area. Even if the *Calhoun*, or any of the other privateers operating out of New Orleans, steamed out and avoided her, which would not have been difficult, they would not have been able to sail their prizes back to the city, for the Federal warship could easily recapture them.

The Confederate States District Court for Louisiana, sitting in New Orleans, condemned Wilson's prizes as legitimate captures in time of war. On July 27, the vessels and their cargoes were sold at public auction, the proceeds being distributed among the owners, officers, and crew of the *Calhoun*. The *Milan* brought $9,000; the *Mermaid*, $8,300; the *Ocean Eagle*, $6,800; the *Panama*, $1,400; the *John Adams*, $1,150; and the *Ella*, $1,050. The court found that the cargo of the *Ella* belonged to an Englishman, and it was restored to its rightful owner and not included in the sale.[9]

While the prospects for success were beginning to look bleak in the Gulf for privately armed raiders, another area along the Confederate coast was becoming a hotbed of privateering activity. Just thirteen miles southwest of Cape Hatteras, that lonely and windswept point of sand that thrusts itself farthest into the ocean off the North Carolina coast, lies Hatteras Inlet. For centuries this channel has provided an avenue of escape from the howling winds and monstrous waves of the turbulent Atlantic. Through this inlet, many struggling vessels and frightened seamen have reached the safety of the placid waters of Pamlico Sound. When the Old North State seceded, Hatteras Inlet and the waters behind the sand dunes in the Sound, soon became a haven for the eager and adventurous privateers.

First to arrive were the hastily-armed vessels of the North Carolina Navy. Upon secession the state had authorized a navy, and the first to arrive at the inlet, under the command of Lieutenant Commander Thomas M. Crossan,

Lieutenant Commander Thomas M. Crossan of the North Carolina Navy. Crossan commanded the NCS *Winslow* in early raids through Hatteras Inlet.
Clark, *North Carolina Regiments, 1861–1865*

was the NCS *Winslow,* a side-wheel steamer mounting two guns. Commander Crossan would remain in the North Carolina Navy when that state's vessels were transferred to the Confederacy, and would later captain the state's own blockade runner, the *Advance.* The *Winslow* was soon followed by the NCS *Raleigh* and the NCS *Beaufort.* Beginning in May, these North Carolina warships began intercepting Northern merchant vessels off shore and bringing them through Hatteras Inlet to New Bern for adjudication. While these vessels acted as privateers, in reality they were not, because they were publicly owned by the state. The first true privateer to arrive on the scene—on July 25, 1861, with a prize in tow—was a speedy side-wheel steamer from Charleston, the C.S. Privateer *Gordon.*[10]

The *Gordon* had been a packet boat before the war, serving between the ports of Charleston, South Carolina and Fernandina, Florida. She weighed 519 tons and carried a crew of fifty men. Armed with three heavy guns, her letter of marque and reprisal had been received only ten days before. She was commanded by the venerable

Thomas J. Lockwood, a sea captain who was destined later in the war to become a household word throughout the South for his many daring and successful exploits as a blockade runner. Shortly after sunrise on July 25, 1861, the Gordon was approximately forty miles off Cape Hatteras when the cry "Sail ho!" rang from the masthead.

The vessel to which the lookout was excitedly pointing, was the brig *William McGilvery* of Bangor, Maine, carrying a cargo of molasses to Boston. The statement of the brig's master, Hiram Carlisle, taken at an inquiry in New York sometime after the event, describes the details surrounding the capture:

Thomas J. Lockwood, captain of the privateer *Gordon.*

On 25th July, about 40 miles E. by S. from Hatteras, was fired at by the privateer steamer, Gordon of Charleston, S.C. The first shot fell short, the second went between the head stays and foresail. We then hove to, when the steamer came up alongside and ordered us to launch our boat and the captain and 4 men to go on board the steamer. This I refused to do, when they threatened to sink us. After being so threatened, (I) ordered out the boat and took four men and went on board. At the same time they sent a boat with six men on board the brig, armed with cutlasses, pistols, and bowie knives. (They) wore the brig around with her head to the westward, took her in tow, and towed her into Hatteras Inlet. Upon anchoring they sent us ashore to the fort, and after about three hours they sent us off to the steamer, where we were put in irons for the night. Next morning the irons were removed and we were sent out to the brig under a guard of four armed men, where we remained four days, when they gave us a pass by (the) steamer Albemarle to New Bern, N.C. Remained there eight days; was at liberty all the time; was provided (for) by the quartermaster. Left there August 10 on schooner Priscilla, of Baltimore, which vessel had been seized as a prize, but afterwards released. The C.S. Government paid our passage to Baltimore.[11]

The *Priscilla* had been seized by one of the North Carolina steamers, but when her Maryland nationality was discovered she was released. Carlisle was very observant while he was a prisoner, and made a careful mental note of all the privateer activity: *At Hatteras Inlet there is 14 feet of water. The privateer force consists of four steamers, sometimes as many as 6, besides several small sailing vessels, sent as pilot boats, etc. When leaving there they had sixteen prizes in all.*[12]

Steaming out through Hatteras Inlet, the *Gordon* was soon prowling for additional victims. On July 28, she apprehended the schooner *Protector* from Philadelphia, which was loaded with tropical fruit from the Cuban port of Mantazas. Lockwood exercised his gun crew again and sent a shot whistling across the *Protector's* bow. The *Gordon* passed a line and the little schooner was towed quickly into Pamlico Sound. Two days later, while searching the rough seas off Hatteras, the *Gordon* was spotted by an American warship which gave chase. Lockwood pointed the privateer's stern toward the enemy, and with the throttles held wide open, ran for Beaufort, North Carolina.

On Saturday, August 4, 1861, visibility was fair to good from the Hatteras lighthouse in spite of the numerous scattered rain showers. As daylight broke over the gray eastern horizon, the lookout on this lofty tower signaled to the numerous privateers in the sound that several sails were in sight. Soon steam hissed in the *Gordon's* engine room, pressure built rapidly in the boilers, and within minutes, Lockwood had the steamer pounding through the swells outside the entrance to the Inlet. Perched high on the mainmast above the deck, the lookout scanned the patches of ocean among the scattered squalls of rain. It was not long before the cry, "Sail ho!" was shouted. Rapidly approaching a small schooner, the morning air was awakened by a roar from one of the *Gordon's* guns. The *Henry Nutt*, from Key West, bound for Philadelphia, quickly rounded into the wind. She carried a rich cargo of logwood and mahogany which would bring a high price on the auction block at New Bern. Placing a small prize crew on board, Lockwood ordered the *Gordon* off toward another sail. Once again the boom of the privateer's gun brought a Northern schooner rounding into the wind. She was the *Sea Witch*, which was returning to New York from Baracoa, Cuba, after picking up a load of tropical fruit. Passing a line to the *Henry Nutt*, Lockwood towed both prizes into the Sound.[13]

Forays by the *Gordon, Winslow, Raleigh, York, Mariner, Teaser,* and many others were becoming an embarrassment and a thorn in the side of the U.S. Navy. As a consequence, preparations were soon under way to put an end to the Hatteras privateers. The alarm had now spread, and Northern merchantmen were giving the Outer Banks of North Carolina a wide berth. As a consequence, even though Lockwood kept the *Gordon* at sea for the next several weeks, not one sail was spotted.

Map of the Outer Banks of North Carolina. Privateers would dash out through the inlets, capture a prize, and return to the sanctuary of Pamlico Sound.

Battles and Leaders

Then on the August 27, while steaming out through the Inlet, ten vessels were sighted on the distant northern horizon. Seven of them appeared to be man-of-war steamers and the other three were sail-driven transports. Lockwood quickly determined that the little *Gordon* was no match for this armada, and so turned the vessel's head southward. That night he put into Wilmington where the privateer remained for two days. Early on the morning of August 30, the *Gordon* left Wilmington, steamed down the Cape Fear River, and set a course for home. Later that same day, she arrived in Charleston. Within a week, after a heroic, but hopeless, resistance by a pitifully small garrison, the forts guarding the entrance to Hatteras Inlet fell to a combined Federal army and naval force—the same force that Lockwood had spotted as he sped southward. With the inlets in the possession of the enemy, and Union gunboats patrolling Pamlico Sound, prizes could not be brought into Confederate ports for adjudication, and privateering abruptly ceased along the Carolina coast.[14]

While the numerous private and public-armed vessels which sallied forth from Hatteras Inlet were enjoying their successes, the most prosperous of all Confederate privateers was gathering up one merchant vessel after another and sending them under the direction of a prize crew into Charleston, South Carolina. On June 18, 1861, a letter of marque and reprisal had been issued to the 230-ton brig *Jefferson Davis* of Charleston. The *Jeff Davis*, as she was commonly referred to, was armed with five old obsolete guns which had been cast in England in 1801. Two 24-pounders and two 32-pounders were mounted in broadside, and one long 18-pounder was mounted on a pivot amidships. The gun room was well stocked, however, with an ample supply of muskets, double-barreled shotguns, cutlasses, and revolvers. The *Jeff Davis* carried a crew of seventy-five, and was captained by Louis M. Coxetter. She had been built in Baltimore about 1845, delivered to New Orleans, and given the name *Putnam* when she was registered as a trader. Later, under the name *Echo*, the sleek sailing brig had entered the disreputable and illegal business of slave trading. In August of 1858, the *Echo* was captured by John Newland Maffitt, commander of the USS *Dolphin* at the time, and taken into Charleston harbor where she was confiscated. Here she remained until the spring of 1861, when she was purchased by a large group of Charleston businessmen for the purpose of privateering. With the English pivot gun visible amidships, and her hull painted a man-of-war black, the rakish *Jeff Davis* now took on the appearance of a bona-fide warship.[15]

Captain Coxetter, like many privateering commanders, would later earn his fame as a daring and resourceful captain of blockade runners.

Among his later commands were the *Herald* and the *General Beauregard*.[16] The first lieutenant and executive officer was W. Ross Postell, formerly of the United States Navy. In 1839 he had resigned from that service in order to enter the navy of the Republic of Texas with the rank of lieutenant. There he commanded the Texas sloop-of-war *Austin* and was highly commended by his superior officer. The remaining offices included R. H. Stuart from South Carolina, who was appointed as second lieutenant; Edward M. Seabrook, first surgeon; W. H. Babcock, second surgeon; and Frederick Sandvrie, who was captain of the marine guard on board. Most of the *Jeff Davis'* officers were smartly dressed in double-breasted blue uniform coats with brass buttons embossed with the raised letters "SC."

On the black night of Friday, June 28, 1861, the *Jeff Davis* crossed the bar at the entrance to Charleston harbor, and with her sails filled by the balmy summer breeze, sped rapidly out into the broad expanse of the dark Atlantic. As daylight broke early the next morning, the saucy Confederate privateer was well out to sea and headed northward before a stiff breeze.

The excitement of the first day kept the lookouts glued to their stations, but they were destined to be disappointed, for no merchant vessels were sighted. The second day out, however, two sails were reported by the excited lookouts, but owing to some problems with the rigging, they could not be pursued. Later another vessel came into view, but because she appeared to be of French nationality, she, too, was allowed to pass. Lulled along by gentle summer breezes, the *Jeff Davis* cruised northward parallel to the Carolina coast for nearly a week without capturing a single prize. On July 4, the Confederate flag was raised, and with the officers and crew at attention, a salute was fired from the old English guns.

Later that same day, the weary and discouraged lookouts spied a sail on the lee bow. With a full spread of canvas, the privateer took up the chase. When within range, the 18-pounder pivot thundered, sending its iron ball splashing across the bow of the fleeing vessel. Obediently she swung into the wind and was rounded to. After an examination of her papers, much to the disappointment of Coxetter and his crew, she proved to be the English brig *Grace Worthington*. With gracious apologies to her master, she was told to proceed on her journey. Still later in the day, another brig was stopped, but because she hailed from Baltimore, and the Confederacy considered Maryland a friendly state, Coxetter released her also.[17]

While the crew was becoming dispirited and griping among themselves about their lack of success, the privateer's fortune was about to change. As the sun broke the eastern horizon on Saturday morning, July 6, an excited cry of "Sail ho!" sounded from the masthead. The *Jeff Davis* was about 300 miles off the Delaware coast and was standing on a heading of due south. The sighted vessel, which appeared to be a brig, was sailing northeast. Fearing that the brig's master would become suspicious, Coxetter ordered a slow turn to port and pointed the ship's head toward the northwest. Captain Fitfield of the Philadelphia brig *John Welsh*, out of Trinidad and bound for Falmouth, England with a load of sugar, later narrated the succession of events to a Northern newspaper:

At 8:30 the privateer tacked and stood N.W., at the same time setting a French ensign, and from the fact of her having French-cut hempen sails we supposed she was a French merchant brig. In answer to her colors we set the Stars and Stripes, and thought no more of the stranger. At 9 o'clock, to our surprise, she fired a shot across our bows, when we took in the studding sails and hove the John Welsh to. We then supposed her to be a French man-of-war brig; but her ports were closed and the guns covered up, while but few men were to be seen on her decks. She came within musket shot of us, and lowered a boat which was manned by expert seamen and contained Lieutenant Postell, late of the United States Navy. Just before the boat came alongside the French flag was hauled down and the Confederate flag run up. In about two minutes afterwards the armed crew was on our deck.

After inquiring after my health, Lieutenant Postell desired me to show him the brig's papers. I invited him into the cabin, and after showing them, I stated (that) the cargo was Spanish property. Said he, "You are our prize, and the Spaniards had no business to ship their cargoes in American bottoms."[18]

Captain Fitfield and his crew were taken on board the *Jefferson Davis*, and a prize crew from the privateer, under the command of J. W. Stevens, was transported to the *John Welsh*. Coxetter instructed Stevens to sail the brig to Savannah, and she soon departed, arriving safely in the Georgia port a few days later. In early September, she was condemned by the Confederate District Court sitting in Charleston, and the vessel and her valuable cargo of sugar was sold at auction.

Captain Coxetter earned a reputation during his tenure as captain of the *Jeff Davis*, as a kindhearted commander who treated his prisoners humanely and with respect. Captain Fitfield attested to this when he continued his narration of the events surrounding his capture:

After the work of transferring the stores had been completed, Capt. Coxetter mustered all hands aft and said to them, "Boys, if you molest the crew of that brig or their things to the value of a rope yarn, I will punish you to the utmost of my power. Do you understand? Now go forward." Turning to his officers he said, "Gentlemen, I desire that you do everything in your power to make the stay of these gentlemen as agreeable as possible." He then invited me to dine with him in his cabin while my mate was taken into the officers' mess.[19]

In the afternoon another prize was taken, this being the schooner *Enchantress* of Newburyport, Massachusetts, bound from Boston to Santiago de Cuba. William W. Smith, a Savannah pilot, was placed on board as commander of the prize crew, and ordered to sail the schooner to that Georgia port. Unfortunately, the fate of the afternoon prize was not as favorable as the one captured earlier. Off Cape Hatteras, the *Enchantress* was hailed by the USS *Albatross* and ordered to heave to. Smith and his men were preparing to pass themselves off as the original crew when the steward, who had been retained on board to cook for the Confederate crew, began shouting, as he threw himself overboard, that they were a prize of the privateer *Jeff Davis*. Picking up the floundering steward, the Federal warship quickly took possession of the *Enchantress* and placed Prize Master Smith and the rest of his men in irons.[20]

Arriving in Philadelphia, Smith and his men were thrown, handcuffed, and ankle chained into Mayamensing Prison and charged with piracy. The case came to trial on October 22, 1861, and after four days of testimony, the jury found Smith guilty and condemned him to be executed. Several days later, the members of Smith's prize crew were tried and received similar sentences. Word of this injustice was not long in reaching Richmond. On November 9, President Davis, outraged at the treatment of Smith and the men from the *Jeff Davis*, ordered Brigadier General John H. Winder, provost marshal of Richmond, *to choose by lot from among the prisoners of war of highest rank, one who is to be confined in a cell appropriated to convicted felons, and who is to be treated in all respects as if such convict, and to be held for execution in the same manner as may be adopted by the enemy for the execution of the prisoner of war Smith, recently condemned to death in Philadelphia.*

Winder was instructed to select thirteen additional high-ranking prisoners, and confine them as felons, each one standing for one of the convicted privateersmen. In the presence of several Northern officers, and a U.S. congressman who had been captured at the Battle of Manassas, names of the highest ranking Union prisoners of war were placed in a can and the drawing commenced. The first name drawn was that of Colonel Corcoran of the 69th New York, who was designated to stand for William Smith. The drawing continued, with each Federal officer whose name was drawn being designated to represent one of the condemned prisoners. Afterward they were hurried off to prison to await their fate which was totally dependent upon the fate of the men they represented. The Lincoln government, finding itself in a bind, at last backed down, and the following February all of the Confederates were accorded prisoner of war status and removed to military prisons. By summer, Smith and his men, totally destitute and in rags, were finally exchanged.[21]

On Sunday, July 7, 1861, when approximately 150 miles off Sandy Hook, the morning's worship services had just concluded on the deck of the *Jefferson Davis*, when an excited cry announced the sighting of a vessel dead astern. Shortly the bark of the old 18-pounder sent an iron ball skipping across the bow of the schooner *S. J. Waring*. She was out of Brookhaven, Long Island and bound for Montevideo. A prize crew, consisting of Prize Master Montague Amiel, First Mate George Stevens, Second Mate Malcom Liddy, and two crewmen, were quickly thrown on board, and the schooner was soon on her way toward a Confederate port. The subsequent tale of the *S. J. Waring*, however, was to have a gruesome ending.

Coxetter had left William Tillman, a Negro cook, and three seamen from the *S. J. Waring's* original crew on board the schooner. Amiel steered the prize toward the south, being careful to avoid all other vessels. By July 16, they were less than 100 miles from Charleston. That night, with Amiel and Stevens asleep in their cabins, and the second mate at the wheel, Tillman stole into the master's cabin and with several mighty swings from an ax, beat Amiel to a bloody pulp. Running to the second mate's cabin, he struck a savage blow to Stevens' head, killing him instantly. With no alarm having yet been given, the steward crept up behind Liddy who was still at the wheel, and with a mighty swing, struck the second mate a heavy bash to the base of the skull. Grabbing him under his arms and dragging him to the rail, he threw the unconscious man overboard. Going below, and finding the bludgeoned Amiel wailing in pain, Tillman swung his bloody ax again and again until the groaning stopped. Dragging the two bodies up on deck, he threw them overboard. The two remaining privateersmen agreed to work the ship if the burly Negro would spare their lives. Knowing nothing of navigation, the steward kept the coast on his left and headed north. Eventually, the blood-soaked schooner arrived outside the harbor of New York.[22]

Following the departure of the prize *S. J. Waring*, Coxetter kept the privateer's head pointed northward, and two days later a sail was sighted in the early morning light. The *Jeff Davis* spread every inch of canvas, and it was noon before she approached within range of her pivot gun. One thunderous shot and the *Mary Goodell*, commanded by Captain McGilvery and bound for Buenos Aires, rounded to. Finding that the merchant ship's captain had his wife on board, Coxetter placed a number of his prisoners aboard the *Mary Goodell* and released the New York vessel. Before she sailed happily away, however, five of her crew members had joined the privateers. McGilvery had given his word that he would continue on course to Buenos Aires, but as soon as the *Jeff Davis* dropped below the horizon, he altered course and sped for Portland, Maine, to spread the alarm. Soon Federal warships were criss-crossing the North Atlantic looking for the "rebel pirate" that was cre-ating havoc off the New England coast.

No sooner had the *Mary Goodell* departed than the brig *Mary E. Thompson* from Searsport, Maine, was apprehended. By this time Coxetter was extremely shorthanded and could not afford a prize crew for such a worthless vessel. Placing his remaining prisoners on board, the *Thompson* was released.[23]

The *Jeff Davis* ranged to within 100 miles southeast of the Nantucket shoals where Coxetter ordered her about and shaped his course for the West Indies. On July 29, when located near latitude 25° 4' north, and 50° west longitude, the bark *Alverado* of Boston was captured. She was 51 days out of Cape Town, South Africa, bound for her home port and carried a valuable cargo of wool, hides, sheepskins, copper, and iron. Captain Coxetter placed Gilbert Hay and nine men on board the bark and dispatched them to the Confederacy. Two weeks later, on August 5, Hay and the *Alverado* were approaching Fernandina, Florida, when they were spotted by the USS *Jamestown* which was blockading the entrance to the St. Mary's River. Hay seems to have panicked, for he ran the bark ashore on Amelia Island, and he and his crew escaped in the vessel's small boat. The *Jamestown* sent a boarding party which proceeded to set the bark on fire, and by morning light of the next day, nothing remained but the charred sternpost.[24]

With water and provisions running low, Coxetter sailed the *Jeff Davis* into San Juan, Puerto Rico. The privateer's stay was brief, however, for by the next day, her larder and water tanks filled, she was again prowl-ing the seas in search of prey. On August 5, two Northern vessels fell into her snare. The schooner *Windward* was brought alongside, but before a prize crew could be placed on board, another much larger vessel was spotted. Coxetter immediately cracked on every inch of can-vas and went in chase of the second ship. She was the brig *Santa Clara* and she was a fast one, but soon the *Jeff Davis* was near enough to send an iron ball from the old pivot gun whistling through her rigging. The *Santa Clara* surrendered to her fate and Coxetter, with the brig in tow, returned to the *Windward*. The brig was a far more valuable prize than the little schooner, so the privateer's captain placed his prisoners from the *Alvarado* and the *Santa Clara* on board the *Windward* and turned her loose.

With no qualified officers left to command prize crews, Coxetter was forced to place the *Santa Clara* in the hands of a crew commanded by a helmsman. A. Stone proved his mettle as a commander and a helmsman, however, for he brought the brig safely into Savannah, where she was condemned by the District Court of Georgia, and her cargo sold at auction on April 24, 1862. The *Santa Clara* herself, however, was seized by Confederate authorities in November of 1861, and along with several other vessels, sunk as an obstruction in the Savannah River.[25]

After the capture and dispatching of the *Santa Clara*, Captain Coxetter shaped his course for the Confederacy. By now provisions and water were running low and the *Jeff Davis* was severely shorthanded. Even if another vessel were captured, it would be impossible to furnish a prize crew to take her into a Confederate port. Several days later, she was approaching the coast of Florida when the merchant ship *John Carver* was overhauled. She had been charted some five months earlier by the Federal government to carry coal to the Union forces at Key West, Florida. With a draft of twenty-two feet, she was much too low in the water to cross the bar at any Southern port, even if Coxetter had had the men to sail her. Removing her twenty-two officers and men, the *Jeff Davis'* commander ordered her scuttled and set afire. As the privateer pulled away in the fading evening light, many of her men watched what would become an all too familiar scene for the Northern merchant fleet that plied the waters of the South Atlantic. The *John Carver*, ablaze from stem to stern, sat motionless on a rising sea. Crackling sticks of flame raced up her slender masts and danced out along her graceful spars. Unfavorable weather was approaching, and the rising winds whipped her cargo of burning coal into a white-hot inferno that lit the turbulent ocean for miles around. Hours later, even after she had dropped below the horizon, the night sky continued to be illuminated with a dull but shimmering glow of orange and red. By morning, the *John Carver* was gone.[26]

By Friday evening, August 16, 1861, the *Jeff Davis* had reached the port of St. Augustine, Florida, but with the rough sea and howling wind, it would have been folly to attempt to cross the bar. During the long stormy night, and all the next day, the privateer stood off St. Augustine while the angry seas broke over her decks, and the gale-force winds tore through her rigging. Clinging to their perches, the unfortunate lookouts strained to see through the driving rain, while Coxetter paced his cabin, praying that no enemy cruiser would stumble upon them.

By Sunday morning, August 18, the storm had abated enough that Coxetter attempted to take her across the bar, but before moving very far, she ran hard aground. A small boat was lowered and Surgeon Babcock, along with Marine Lieutenant Baya, escorted the prisoners ashore. Although the sea was rough, Coxetter managed to success-fully launch the privateer's remaining boats, and all the officers and crew managed to make it safely to shore where they were greeted en-thusiastically by the townspeople. Later, at approximately 9:30 a.m., Coxetter and some of his officers returned to the stranded *Jeff Davis* in two lightboats. The starboard guns were thrown overboard in an ef-fort to lighten the brig and clear her deck of water, but she remained hard aground. Coxetter later surmised that the guns which had been thrown overboard stove in her sides and flooded her.

While the breakers continued to pound the stranded vessel, the of-ficers filled the two boats with provisions and baggage, and hurriedly cast off. Rowing back to the town, they were received by cheer after cheer and accorded the status of Southern heroes by the ladies of St. Augustine. Meanwhile, the *Jefferson Davis*, still hard aground on the bar, began to break apart from the constant pounding of the surf, and in a few days, she had broken up and disappeared beneath the waves.[27]

The *Jefferson Davis* was not the first Confederate privateer, and she would not be the last. She had, however, been the most successful. Augmented by an ever increasing number of warships, the Union block-ade soon began to make it almost impossible for any vessel but the swiftest steamer to enter a Southern port. With no harbor accessible in which to safely deliver their prizes, the role of the privately armed vessel in Confederate service slowly came to an end. (See Appendix A for a list of commissioned privateers.) The far off columns of black smoke and the dull orange glow of burning ships on the distant hori-zon would continue, however. Commissioned cruisers of the Confed-erate States Navy, with such names as *Sumter, Florida, Alabama, Geor-gia, Shenandoah*, and others, would soon take the war to the enemy's commerce. In the process, they virtually drove the American merchant marine from the high seas—a blow from which it would not recover until the advent of World War II. But until these now famous South-ern cruisers could be built or purchased, fitted out and deployed, it was the privateers that struck the first blow.

JEFFERSON DAVIS,

President of the Confederate States of America.

To all Who shall see these Presents---Greeting:

Know Ye, That by virtue of the power vested in me by law, & have commissioned, and do hereby commission, have authorized, and do hereby authorize the _____ _____ (now particularly described in the schedule hereunto annexed) whereof _____ is Commander, to act as a private armed vessel in the service of the CONFEDERATE STATES, on the high seas, against the United States of America, their Ships, Vessels, Goods and Effects, and those of their citizens, during the pendency of the War now existing between the said CONFEDERATE STATES and the said United States.

This Commission to continue in force until revoked by the President of the CONFEDERATE STATES for the time being.

Schedule of Description of the Vessel.

Name, _____
Tonnage, _____
Armament, _____
No. of Crew, _____

BY THE PRESIDENT.

Given under my hand and the Seal of the CONFEDERATE STATES at Montgomery, this _____ day of _____ A. D. 1861.

_____

Secretary of State.

A commission blank used for authorizing a privateer to operate in the name of the Confederate States.

Chapter Two

The Stars and Bars in the English Channel

In spite of the fall chill permeating the air on Thursday, November 21, 1861, the docks and wharves of Southampton, England were swarming as usual with a mass of humanity. All eyes were straining in excited expectation, as each person attempted to catch a glimpse of a distant steamer with an unfamiliar flag that was just entering the harbor. She was a side-wheeler, they could see, and flying from her main gaff streamed a bright red and white ensign with a blue canton containing eleven stars. Wisps of black smoke trailed from her funnel, as her slowly revolving paddle wheels drove her cautiously through the maze of shipping in the anchorage. Finally, after reaching a spot designated by the harbor master, the command was given, and the iron anchor splashed into the cold waters of the port. Those who were close to her mooring could discern two small pivot guns, one forward and one aft, mounted on her deck. Bells clanged and excess steam was blown off, as officers in double-breasted blue uniforms scurried about giving last minute instructions to the crew. For those English citizens who were still ignorant of the rakish visitor's nationality, the *London Times* provided their enlightenment: *Great excitement has been created here by the arrival in our waters this morning of a steamer of war bearing the flag of the Confederate States of America.* The "steamer of war," heralded by the

Times—the first warship to carry the flag of this new nation to European waters—was the CSS *Nashville*.[1]

***

On May 4, 1861, C. H. Stevens of Charleston, addressed a letter to Treasury Secretary Christopher G. Memminger requesting that a letter of marque be granted him for the steamer *Nashville* which was then lying at Charleston. A second letter, written the same day, was addressed to Navy Secretary Stephen R. Mallory in Montgomery. Immediately, Mallory began to develop a special interest in Mr. Stevens' side-wheel steamer.[2]

The *Nashville* was launched from the Thomas Collyer Shipyard in New York on September 22, 1853. She was 215 feet in length; 34 feet abeam, and drew almost twenty-two feet of water. She weighed 1,221 tons, but after being lightened by the removal of her passenger saloons and luxury appointments, her single side-lever engine could drive her through the water at over 16.5 knots. She had been used in the New York to Charleston passenger run, and happened to be at the South Carolina city when the attack on Fort Sumter signaled the beginning of hostilities. Seized by South Carolina authorities, she was purchased by a group of Charleston businessmen who hoped to convert her into

The CSS *Nashville*.

a privateer. The *Nashville* was in excellent condition, having just undergone a complete overhaul which included the installation of new boilers. Stevens believed, correctly so, that she would make an excellent privateer, but Secretary Mallory had other plans for the speedy vessel.[3]

President Davis had given Mallory the responsibility of conveying Confederate commissioners John Slidell to France and James M. Mason to Great Britain. It was an important assignment, for recognition of the new Southern nation by the European powers could bring military intervention on behalf of the Confederacy. Mallory wanted to be certain that Slidell and Mason would be able to elude the Federal blockade, and the speedy *Nashville* appeared to be the best choice available to accomplish this mission. Rejecting the application for a letter of marque and reprisal, Mallory purchased the steamer for $100,000.[4]

Stephen R. Mallory, Secretary of the Confederate States Navy.

On September 27, 1861, Lieutenant Robert B. Pegram took command of the *Nashville*. Finding her unarmed, he appealed to the state of South Carolina to lend to him two small English-made 6-pounders, which he had mounted on pivots fore and aft. Pegram, who was from Virginia, had resigned from the U.S. Navy and was appointed a lieutenant in Confederate service on June 10, 1861. Assigned to Norfolk, he was commanding the naval batteries along the Elizabeth River when Mallory tapped him for the important mission with the *Nashville*.[5]

Pegram reported to Mallory that: *From the time that I arrived at Charleston, I informed myself by frequent reconnaissances of the exact position of the enemy's blockading squadron....* To effect his observations, Pegram employed the services of the former privateer *Gordon*, the fast steamer which was still under the command of Thomas J. Lockwood. The *Gordon* was now chartered by the Confederate Navy to act as a coast and harbor patrol boat, and her appearance outside the bar had become a regular occurrence to the Federal blockaders. Knowing that they could not overtake her because of her great speed, the Union commanders had come to ignore her. She was the ideal vessel, therefore, for Pegram to study the positions of the Federal warships, and he continued to plan and postulate his escape. The *Nashville's* commander was aware that because of his vessel's deep draft, he would be confined to the known channels in order to cross the bar, and these were being closely watched. Growing weary of Pegram's seemingly excess caution, Mason and Slidell chartered the *Gordon* for $10,000 to slip through the blockade and deliver them to a port in the West Indies. With her armament removed, and renamed the *Theodora*, Lockwood slipped her out of Charleston on the dark, rainy night of Friday, October 11, and soon arrived uneventfully in Cardenas, Cuba. From there the commissioners traveled by train to Havana, where they boarded the British Royal Mail steamer, *Trent*, setting the stage for the famous "Trent Affair."[6]

Even though the Confederate commissioners had departed in the *Theodora*, Pegram continued to watch for an opportunity to take the *Nashville* to sea. In his report to Secretary Mallory, Pegram noted that: *...being directed to carry out the remainder of my instructions, I awaited a favorable opportunity for running the blockade.* Scholars and historians have speculated on the exact mission of the *Nashville*. Now that Slidell and Mason were on their way, why was the *Nashville* still preparing to sail to Europe? Evidence indicates that her assignment was twofold: First, it was known that Federal authorities expected Slidell and Mason to sail in the *Nashville*, and every effort was being made to apprehend them. Their early departure in the *Theodora*, however, was not known. It was considered imperative, therefore, that the *Nashville* maintain the "appearance" of transporting them in order to cover their real voyage. Secondly, the Confederate government was extremely eager to establish itself before the courts of Europe as a legitimate member

Lieutenant Robert P. Pegram, commander of the CSS *Nashville*.

of the world of nations. What better way to convince the heads of these states, than to dispatch a speedy warship flying the nation's flag! The very appearance of this vessel, it was thought, would lend credibility to the mission of Slidell and Mason, as they sought recognition for the new Confederacy.

Finally, Pegram felt that conditions were favorable. *This opportunity appeared to have arisen on the 26th of October,* he wrote, *and on the night of that day, having again carefully reconnoitered the position of the enemy and placed boats on the bar for my guidance, I left Charleston Harbor. One of the boats placed upon the bar, through some unseen circumstances, however, drifted from its place, and the Nashville struck rather heavily upon a reef, from which she was got off without injury. It had been my intention to run out before the rising of the moon, but, as a consequence of the detention caused by running aground, the moon had already risen above the horizon as we were crossing the bar, enabling us to clearly perceive the enemy's vessels, while the Nashville, lying in the shadow thrown by the land, was completely hidden from hostile observation. Having thus baffled the vigilance of the blockading fleet, I shaped our course for the Bermuda Islands, which we reached on the 30th of October.*[7]

Also at St. George, Bermuda, was the British steamer *Fingal* under the overall command of James D. Bulloch, Confederate naval agent to Europe. Bulloch was on his way to the Confederacy with a huge load of arms and munitions, and Pegram was able to supply some coal to the blockade runner. In addition Pegram transferred his Savannah pilot to the *Fingal,* and with the *Nashville's* bunkers filled to capacity, the cruiser was ready to sail.

On the 5th of November we left Bermuda, Pegram recorded, *and in order to elude pursuit, took a track across the ocean but little frequented by other vessels.*[8] Like most side-wheelers, the *Nashville* was a poor sailer and had to depend mostly on steam. For the first part of the voyage she made reasonable time with calm seas and fair winds. As the trip progressed, however, the weather began to worsen, and soon the cruiser was plowing through angry seas and burning coal at an alarming rate. Strong head winds battered her frail hull; huge waves crashed over her bow, smashing her wheelhouses and carrying away her bulwarks and part of the hurricane deck. The forty exhausted crew members lashed themselves to the deck and fought against the biting wind and flying spray just to keep the *Nashville* struggling eastward.

While the Confederate cruiser fought the howling winds and battering waves of the North Atlantic, another drama was taking place in the Bahama Channel. It was Friday, November 8, and the British Royal Mail steamer *Trent* was stopped dead in the water, while the USS *San Jacinto* lay nearby, her heavy guns trained on the English vessel.

American naval officers were in the act of forcibly removing Slidell, Mason, and their secretaries from Her Majesty's ship, while enraged British officers were held at bay by the leveled bayonets of United States Marines. Captain Charles Wilkes of the *San Jacinto* hustled the prisoners aboard his warship, and immediately headed for Boston where he was initially hailed as a hero. The illegal abduction of the Confederate delegation on the high seas from a British ship would soon bring the United States and England to the very brink of war.[9]

At 9:00 a.m. on the morning of November 19, the *Nashville* was approaching the western coast of Ireland, when a sail was spotted over the bow standing toward the cruiser. The two ships approached one another, with the captain of the oncoming vessel expecting to exchange the customary salute with the strange side-wheel steamer. Just as they arrived abeam, Pegram ordered the Confederate flag raised, the little 6-pounders uncovered, and demanded the immediate surrender of the ship. Not knowing what was in store for him or his craft, Captain Nelson of the 1,482-ton *Harvey Birch* lowered the United States flag and ordered her rounded to. She was a beautiful clipper ship, bound from Le Havre to New York, but was running in ballast.

I then ordered the captain to come on board with his ship's papers, Pegram wrote, *and after a careful examination of these, one of the officers of the Nashville went on board of the Harvey Birch, and after transferring the officers and crew (thirty-one in number) on board the Nashville, with their personal effects, set the Harvey Birch on fire. Before she was lost to our sight, her masts had gone by the board and she had burned to the water's edge.*[10]

With the black smoke from the *Harvey Birch* spreading across the western horizon, the *Nashville* turned her head eastward and continued on course toward Southampton. News of the destruction of the *Harvey Birch* made sensational news in the English press. Almost overnight, insurance rates for American shippers skyrocketed, and many companies advised their captains to remain in port. None realized that the destruction of this one clipper signaled the beginning of a long and successful war against American commerce—a war that would see American merchant vessels virtually driven from the sea.

The *Nashville* dropped anchor at Southampton on November 21, 1861, and Pegram immediately released the 31 crewmen and passengers from the *Harvey Birch*. The mystery of the *Nashville's* visit to England is only deepened by the next paragraph in Pegram's report to Mallory: *Immediately upon my arrival at Southampton I communicated, as instructed, with Lieutenant North, C.S. Navy, and the Hon. William L. Yancey, and apprised them of your instructions, having previously shown these to Captain Bulloch, C.S. Navy, at Bermuda.*[11]

The CSS *Nashville* burning the *Harvey Birch* off the coast of Ireland, November 19, 1861.

Lieutenant James H. North had been appointed as a naval purchasing agent by Mallory on May 17, 1861, and was immediately dispatched to Europe. North's responsibilities included contracting for and overseeing the construction of ironclad warships in Europe. His slowness in arranging these details irked Mallory, and when Bulloch arrived in England as the navy's "Chief" purchasing agent, North was made subservient to him. Yancey had been dispatched by President Davis as part of a three-man team which included Pierre A. Rost and A. Dudley Mann, to seek recognition of the Confederacy from the European powers. Yancey was not a good choice, given his quick temper, impatience, and rhetorical outbursts, and the mission in the final analysis was a failure.

It is most likely that Pegram carried, first of all, more specific instructions for North relative to the construction of warships in Europe. Having left the Confederate States so soon after its formation, it is reasonable to assume that Mallory had now formulated more specific directions for North, and that the *Nashville* provided a convenient means of transmitting these to him. Knowing that Bulloch would soon return to England, could also explain why he was shown these instructions when Pegram met him in Bermuda.

In addition to the instructions for North, it appears that Pegram delivered orders relieving Yancey of his post and ordering him home to the Confederacy. Pegram wrote in his official report that he offered passage on board the *Nashville*, but that the fiery Yancey declined. Whatever the exact mission of Pegram and the *Nashville* might have been, it soon became of little consequence, however, for the "Trent Affair" now burst upon the scene.

The news reached England on November 28, and bitter anti-Union emotions erupted all across Great Britain. The press raged at the thought of the arrogant United States holding its vessel at bay with loaded guns, while armed marines dragged the Southern dignitaries off the ship. The British government demanded an immediate apology from the Lincoln government, and coupled this with the insistence that Mason and Slidell be released without delay. Foreign Minister Lord John Lyons called for a severance of diplomatic relations with the United States within seven days if corrective action was not taken. There was talk of war, and 8,000 British troops trudged aboard fast steamers and were dispatched posthaste to Canada.[12] Pegram observed that: *In consequence of the seizure of the Confederate commissioners, Messrs. Mason and Slidell, there then appeared to be a great probability of an early rupture between England and the United States, I determined to await the results.*[13]

The stormy Atlantic crossing had taken its toll on the frail *Nashville*, and while awaiting the outcome of the "Trent Affair," Pegram partitioned the authorities for the use of government repair facilities. The cruiser's commander wrote that: *Upon examination (I) found that the Nashville required thorough overhauling, and she was taken accordingly into the dry dock at Southampton on the 5th of December. There I was allowed by the admiralty agent to have the ship placed in the condition in which she was when we left Charleston, but I was not permitted in any way to alter or strengthen her, the British cabinet having determined to maintain a strict neutrality, in accordance with the tenor of the Queen's proclamation.* Unfortunately for Pegram, the *Nashville* was taken into dry dock with another vessel which meant that neither could leave until the repairs were completed on both.[14]

At about this time, on a dark winter night around midnight, someone attempted to set fire to the *Nashville*. Pegram, who seems to have never trusted his crew, was convinced it was one of his men, for several of them deserted shortly afterwards. The perpetrator, whoever he was, was never discovered. The cruiser's commander was anxious to leave, but with the Mason and Slidell situation still unresolved, and his ship consigned to dry dock, he had no choice. Two days before Christmas he wrote to North: *I wish with all my heart that I could get away from this place, but I see no alternative but to await the decision of the Government respecting the affair of the Trent.*[15] Within a few days, Pegram would have another problem to contend with.

John Slidell and John M. Mason, Confederate envoys to Europe. The forced removal of these two ministers from the British Royal Mail ship *Trent* by the USS *San Jacinto* triggered the "Trent Affair."

Under orders to avenge the burning of the *Harvey Birch* by the "rebel pirates," Commander T. Augustus Craven had dashed across the storm-buffeted Atlantic with the United States sloop-of-war, the USS *Tuscarora*. The Federal cruiser was a 1,457-ton screw steamer carrying nine heavy guns. Battered by fierce winter gales, she finally limped into Southampton on January 8, 1862, arriving just as Pegram was finalizing preparations to sail. *The pirate steamer is ready for sea and is lying at the docks, about a mile from where I have anchored;* Craven reported, *there being two outlets to this port, I can keep watch for the vessel by lying at anchor inside.*[16]

Desperate to apprehend the *Nashville* when she sailed, Craven sent a boat's crew ashore to spy on the Confederate cruiser, but they were discovered by British authorities and ordered back to their ship. Fearful of a confrontation within their home waters, the government notified both Pegram and Craven that, according to international law governing belligerent vessels in a neutral port, one vessel could not sail within twenty-four hours after the other ship had departed.

The day after the arrival of the *Tuscarora*, word reached Great Britain that the Lincoln government had backed down and had released Mason and Slidell. It would be near the end of January, however, before they finally reached England. In the meantime, Pegram fretted about possible sabotage and bided his time waiting for an opportunity to slip by the *Tuscarora*. Craven, too, was busy. His surveillance party ashore having been discovered, the Union captain hired a pilot boat to keep an eye on the "pirate," and to report any observed activity to him. This, too, was discovered by the authorities, and Craven ordered the pilot boat discharged.

The presence of the two belligerent vessels in the same port was a cause for another concern by the British authorities. Both Pegram and Craven felt it necessary to grant liberty to their officers and seamen in order to maintain morale among the crew, and inevitably these men would meet one another as they made their rounds in Southampton. William R. Dalton, wrote: *To us "youngsters," however (the midshipmen, there were eight of us), our stay there was a source of delight, for we went sight-seeing in England and over to Paris, where we had good times generally. Occasionally our respective crews would meet at the theaters or other places of amusement in town, when trouble arose, and fights galore ensued until the participants were restrained by the authorities and "jugged" in jail, which cooled their warlike ardor considerably.*[17]

Not only did the British officials make it clear that they intended to enforce the 24-hour rule, but on January 26, 1862, Captain Charles G. Patey, senior British naval officer at Southampton, notified both Craven and Pegram that they must give 24 hours' notice of any intention to depart. The following day, Craven notified Patey that he intended to proceed to sea the next day, Tuesday, January 28. Unknown to the admiralty, was the fact that Craven intended to return immediately and announce his intention of sailing again within 24 hours. By this stratagem, he hoped to keep the *Nashville* confined to port.[18]

By this time the English port officials were growing weary of both vessels, and fearful that hostilities might erupt within their waters, ordered the *Tuscarora* to depart, with the *Nashville* to follow in 24 hours. Pegram, knowing that the Federal warship would wait outside the three-mile limit to engage him, appealed to the Duke of Somerset for concessions:

My ship not being originally designed to cross the Atlantic, much less as a war vessel, I have not been able to strengthen her sufficiently to sustain the light 6-pounder guns which had been put on board of her, and to leave within the fatal delay specified in the above order would be to subject me to inevitable capture. So obvious is this, indeed, that I am driven to the conclusion that there has been some strange misconception in regard to this sudden summons, and this, in connection with the very brief time allotted me, urges me to address your grace in person, and to submit the enclosed copies of the communications I have received from Captain Patey.

Your grace cannot fail to observe, from these orders, that my movements are made subordinate to those of the Tuscarora, and that the commander of that vessel is absolutely empowered to force me into a collision with him upon his own terms.[19]

Pegram assured the Lord Duke that, if necessary, he would yield to the order, but he entered his protest in the name of humanity and the Confederate government. Heeding the Southern commander's plea, the British government reversed its ruling, and Craven, having again anchored in English waters, was ordered to remain where he was, while the *Nashville* put to sea.

Finally, on February 3, 1862, all preparations were complete and all hands were on board. At 5:00 p.m., escorted by the British frigate H.M.S. *Shannon*, the *Nashville* steamed triumphantly past the *Tuscarora*, and headed for the open sea. As the Confederate cruiser surged by within hailing distance, Captain Patey stood on the bridge of the *Tuscarora*, reminding the chagrined Craven that Her Majesty's government would tolerate no infringement of the 24-hour rule. To add insult to injury, Pegram hoisted signals as he steamed past, challenging the Federal captain to catch him if he could. The next day, a disgusted and angry Commander Craven, hoisted the *Tuscarora's* anchor and headed for Gibraltar in search of Semmes and the CSS *Sumter*.[20]

The arrival of the *Nashville* at Southampton had caused a stir among the public and the British press. The seizing of Mason and Slidell from the Royal Mail steamer *Trent*, while the *Nashville* was in port, only heightened the excitement concerning her. While her exact mission is to this day somewhat clouded, the presence of the speedy Confederate cruiser in a British harbor had several precedent setting ramifications. Although the lightly-armed vessel was not much of a warship, she still provided proof that the Confederate government had created a navy and was serious about gaining its independence. The most important consequence of her visit, however, was a statement by Lord John Russell, British Foreign Secretary, that according to the terms of the Foreign Enlistment Act, the *Nashville* was not a "pirate," but a regularly commissioned man-of-war. This, over the severe protests of the American consul, assured the Confederate government of belligerent status for their vessels, with the rights of safe passage into British ports for coal, supplies, and repairs. Still, it had been a vexatious stay for Lieutenant Pegram. With the *Nashville's* big paddle wheels now driving her westward through the biting spray of the cold North Atlantic, Pegram must have wondered if it had all been worth it.[21]

Upon leaving England I had determined to make direct course for one of our Southern ports, wrote Pegram in his report to Mallory, *but finding that the Nashville could not weather in safety continued northerly gales, and that far more coal had been consumed than was anticipated, I shaped our course for Bermuda, anchoring in the harbor of St. George on the 20th of February. Whilst receiving on board a supply of coal, I learned that the owner and master of the Confederate schooner Pearl, which had run the blockade from Beaufort, N.C., and had run aground on the northern part of the Island of Bermuda, was then at Hamilton, and I determined on seeking an interview with the person in charge. Before, however, I could carry out this resolution, Captain J. Pender, the owner of the Pearl, came on board the Nashville, and in the most patriotic and praiseworthy manner volunteered his services, and those of his master, Mr. J. Beveridge, a practiced pilot, to pilot the Nashville into Beaufort, N.C., speaking with the utmost confidence of our ability to run into that port.*[22]

Four days after touching at Bermuda, the *Nashville* steamed out of the harbor of St. George, bound for Beaufort, North Carolina. With pilot Beveridge on board for the run into the Southern coast, Pegram was confident that they would have no trouble reaching the Carolina port. A sharp lookout was kept, for they were now entering the waters patrolled by the Federal blockaders, and although Pegram was not actively searching for Northern merchant ships, neither would he turn down a chance meeting with an American vessel. At dawn, on February 26, two days out of St. George, the lookout spotted a schooner off the port bow. Pegram ordered the helmsman to maintain the *Nashville's* course, and as the two vessels approached one another, he ordered the

First Lieutenant Charles M. Fauntleroy, executive officer on the CSS *Nashville*.

Lieutenant Robert P. Pegram, in civilian attire.

Midshipman William H. Sinclair of the CSS *Nashville*.

First Lieutenant John W. Bennett, an officer on the CSS *Nashville*.

American ensign raised. Captain Smith of the *Robert Gilfillan*, en route from Philadelphia to Santo Domingo, mistook the Confederate cruiser for the USS *Keystone State*, which was similar in appearance, and he, too, hoisted the Stars and Stripes.

The *Nashville* and the schooner hauled up opposite one another, and Smith signaled, inviting a landing party from the *Keystone State* to come aboard. Master John H. Ingraham, the *Nashville's* boarding officer, climbed onto the schooner and was promptly entertained by a boisterous Smith with stories of glorious Union victories. Growing impatient, Ingraham tersely terminated the

Midshipman James W. Pegram served on the CSS *Nashville*.

Master John H. Ingraham, of the CSS *Nashville*. Promoted to first lieutenant, Ingraham later commanded the ironclad CSS *Chicora* at Charleston.
Scharf's *History of the Confederate States Navy*

conversation, announced that Smith and his crew were now prisoners of the Confederate States steamer *Nashville*, and ordered him to secure his ship's papers and to report on board the cruiser. The stunned captain probably noticed by this time that the Stars and Stripes fluttering over the *Keystone State* had been replaced with the Stars and Bars. The sea being too rough for the transfer of any provisions, Smith and his seven-man crew were rowed to the side of the *Nashville*, and soon the *Robert Gilfillan* was a mass of flames.[23]

In heavy seas, the *Nashville* continued on her course for the North Carolina coast. Pegram described their arrival in his report to Mallory: *At daylight on the morning of the 28th of February we found ourselves near the harbor of Beaufort, N.C., and the first thing seen was the enemy's ship blockading the port. I stood directly toward her, hoisting the American flag and the ship's private number. This was replied to by the enemy. As soon, however, as I had passed her, I ordered the United States flag to be hauled down and hoisted the Confederate flag at the foremast head and at the peak, while my pennant was run up the main. When the United States flag was hauled down on board the Nashville, the Federal vessel's captain endeavored to bring her broadside to bear, but before the ship could be swung we were out of range of his guns.*

This Federal vessel was the USS *State of Georgia*, commanded by James F. Armstrong. He, too, was deceived by the *Nashville's* close resemblance to the *Keystone State* and allowed the Confederate cruiser to pass him by, thinking she was in the process of delivering the mail. Pegram continued his narrative: *In spite of this the enemy fired twenty-one shots, but without the slightest effect. I answered the enemy's salute by firing one gun, finding it useless to waste more powder. At shortly after 7 a.m. we had passed the lines of Fort Macon and were safely moored alongside of the railroad wharf at Morehead City.*[24]

The arrival of the *Nashville* in Southern waters signaled the end of her career as a Confederate naval warship. When Pegram arrived in Richmond, he was informed that she had been sold to Fraser, Trenholm and Company, the Charleston and Liverpool-based banking firm, which intended on operating the speedy steamer as a blockade runner. Returning to Morehead City, Pegram ordered all government property removed, and the vessel prepared for movement to Charleston where the new owners would take delivery. After braving the guns of the *Tuscarora* and the winter storms of the North Atlantic, however, the *Nashville* was now threatened with destruction from another quarter. Lieutenant William C. Whittle, who had been placed temporarily in command, described this new danger:

General Burnside's movement upon New Bern, N.C., was then being executed, and Captain Pegram, with the officers and crew of the Nashville, went through on one of the last trains that could escape, after which all communication inland was completely cut off. Burnside's expedition was moving upon Morehead City, and the capture of the Nashville seemed inevitable. The blockading fleet had been increased to two steamers and one sailing vessel, and the Federal troops were on the march to seize the vessel as she lay tied up at the wharf.[25]

Union General Ambrose Burnside had launched his amphibious assault against the North Carolina coast in late January, and one by one the weakly-held Confederate positions had fallen to the enemy. After taking New Bern on March 14, Burnside sent his troops on an overland campaign to envelop and capture Fort Macon, which sat on

The CSS *Nashville* running into Beaufort, North Carolina, February 28, 1862.

the eastern tip of Bogue Banks and guarded the water approaches to Beaufort and Morehead City. While Federal infantry inched closer and closer, siege batteries were constructed on the mainland to batter the masonry fort into submission, and Union navy guns shelled the fort from off shore. With Federal warships off the bar, and heavy guns in their rear, the plight of the now unarmed *Nashville* looked dark indeed.[26]

Without a crew or means of defense, without even a chart or chronometer, short of coal and provisions, the idea of saving the ship was simply vain, Whittle continued. *There seemed a single chance, however, and I determined to take the chance. The fall of Fort Macon was only a question of time, and a very short time at that; the blockade must therefore, be broken. Quietly and secretly we set to work, and being assured by my chief engineer* (James Hood) *that with his small force and assistance of the deck hands he could keep the vessel under steam, we made ready to run through the blockading fleet. I was fortunate in securing the services of Captain Gooding, an excellent coast pilot, who was then in command of a sailing ship blockaded in the harbor. He brought with him a chart, chronometer and sextant, and such instruments as were deemed absolutely necessary for navigation, with the promise that if his efforts were successful the ultimate command of the ship would be given him by the purchasers.*

Whittle and his men worked feverishly to get the *Nashville* ready. The young lieutenant was determined that the Confederate steamer would not fall into the hands of the enemy, and accordingly made preparations on board to destroy her if it became necessary. When all was ready, Whittle dropped down under the guns of Fort Macon, and there, planned the final steps of his intended escape. Lieutenant Colonel Moses J. White, commander of Confederate forces at the fort, came on board and apprised Whittle of the Federal schemes to capture the *Nashville*. Whittle informed the colonel that he had no intention of allowing the enemy to lay hands on the cruiser, and divulging his plans for running out, asked that White make sure that his men did not fire on them as they passed in the dark. White assured him that he would forward the message and wished him Godspeed.[27]

On the evening of March 17, 1862, between sunset and moonrise, the moon being nearly full, I tipped my anchor and ran out. As soon as I was under way a rocket was sent up from the lower side of Bogue Island, below Fort Macon, by an enemy's boat, sent ashore from the blockaders for the purpose of watching us, giving me the assurance that our movement had been detected.

Steaming toward the entrance at the bar, I found the three vessels congregated close together under way and covering the narrow channel.... We were going at full speed, say fourteen knots per hour. I was in the pilothouse with Gooding, and two others were at the wheel. The blockaders, under way and broadside to me, were across my path. I ran for the one fartherest to the northward and eastward, with the determination to go through or sink both ships. As I approached rapidly I was given the right of way and passed through and out under a heavy fire from the three vessels. They had commenced firing as soon as I got within range and continued until I passed out, firing in all, as well as we could determine, about twenty guns. The moon rose clear and full a short time afterward and found us well out to sea, no attempt being made to pursue us that we could discover.[28]

Whittle ran the *Nashville* out to the Gulf Stream and turned her south. His intentions were to enter Charleston, but upon arriving there before dawn on the 19th, found the entrances too well-guarded to hazard an ap-

Lieutenant William C. Whittle, of the *Nashville*. Whittle later served on the CSS *Shenandoah*.

proach. With Federal rockets lighting the sky to alert the blockaders of his presence, Whittle turned the cruiser around and withdrew northward along the coast. The next favorable port was Georgetown, and the *Nashville*'s head was swung in that direction. Approaching the small South Carolina port at sunrise, two plumes of black smoke were spotted on the northern horizon. With his few crew members totally exhausted, low on fuel, and no means of defense, Whittle made hasty preparations to destroy the cruiser. Happily, however, the columns of smoke disappeared over the horizon, and the *Nashville* ran for the entrance to the harbor.

Suddenly, with a moaning and creaking of her timbers, the *Nashville* lurched to a stop. Not being familiar with the entrance to Georgetown, the pilot had run the cruiser aground on the bar. Whittle had just lowered a boat and ordered a party to take soundings to determine if they could free the vessel, when a body of cavalry appeared on the beach. Not knowing if they were Federal or Confederate, Whittle once again prepared to destroy the *Nashville*. Fortunately the horsemen were a company of South Carolinians, and after freeing the *Nashville* from the bar and taking on board an additional pilot, the cruiser steamed on up to Georgetown.[29]

The Federal Navy, much to its consternation, had lost track of the *Nashville* and was not even aware that she was at Georgetown. While Union warships prowled the ocean looking for the vanished "pirate," Whittle traveled to Richmond to confer with Secretary Mallory, and then to Charleston to finalize the sale of the cruiser to the Fraser, Trenholm and Company. On March 27, after taking on coal and a few additions to the crew, the *Nashville*, with Captain Gooding in command as promised, sailed out of Georgetown in broad daylight with flags flying. Running in ballast in order to cross the bar, Gooding set her course for Nassau. Upon arrival in the Bahamian port, the first warship to fly the Stars and Bars in the English Channel, the *Nashville* was placed under British registry and her name changed to the *Thomas L. Wagg*.[30]

The *Thomas L. Wagg* left Nassau, according to Confederate agent Louis Heyliger, on April 5, 1862, loaded with "1,000 kegs of powder, some 5,000 rifles, bales, blankets, boxes, tin pans, etc." Gooding cruised the Southern coast from Charleston to Wilmington, North Carolina, but could not find an opportunity to successfully run the blockade. Running low on coal, the *Wagg's* commander brought the blockade runner back to Nassau. Sailing again, she finally arrived safely at Wilmington on April 24, where she promptly ran aground. Small boats were sent out to unload her cargo of 60,000 rifles and 40 tons of powder. Once lightened by the removal of her cargo, she floated free and was towed up to Wilmington for repairs.[31]

On April 30, the *Thomas L. Wagg*, carrying a cargo of cotton, departed Wilmington without incident. Discharging her payload in Nassau, she was loaded with a cargo of arms which had been off-loaded from the steamer *Southward* and prepared for her return trip. Arriving off the South Carolina coast in the darkness of the early morning hours of June 23, Gooding tried once more to enter Charleston, but was spotted by the blockaders. Ordering the *Wagg* put about, Gooding headed back out to sea, but three Union vessels broke away from the blockading squadron and took up the chase. Two of the Federals soon fell behind and returned to the fleet, but the third, the *Nashville's* old look-a-like, the USS *Keystone State*, hung on and continued to pursue the fleeing blockade runner.

Daylight found the former *Nashville* in a race for her life. Gooding watched anxiously as the *Keystone State* continued the chase, and ordered the *Wagg's* engine room to do everything possible to increase her speed. The exhausted engineers responded, and soon the cast of the lead showed that they were pounding over the waves at twenty knots. Still the Federal warship hung on. All day, for over 300 miles, the chase continued. By evening the *Keystone State* was gaining, and the *Thomas L. Wagg* was just about out of coal. Desperate to maintain steam pressure, Gooding ordered his crew to begin dismantling hatches and bulkheads, and to throw the pieces into the roaring furnace. Axes flashed and splinters flew as the men rushed to cut away anything that would burn.

Darkness settled over the scene, as Gooding continued to drive the vibrating steamer through the heavy seas. Black smoke, mixed with sparks and burning embers, spewed from her funnel, and as Gooding looked back, he could see that the *Keystone State* was now definitely gaining on them. The night grew stormy, with thick rain showers, thunder, and lightning. The *Wagg's* commander shouted for the helmsman to steer toward a threatening squall line, and within minutes the blockade runner was enveloped in pouring rain and biting spray. Visibility went to zero. Gooding ordered a course change and kept the *Wagg* plowing ahead. The *Keystone State*, her target lost in the black clouds and torrential rains, slowed, turned, and began the long trek back to the blockading squadron. The next morning, the *Wagg* wheezed into the tiny fishing village of Abaco on one of the northern-most islands in the Bahamas. Her upper works were in shambles; bulkheads, deck panels, railings—anything combustible—had been fed into her furnace. She was afloat, however, and her cargo of arms and munitions was safe. After repairs and refueling, Gooding would try again.[32]

On July 6, 1862, the *Thomas L. Wagg* entered the Ogeechee River south of Savannah, Georgia, and unloaded her cargo of 2,600 stand of arms at the railroad bridge near King's Ferry. It would be the last service she would render for the Confederacy, for her luck was about to run out. Stung by public criticism, the Union Navy was determined this time not to allow the former Confederate cruiser to escape and, therefore, stationed every available warship off Ossabaw Sound. Fraser, Trenholm and Company, seeing that their vessel was bottled-up in the river, sold her to a group of private citizens who intended to turn her into a privateer. A civilian, Captain T. Harrison Baker took command, and securing a letter of marque and reprisal on November 5, mounted six guns, painted the entire ship a battleship gray, and renamed her *Rattlesnake*.

Although several attempts were made, Captain Baker could never find an opportunity to run safely past the blockaders. Tired of waiting, and learning that the privateer had been moved down river to just behind Fort McAllister, the Federal forces determined to go upriver to get her. On February 28, 1863, at 7:07 a.m., the Union ironclad monitor *Montauk*, captained by Commander John L. Worden, maneuvered into position just 1,200 yards from the *Rattlesnake*. Ignoring the return fire from Confederate forces in Fort McAllister, Worden opened fire on the *Rattlesnake* which had run aground, and whose masts he could see behind a spit of land. Finding the range with the 11-inch gun, the Federal commander unleashed his huge 15-inch smoothbore. Shells were seen to burst over the Confederate vessel, and soon dense black smoke began to roll skyward. A gun exploded from the heat of the fire that now blazed on her deck, and then a thunderous blast rocked the countryside as the *Rattlesnake's* magazine exploded, tearing to pieces, the one-time CSS *Nashville*.[33]

The *Rattlesnake* burns in the Ogeechee River south of Savannah, after being attacked by the USS *Montauk*.

The USS *Montauk* firing on the *Rattlesnake* near Fort McAllister, Georgia, February 28, 1863.

Chapter Three

The "Mosquito Fleet"

The three small steamers had begun preparations earlier in the morning, and now sat tied to the boat landing at Fort Huger on Roanoke, Island, North Carolina. Wisps of wood smoke curled upward from their stacks as steam hissed through their pipes and valves. It was a beautiful autumn day, October 1, 1861, and the calm waters of Croatan Sound fairly shimmered in the early morning sun. Waiting in line to board the vessels over rickety gangplanks were three companies of the Third Georgia Regiment with the imposing names of "Dawson Grays," "Governor's Guards," and the "Athens' Guards." Excited over their upcoming "cruise," the Georgia troops laughed and sang like school boys going on a Sunday school picnic. Except for their trip through the Dismal Swamp Canal from Norfolk aboard an old leaky barge, most of the tall lanky Georgians had never set foot on a steamboat.

While the men from the red clay state may have stared in wonder at the water-borne monsters with their roaring furnaces and hissing engines, experienced navy men on board were not very impressed. In fact, their vessels were so small and so weak, so pathetically armed, that they had begun derisively referring to themselves as the "Mosquito Fleet." But for the Confederate Navy, guarding the inland waters of North Carolina on this sunny Tuesday morning, it was all that was available.

42

Federal troops land on the beach to attack Forts Hatteras and Clark (right), August 28, 1861.

Captain William F. Lynch, commander of the "Mosquito Fleet."
Bendann Brothers, Baltimore, Md.

Although the Mosquito Fleet would eventually number some seven or eight vessels, only three were being loaded this morning with the men from Georgia. Captain Lynch, commander of all Confederate naval forces in the coastal waters of North Carolina, had chosen these three for the expedition because they were the best. Lynch's objective was to find out just what the Federal forces were up to in Pamlico Sound since their easy conquests of Forts Hatteras and Clark on August 29. Word had reached Lynch and Colonel A. R. Wright, senior army commander on Roanoke Island, that the Federals had established a camp at the desolate village of Chicamacomico, approximately twenty-six miles north of the Hatteras light on the Outer Banks. It was rumored that this camp was to become a jumping off point for an attack on Roanoke itself, and Lynch was determined to investigate it.

William F. Lynch was a naval officer of the "old school," having entered United States service in 1819 at the age of eighteen. Born and reared in Virginia, Lynch had served his entire adult life in the service of his country, rising to the rank of captain before he resigned on April 21, 1861, to offer his sword to his native state. He had served in the Virginia Navy until that state's forces were transferred to the Confederacy, and then had been in charge of the naval batteries along the Aquia Creek until tapped by Secretary Mallory for the defense of North Carolina. Lynch's predecessor, Captain Samuel Barron, had been taken prisoner when Fort Hatteras capitulated. With the Richmond government's eyes focused on the Virginia front, Lynch's task was destined to be a frustrating one, for there was never enough of anything—men, ships, or guns—to adequately defend the Carolina coastal region.[1]

Captain Lynch flew his flag from the CSS *Curlew*, the largest of the three steamers which were now about to cast off their lines at Roanoke Island. Commanding the *Curlew* was another Virginian, Thomas T. Hunter, who, having acheived the grade of commander in the United States service, resigned and was appointed a commander in the Confederate Navy on June 10, 1861. The *Curlew* had been constructed as a tug at Wilmington, Delaware, in 1856, and had been purchased at Norfolk in 1861 by the Confederate government. She was a 260-ton side-wheel steamer, 150 feet long, and could make about 12 knots. Her draft of 4.6 feet meant that she was well suited for the shallow waters of Pamlico Sound. A 32-pounder that had been rifled and banded at the Gosport Navy Yard opposite Norfolk, was removed from Fort Bartow and installed on a makeshift pivot in her bow. An old 12-pounder smoothbore was mounted on a field carriage and positioned on her stern.[2]

The *Raleigh*, under the command of Lieutenant Joseph W. Alexander, was a small propeller-driven steamer that had seen service with the North Carolina Navy until transferred to Confederate service in July of 1861. The 65-ton steamer had operated as a towboat on the Albemarle and Chesapeake Canal, and had been armed with one 32-pounder on her bow when she was taken over by the state of North Carolina in May of 1861. Alexander, the son of the distinguished Judge Julius Alexander of Charlotte, North Carolina, had been graduated from the Naval Academy at Annapolis in 1861 and had commanded the *Raleigh* ever since the early days of her commissioning in the North Carolina Navy.[3]

The third vessel of Lynch's expedition was another small screw-propeller that had operated on the inland waters and canals of North Carolina before the commencement of the war. The 79-ton *Junaluska* had been built in Philadelphia in 1860, and like the *Raleigh*, had been purchased by the Confederates while she was at Norfolk. Two 6-pounder howitzers were mounted on her narrow deck, and she was under the direction of Midshipman William H. Vernon, assisted by Midshipman James M. Gardner.[4]

Now that the frolicking troops were on board, and the inexperienced gun crews, comprised of army details from 3rd Georgia, were at their stations, Captain Lynch gave the signal to cast off. With the men cheering and the captains blasting their steam whistles, the Mosquito Fleet chugged out into Pamlico Sound and headed south. Just over forty miles in that direction, another steamer, the USS *Fanny*, flying the Stars and Stripes, was on its way north.

Several days before, Colonel Rush C. Hawkins, Federal commander at Fort Hatteras, had dispatched Colonel W. L. Brown's 600-man 20th Indiana Regiment to the northern end of Hatteras Island near Loggerhead Inlet. There, on the wind-swept dunes near the village of Chicamacomico, they established an outpost to guard against any possible Southern attacks from Pea Island to the north. Early on the morning of October 1, while the Georgia boys were clambering aboard the Mosquito Fleet to the north, Hawkins dispatched the army tug *Fanny*, loaded with supplies for the regiment, to Loggerhead Inlet.[5]

The *Fanny*, armed with a rifled 32-pounder, an 8-pounder rifle, and under the command of J. H. Morrison, arrived opposite Chicamacomico at around 1:00 p.m. and dropped anchor in eight feet of water. There, twenty-five members of the 20th Indiana, who were on board as reinforcements, and the *Fanny's* gun crews lounged about the deck waiting for Colonel Brown to send a lighter to off-load the supplies. It was two and one-half hours before the first boat pulled alongside. Once loaded, the small craft started for shore when suddenly someone shouted that there was a vessel rapidly approaching from the west.

Captain Lynch had spotted the anchored Federal steamer and had turned his flotilla of three ships directly toward her. Bells rang in the Confederate steamers' engine rooms as engineers opened the valves and threw the levers for full speed. The *Curlew* was in the lead, and her army gun crew scrambled to load and train their cannon on the distant target. The soldiers had spent two days practicing with the 32-pounder before it was mounted on the *Curlew*, but because of the shortage of powder, they had yet to fire the weapon. At a range of a mile and one-half, the firing lanyard was pulled, and the Confederate gun responded with a thunderous blast. The startled Georgia troops had never seen anything like it. Smoke, which initially shrouded the bow of the boat, quickly blew to the rear as an explosive shell streaked low over the Sound and splashed near the *Fanny*.

The *Raleigh* and the *Junaluska* now joined in, their excited gunners sending shells splashing near and far but not hitting the Federal steamer. The Union gunners were not idle. Swinging their two pieces around, they opened a brisk and accurate fire on the approaching Mosquito Fleet. Morrison later claimed that one shell exploded on the bow of the lead vessel, but there is no mention of a hit in any Confederate reports. Steadily the Confederate flotilla advanced, their enthusiastic gunners firing wildly. Geysers of water, thrown up by near misses from the return fire, cascaded down on the little steamers, drenching everyone on board. The range had diminished by now, and presently a shell from the *Curlew* was seen to explode on the *Fanny's* deck. A few moments later a white shirt knotted to the halyards, was run up, and Lynch shouted for his gunners to cease firing. The *Fanny* had surrendered, and within a few minutes Colonel Wright's men were tumbling aboard the Union steamer. When the Stars and Bars were run up, the ecstatic Georgians shouted until they were hoarse. Compared with what was to come later in this long and brutal war, it was not a very impresive victory. But after the disasters at Hatteras Inlet and the loss of Forts Hatteras and Clark, it was a sweet victory, indeed, for those Southerners who were there, and the first victory of the war for the Confederate Navy.[6]

In addition to the 49 prisoners, the *Fanny* yielded a large cache of ammunition, 1,000 overcoats (which were distributed to the 3rd Georgia), 1,000 dress coats and pants, and 1,000 pairs of shoes. The 3rd Georgia might look like a regiment of "Yankees" during the coming winter, but at least they would be warm! Putting a crew on board, Lynch's men hoisted the captured steamer's anchor and triumphantly steamed the now CSS *Fanny* back to Roanoke Island in company with the Mosquito Fleet. Along the way, illustrating yet another example of the many shortages with which Lynch was faced, the Confederate vessels stopped along the shore to allow the crews to gather firewood for fuel, there being no coal available.

The Union outpost at Chicamacomico posed a serious threat to the entrenched Confederates on Roanoke Island. Lieutenant Colonel Claiborne Snead of the 3rd Georgia explained: *The situation of the Confederates was alarming. It was evident that the new position taken by the enemy was intended as a base of operations from which to assail Roanoke Island and capture the small garrison thereon. The Third Georgia Regiment and Col. Shaw's North Carolina regiment* (8th North Carolina), *with Commodore Lynch's "Mosquito Fleet," comprised our entire defense, while reinforcements could not be obtained nearer than Norfolk by a long and difficult route through Albemarle Sound, Dismal Swamp Canal, and the Elizabeth River. On the other hand, the Federal forces, daily accumulating at Fort*

The USS *Fanny* being attacked by the *Curlew*, the *Raleigh*, and the *Junaluska*, at Chicamacomico, October 1, 1861.

Hatteras, had behind them on the open sea, a powerful navy, efficient both in attack and in the transportation of troops.[7]

The capture of the *Fanny*, and the intelligence concerning the Federal outpost at Chicamacomico, set into motion one of the most confusing and bizarre campaigns of the war. Wright and Lynch formulated a plan whereby all available Confederate troops would be transported by the Mosquito Fleet to a point just north of the Union camp. There the 3rd Georgia would splash ashore and attack the enemy, driving him down the island to the south. Meanwhile, Colonel H. M. Shaw's 8th North Carolina would proceed down the Sound and effect a landing near the Hatteras lighthouse, thus acting as a blocking force. Once the Indiana regiment was disposed of, the Confederate troops would destroy the Hatteras light, and in conjunction with the Mosquito Fleet, attack and attempt to retake Forts Hatteras and Clark. It was an ambitious plan.[8]

By October 4, Lynch had his fleet ready. A visitor to the island described the scene where he found the Mosquito Fleet ...*all very busy in making preparations and embarking troops.... I remained with them until just before they left. The scene was very animating. The evening was calm and the Sound smooth as glass. Steamers and barges crowded with troops were anchored off from the shore. Cheers of welcome arose from the troops on board, as new companies marched down to embark. I went on board a schooner to return to N. H. (Nags Head) and remained near the steamer and barges until about 10 o'clock at night. Everything was animate with excitement. From my position and the favorable state of the atmosphere you could hear every word that was said. From one steamer the lively notes of Dixie filled the air; from another the notes of the violin floated on the air and from others the solemn service of praise and prayer to God, rendered more solemn by the circumstances, went up from the mingled voices of a large and apparently devout congregation of worshippers.*[9]

In addition to the *Fanny*, now under the command of Midshipman James L. Tayloe, Lynch had rounded up two more of his steamers, making six in all for the mission. They included the 120-ton sidewheeler *Empire*, armed with two guns and the 85-ton *Cotton Plant*, another side-wheel steamer which may have been unarmed. The *Empire*, whose name was later changed to *Appomattox*, was under the command of First Lieutenant Charles C. Simms, while the name of the *Cotton Plant's* captain is unknown. At approximately 1:00 a.m., amid the flickering glare of pine torches and the blasting of steam whistles, the Mosquito Fleet got under way.[10]

Colonel Snead described their arrival at Loggerhead Inlet: *Passing through Croatan Sound into and down Pamlico Sound, the little fleet arrived off Chicamacomico, and about three miles therefrom, just after sunrise. All the vessels were of too deep a draft to get nearer this point of the island, except the Cotton Plant, which was enabled to advance a mile farther on. Upon her, Colonel Wright, with three companies of the Third Georgia, and two six-pound boat howitzers, ...proceeded toward the shore, the officers and men wading in the water up to their middies for three-fourths of a mile, and opening a rapid fire upon the enemy, who stood in line of battle on the beach, twelve hundred strong according to their muster rolls.* (Only 600 men from the 20th Indiana were present.) *Soon after the firing commenced they began a retreat, moving hastily and in great disorder toward Fort Hatteras.*[11] Thus ensued what would be fittingly referred to later as, the "Chicamacomico Races."

While the remainder of the 3rd Georgia waded ashore, Lynch pulled his Mosquito Fleet out and headed south with the 8th North Carolina. The Confederate fleet would attempt to land them near the Hatteras light, and if successful, they would trap the 20th Indiana. While Lynch's steamers raced south to set up the blocking force, the chase went on. Neither side was accustomed to forced marches, let alone a hectic pace in loose sand. Colonel Snead remembered that: *The attacking party scarcely numbered seven hundred men, some of whom, with their own hands, drew the two howitzers through the deep sand, (and) pursued the retreating foe flying pell-mell for twenty-six miles, killing eight and capturing forty-two men.*[12]

Man after man, Confederate and Union, fell from the ranks, but the majority kept going. It was a hot day for October, and the sun beat down unmercifully upon the heads of friend and foe alike. It was maddening; the roaring surf only a few feet away and yet not a drop of water to drink. The chase continued all day, while farther down the Sound, the 8th North Carolina was not faring very well. By late afternoon the Mosquito Fleet was in position, but because of the shallowness of the Sound at this location, none of the vessels could approach the landing nearer than two miles. Determined to give it a try, the Tarheels jumped overboard and began splashing toward shore. After wading about a mile, the bottom of the Sound dropped off so sharply that they could not keep their heads above water, and reluctantly, the North Carolinians returned to their boats.

Finally, near midnight, the weary 20th Indiana reached the lighthouse, and using it as a rough-and-ready fortification, dropped down in the sand to get some rest. The weary 3rd Georgia, unaware of Colonel Shaw's failure to land the 8th North Carolina, fell exhausted in the sand just south of the village of Kinneket. But the Chicamacomico Races were not over. The next morning, when it was learned that there was no blocking force to cut off the fleeing Federal troops, Colonel Wright gave the order for his 3rd Georgia to return to Chicamacomico.

The disgusted and bone-tired Georgians, many with blistered feet, had just begun their countermarch when the 9th New York, having hurried up from Fort Hatteras during the night, suddenly appeared in their rear. Now it was the Confederates who were being chased. Back they went pell-mell over the loose sand dunes and rough scrub that characterized the bleak island. Soon, as an officer of the Georgia regiment recalled, they had another problem: *After marching only a few miles upon our return, a Federal steamer anchored off the coast and opened upon us with shell, shot, and grape shot. They fired the first gun at 5 minutes after 1 o'clock, and continued the fire till dark, throwing by Commander Lynch's count 441 shot. It was a miracle that numbers of us were not killed.*[13]

It was the USS *Monticello* that was lobbing the shells at the harried Confederates, and to avoid her fire as much as possible, the men marched on the Sound side of the island. This necessitated their wading across the numerous little inlets that dot the western shore, but even here, because of the narrowness of the island, the *Monticello* and her thundering guns were at times only 500 yards away. At last the panting Southern troops arrived at their starting point and hurriedly began re-boarding the steamers which had returned from their abortive part of the mission. Shooting over the island, Lynch opened fire on the *Monticello* with several of his rifled guns, but the distance was too great and the shells fell short. The Chicamacomico Races were over, and with each side contending that that they had won a great victory, the Confederates returned to Roanoke Island, and the Federals to Fort Hatteras.[14]

Federal authorities in Washington were now keenly aware that the seizure of Hatteras Inlet was a barren victory unless they could control all the inland waters of eastern North Carolina. Preparations were soon under way in the Federal capital to secure once and for all this important inroad into the heart of North Carolina. Rear Admiral Louis M. Goldsborough and Brigadier General Ambrose E. Burnside were busily planning what would be styled in February, the "Burnside Expedition."

Confederate officials, too, were worried, but with Union forces pushing into Virginia and Tennessee, there seemed little that the Richmond government could or cared to do. Governor Clark of North Carolina continually stressed to Richmond the importance of the North Carolina Sounds and the absolute inability of the state to defend them. One immense problem was the shortage of arms, and Clark reminded the War Department that in addition to arming all of the North Carolina troops, which were now in Virginia, the state had also "loaned" to the Confederacy 13,000 stand of arms for the equipping of troops from other Southern states. Because of this generosity, the harried governor was now attempting to purchase arms from private citizens.

We feel very defenseless here without arms, Clark wrote, and I will not again report to you that this has been affected by our generosity to others.... We see just over our lines in Virginia, near Suffolk, two or three North Carolina regiments, well-armed, and well-drilled, who are not allowed to come to the defense of their homes—and two of them posted remote from any point of attack....

Our forts might resist their attack and landing, but out of reach of the forts we cannot concentrate a force of any magnitude. We have now collected in camps about three regiments without arms, and our only reliance is the slow collection of shotguns and hunting rifles, and it is difficult to buy (these) because the people are now hugging their arms to their own bosoms for their defense.[15]

Captain Lynch, too, could expect little in the way of reinforcements for his Mosquito Fleet. Although a plan for the construction of 100 gunboats to serve on Pamlico Sound was approved, few boats were actually completed, and none before the attack on Roanoke Island. The resources of the state were sadly lacking, and the few vessels that were later constructed were mostly built at makeshift shipyards, sometimes no more than cornfields along a riverbank. Lynch was also not satisfied with the preparations made by the army, and in correspondence with the Navy Department, suggested ways of strengthening the Roanoke defenses. In a letter to Brigadier General Benjamin Huger, theater commander, on September 17 prior to the Chicamacomico Races he wrote: *So great is the breadth of Croatan Sound* (between the island and the mainland) *with a channel of 6 feet near the mainland, 3 miles distant, that I am reluctantly forced to the conclusion that but little dependence can be placed upon the batteries for its defense. After a careful reconnaissance, I am persuaded that the defense of this sound must be made at the marshes, 7 miles below, with floating batteries and gunboats, there being no soil wherewith to construct redoubts.*[16]

Roanoke Island, which divides the waters of Pamlico Sound from those of Albemarle Sound, was the key to the defense of North Carolina. If it fell to the enemy, the whole eastern third of the Tarheel state would be open to the invader. Of major concern was the Weldon Railroad which linked the upper Confederacy and the war front in Virginia, with the supplies from the deep South. If the sounds and rivers were captured, Union troops would be only a day's march from this all important lifeline. The ever-popular Brigadier General D. H. Hill, who had been placed in charge of the defenses of Pamlico and Albemarle Sounds, completed an inspection tour of his district in early

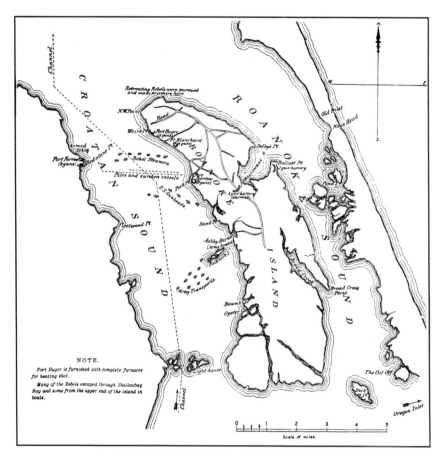

Map of the Battle for Roanoke Island, and the position of the "Mosquito Fleet."
Official Records Navy

October, and in a letter to Secretary Mallory, he described the deplorable condition of the state's defenses. After describing the lack of guns and the shortage of powder at such places as Fort Macon, New Bern, and Washington, North Carolina, Hill got to the crux of the problem:

Roanoke Island is the key to one-third of North Carolina, and its possession by the enemy would enable him to seize the great railway connection between north and south of the Confederacy. This all important island is in want of men and guns. It should have at least 6 more rifled cannon. Feeling that everything depended upon holding it, I came up last night (to Portsmouth, Virginia) to apply to the Navy Department for ordnance and ordnance stores. I found Commodore Forrest, Captain Fairfax, and General Huger fully as much concerned about the island as I was, but they could do nothing for me without your order. Under these circumstances I most earnestly appeal to you for 6

**First Lieutenant William H. Parker was in command of the
CSS *Beaufort* in Lynch's "Mosquito Fleet."**
Scharf's *History of the Confederate States Navy*

*additional rifled cannon—4 for Fort Macon and 2 for Roanoke Island. There
ought to be, however, 4 at least for the latter place. I am confident that Manassas
itself is not more important than it.*[17]

By the end of the year, with the constant demand for men in other
theaters siphoning off what few good troops the state could muster, there
were, exclusive of the garrisons in the three forts, only 1,473 Confederate
soldiers on Roanoke Island. These included 475 men of the 31st North
Carolina, 568 men of the 8th North Carolina, and 450 soldiers of Wise's
Legion, a Virginia unit which had been formed by Brigadier General Henry
A. Wise, now immediate army commander on the island. This was a pitifully small force that was expected to defend and hold the island against
the storm that was about to break.

Lynch's Mosquito Fleet was no better off, for only eight light steamers would be all that was available for the coming battle. The *Seabird*,
commanded by First Lieutenant Patrick McCarrick, was a wooden side-
wheel steamer which mounted two guns. The only other side-wheeler

**Commander James W. Cooke was commander of the CSS *Ellis*
in the "Mosquito Fleet."**
Scharf, *History of the Confederate States Navy*

was the iron-hulled *Curlew*, still under the direction of Commander
Hunter, while all the rest were small screw steamers. They included:
the *Ellis*, captained by Lieutenant James W. Cooke; the *Beaufort*, First
Lieutenant William H. Parker; the *Raleigh*, still commanded by Alexander;
the *Forrest*, Acting Master James L. Hoole; the *Fanny*, Midshipman Tayloe;
and the *Appomattox*, under Simms. All the small propeller steamers each
carried one gun. Lynch also had available an excellent schooner, the
Black Warrior, armed with two 32-pounders and under the command
of Master Frank M. Harris. In addition to the weakness of his vessels,
Lynch had another problem: *...But my greatest difficulty is in the want of
men,* he wrote Mallory on January 22, 1862. *So great has been the exposure
of our crew that a number of them have necessarily been invalided; consequently the complements are very much reduced, some of them one-half. I
have sent to Washington, Plymouth, Edenton, and Elizabeth City for recruits
without success, and an earnest appeal to Commodore Forrest brought me*

only four. To meet the enemy I have not more than sufficient number of men to fight half the guns.[18]

Burnside's forces rendezvoused at Annapolis in early January, and on the night of the eleventh, Goldsborough led his fleet to sea. By February 4, 1862, all of the Federal warships and transports, after much difficulty fighting gale force winds and heavy seas, had managed to cross the bar at Hatteras Inlet and anchor in the Sound. The "Burnside Expedition" consisted of 20 warships of Goldsborough's fleet mounting 62 guns, with 15 of these being the new and deadly nine-inch rifles. Burnside, in addition to the numerous army transports carrying his soldiers, had assembled his own fleet of gunboats which added an additional 108 pieces which could be brought to bear. Early on the morning of February 5, this grand armada of 170 guns and 13,000 troops headed north up Pamlico Sound. The largest amphibious landing in American history, up to that time, was about to take place.[19]

Roanoke Island is approximately 12 miles long and about three miles across at its widest point. Badly situated on the western shoreline guarding Croatan Sound, and running from north to south, were three turfed, sand forts—Huger, Blanchard, and Bartow. These fortifications mounted a total of twenty-five guns, few being rifled. Ammunition was in short supply, and the demoralized and untrained troops who manned them had never seen a large gun until a few days before. Fort Bartow, located midway down the western shore, would be the only bastion to offer resistance, the others being out of range. Across the sound on the mainland was Fort Forrest. Constructed on two old barges which had been hauled up in the mud, Fort Forrest contained seven 32-pounders. The east side of the island was defended by a two-gun battery positioned on Ballast Point, and an eighty-foot redoubt in the middle of the island commanded the only road which ran the length of Roanoke. This three-gun emplacement was flanked on both sides by breastworks and deep cypress swamps which were thought to be impassable. Just to the north of Fort Bartow, a double row of derelict ships and barges, stretching between the island and the mainland, had been sunk to provide obstructions to any invading flotilla. Behind the sunken vessels, a row of pylons was in the process of being put down, and behind these protective obstructions, Captain Lynch positioned his tough little Mosquito Fleet.[20]

At 6:00 p.m., the Burnside Expedition anchored ten miles south of Roanoke Island. The next morning, Thursday, February 6, dawned cold and rainy with poor visibility. At 7:45 a.m., the armada was gotten under way, and a little after 10:00 a.m., had entered Croatan Sound. By noon, however, a thick fog had shrouded the invasion fleet. Goldsborough ordered the advance stopped, and further operations for the day were canceled. Confederate officers on Roanoke Island had been well informed concerning the Burnside Expedition, and now the Federal armada's final objective was clear. At 1:00 p.m., navy Lieutenant Benjamin P. Loyall, commander of Fort Bartow, scratched an urgent message to Colonel Shaw: *The fog has cleared away from below, and I can distinctly see that the enemy is about 8 miles from us, in full force. I can make out more than fifty vessels, either at anchor or under way, in tow of steamers. I believe that they are at anchor. I am of the opinion that they have stopped to consider, but it requires a bright lookout to keep the run of them.*[21]

Lieutenant Parker of the *Beaufort* remembered well this calm before the storm. He and Lynch were warm friends, and he poignantly recalled their evening together before the battle: *At sunset, as we saw no disposition on the part of the enemy to move, we anchored and all hands went to supper.... After getting something to eat I went on board the Seabird (the flagship) to see Commodore Lynch. I found him in his dressing gown sitting quietly in his cabin reading Ivanhoe. He expressed great pleasure at seeing me and said he had thought of signaling me to come aboard, but knew I must be very tired and he did not wish to disturb me;.... We talked for a long time of what the next day would probably bring forth, and our plans for defense, etc. Neither of us believed that we would be successful, nor was there a naval officer in the squadron who thought we would. The force opposed to us, both naval and military, was too overwhelming. Ten thousand men to our two thousand on land, and nineteen vessels and 54 guns to our eight vessels with 9 guns on the water.*

After talking some time on the subject, we insensibly got upon literature. Lynch was a cultivated man and a most agreeable talker.... We commenced on Scott's novels, naturally, as he held one of the volumes in his hand; incident after incident was recalled and laughed over, and I never spent a more delightful evening. We were recalled to our senses by the ship's bell striking 8 (midnight). I jumped up exclaiming that I did not know it was so late and that I had not intended keeping my gig's crew up so long. The Commodore's last words to me at the gangway were: "Ah! if we could only hope for success," "but," said he, "come again when you can."[22]

In the still air of the following morning, tiny plumes of smoke spiraled skyward from the Mosquito Fleet as the galley fires were lit and the crews piped to breakfast. Looking south across the line of obstructions, the anxious Confederate sailors could clearly see a forest of masts and spars which comprised the enemy fleet. It was impossible not to comprehend the tremendous odds arrayed against them. With grim determination, however, the Southern crews were soon busy preparing their boats for action. The overwhelming Union force was also visible from Fort Bartow. After a sparse morning meal, Lieutenant Loyall marched his men to their guns at 10:00 a.m., their usual hour for instruction. Within thirty minutes of reaching their positions, the horizon to the south went black with smoke. The Federal assault was coming.

The men hurried to load their 32-pounders, knowing that this time it was no drill. A sudden boom out on Croatan Sound announced the opening shot from one of the Federal steamer's rifled guns. The green Confederate gunners watched as the shell with its sputtering fuse streaked low over the Sound and impacted on the sand parapet, exploding into a thousand fragments. Someone shouted, "Fire!" and the 32-pounders thundered in response, their shells screaming toward the Federal armada, only to splash short of their targets. The firing now became general with approximately 22 of Goldsborough's fleet opening up on Fort Bartow. Only three guns in the fort could be brought to bear, and Lieutenant Loyall instructed his gunners to fire conservatively and with precise aim, for powder was in very short supply.

Meanwhile, Lynch and his Mosquito Fleet had moved into line of battle behind the barricades. The *Appomattox* had been dispatched to Edenton in search of powder, and the *Black Warrior* was anchored near Fort Forrest and was out of range. This reduced the Mosquito Fleet to seven vessels and only eight guns that could be brought to bear on the enemy. Lieutenant Parker well remembered this opening of the battle:

At 11:30 the fight commenced at long range. The enemy's fire was aimed at Fort Bartow and our vessels, and we soon became warmly engaged. The commodore at first directed his vessels to fall back in the hope of drawing the enemy under the fire of Forts Huger and Forrest, but as they did not attempt to advance, and evidently had no intention of passing the obstructions, we took up our first position and kept it during the day. At 2 p.m. the firing was hot and heavy and continued so until sunset.[23]

Whenever the vessels of the Mosquito Fleet drew near, the Federal gunners would switch their fire from Fort Bartow to concentrate on the Confederate boats. When this happened, the Southern steamers would be almost smothered with whizzing and screaming shot and shell. In spite of the firestorm tearing into their boats and splashing around them, Lynch's inexperienced crews kept their guns hammering away at the enemy. It was not without a price, however. A Federal shell exploded on the *Forrest*, the spinning fragments striking Master Hoole in the head, blinding him in one eye and leaving what was thought at the time, a mortal wound. Fortunately, Hoole recovered. Another shell slammed into the *Ellis*, taking off Midshipman Robert A. Camm's right arm at the shoulder and injuring several others.

Thick gray smoke spread over the Sound, as the air shook from the concussion of the guns and the bursting of shells. The *Forrest* became disabled and had to be towed out of action, and then the flag ship, the *Curlew*, took a mortal hit. *Towards 4 o'clock in the afternoon,* Parker recalled, *a shot or shell struck the hurricane deck of the Curlew in its descent, and went through her decks and bottom as though they had been made of paper. Her captain* (Hunter), *finding she was sinking, started for the shore and as he passed me, hailed; but I could not make out what he said, and he being a very excitable fellow (the North Carolinians called him "Tornado Hunter") I said to Johnson that I thought there was nothing the matter with him. "Oh yes there is," said J., "look at his guards." And sure enough he was fast going down. I put after him in the Beaufort, but he got her ashore in time.*[24]

Unfortunately Hunter beached the sinking *Curlew* right in front of Fort Forrest, completely masking its guns. The crew of the sunken gunboat scrambled to safety in the marshes, but the vessel could not be fired for fear of burning the battery on the canal barges that comprised Fort Forrest. Hunter was indeed an excitable fellow, and Parker remembered that: *He told me afterward that during the fight this day that he found to his surprise that he had no trousers on. He said he could never understand it, as he had certainly put on a pair in the morning. I told him I had heard of a fellow being frightened out of his boots, but never out of his trousers!*[25]

Ammunition was running low and Lynch sent an urgent message to Fort Huger requesting more, but they could spare only ten charges. The entire Federal force now concentrated its fire on Fort Bartow, and the sand fort was literally smothered in bursting shells. Adding to the carnage, the fort's barracks caught fire, and thick black smoke rolled skyward mixing with the blue-gray gun smoke that drifted in from off shore. Around 4:00 p.m., Lieutenant Loyall spotted what he feared most. Union troops were splashing ashore south of him at Ashby's Landing and were pushing inland against no resistance. If they succeeded in passing the redoubt guarding the center of the island, Loyall's position would be turned.[26]

As the afternoon sun mercifully began to disappear over the horizon, one by one the roaring guns of the Mosquito Fleet fell silent. They were out of ammunition. Fortunately, the Federals ceased firing also. *A little after sunset the firing ceased on both sides,* Parker wrote, *and as we felt sure the enemy would not attempt to pass the obstructions by night as he had declined them by day, we ran in and anchored under Fort Forrest. We lit our galley fires, and as we had been fighting all day, were glad enough to get something to eat. Upon the whole I was rather surprised to find myself alive, and congratulated myself upon having one more night before me. I directed my steward to serve out the cabin stores to the men and let them have a good supper.*[27]

Parker was well pleased with the behavior of the men and officers of the *Beaufort*. He was exceptionally proud of his gun captain, Jack

Robinson, and his gunner's mate, John Downard. Both men had trained on the British gunnery ship H.M.S. *Excellent*, and both wore the Crimean Medal which they had earned during that conflict. Some men needed a little extra persuasion, however, and Parker related an amusing incident that occurred during the battle:

During the afternoon, when the battle was at its height, I ordered the engineer to send me all the men he could spare from the fire-room to work at the gun. One of the men sent up was my green coal-passer, who evidently did not like the appearance of things on deck. However, he went to the side tackles of the gun as ordered. After awhile, (with) a shell bursting overhead, I called to the men to lie down, and when it was over I ordered them to jump up and go at it again. All promptly obeyed but the coal-passer, who still lay flat on his stomach. "Get up," I called to him from the hurricane deck just above him. He turned his head like a turtle and fixed his eye on me, but otherwise did not move. "Get up," I said, "or I will kill you!" at the same time drawing a pistol from my belt and cocking it. He hesitated a moment, and then sprang to the gun and behaved well during the rest of the engagement.

As I went aft to my cabin after the battle, my steward being busy forward, I called to the engineer to send a man to make a fire in my stove. I had just seated myself before it when who should come in but my friend the coal-passer. He kneeled down in front of me and commenced blowing up a fire. Knowing that the man had not the slightest idea of the discipline of a man-of-war, and wishing to encourage him, I remarked, "Well, my man, I am glad you did your duty so well at the gun after I spoke to you." He blew awhile, and then looking back he said, "I tell you what, captain, I was mighty skeered;" "but," he said after another blow, "I saw you were going to kill me, so I thought I might as well take my chances with the enemy." After a few minutes more of blowing, he said, "I warn't much skeered after that; it's all in getting used to it, Cap." Well, I thought, you have the philosophy of it after all![28]

With no ammunition for his guns and no additional ordnance supplies available, Lynch was in a dilemma. It would be useless to expose his vessels and their crews to enemy fire in the morning if they had no way of defending themselves, and yet, to leave would appear as though they were abandoning the army. Later that evening, Lynch called his commanders to the flagship and explained his decision. After the conference, one by one, the Confederate vessels pulled out, and with no lights showing, headed north. *I felt sure that Pork Point battery* (Fort Bartow) *could hold out,* Lynch reported, *and earnestly hoped that, profiting by the mistake at Hatteras, the enemy, who had landed on a point of the marshes, would be attacked and defeated during the night. With this conviction and in this hope, with the Forrest in tow, I proceeded with my little squadron to Elizabeth City, 35 miles distant, for ammunition, but finding only a small quantity there, dispatched Commander Hunter express to Norfolk for it.*[29]

Back on Roanoke Island, Union troops continued to wade ashore at Ashby's Landing, and by midnight there were nearly 10,000 of them huddled around their blazing campfires trying to stay warm. Confederate authorities would sorely regret not contesting this landing when they had had the opportunity, for at daylight these troops pushed inland, and soon Colonel Shaw and his North Carolinians were hotly engaged. During the morning the weary gunners in Fort Bartow waited for the Federal fleet to resume the attack, all the while listening to the sound of heavy musketry fire growing closer in their rear. Around noon the redoubt covering the island road was flanked, and the demoralized Tarheel troops pulled out and retreated toward the north end of the island. With the defeat of this line, Roanoke Island was lost, and Shaw sent messengers to the forts advising their abandonment.[30]

Loyall's gunners were incensed. They still had ammunition left and were ready to continue the fight with the Federal fleet, but with Union troops surging up the center of the island, it was time to retreat. Angrily throwing their remaining sacks of powder into the watery sand, they destroyed what equipment they could, spiked the guns, and headed north. Hastily they marched along the sandy paths until they came to the camp of the 8th North Carolina. When they arrived, a white flag was flying from Colonel Shaw's tent pole. It was all over. A battalion of men from Wise's Legion, who had landed on the northern end of the island as a relief force, arrived just in time to be included in the approximately 2,500 Confederate soldiers who laid down their arms.[31]

At Elizabeth City, meanwhile, unaware of the catastrophe that was happening on Roanoke Island, an exasperated Captain Lynch was still searching for enough cartridges to supply his vessels. Finding little at Elizabeth City, Lynch had dispatched Commander Hunter overland to Norfolk, and now sent Lieutenant Alexander and the *Raleigh* up the Dismal Swamp Canal to the same place, where it was hoped he could acquire an adequate amount of powder. Not wanting to lose any more time, however, Lynch decided to take two boats and return to the scene of the battle: *Having procured fuel and ammunition sufficient for two steamers, I left Elizabeth City in the Seabird, with the Appomattox in company, on the 9th instant for Roanoke Island with the purpose of rendering what assistance we could. At the mouth of the river we met a boat, from which we learned that our forces on the island had capitulated. We then continued on in the hope of rescuing the men stationed at the Croatan floating battery* (Fort Forrest), *but were forced to retire upon the appearance of a division of the enemy's fleet, steering toward the river.*[32]

The Union flotilla that was now chasing the *Seabird* and the *Appomattox* back up the river consisted of thirteen warships of Admiral Goldsborough's fleet commanded by Stephen Rowan. The Federal captain's instructions were to find Lynch's Mosquito Fleet, attack, and destroy it. Arriving back at Elizabeth City after dark, Lynch noted with relief that the enemy had anchored for the night about ten miles below the town. The Confederate commander was well aware that he had only the remaining hours of this cold February night to prepare for their arrival.

Elizabeth City is situated on the western shore of the Pasquotank River, approximately twelve miles from its mouth. Between two and three miles below the city, at Cobb's Point, was located a battery consisting of four 32-pounder smoothbores. These guns were under the charge of an army engineer and several North Carolina militiamen. Lynch arranged his vessels, the *Seabird*, *Ellis*, *Appomattox*, *Beaufort*, and *Fanny*, in line abreast across the river opposite the battery. The schooner *Black Warrior* was positioned across the river and slightly below the fort. During the night the men worked feverishly distributing the small amount of ammunition available among all the vessels. Well after midnight preparations were as complete as could be expected. Lynch believed that the enemy flotilla, as they had done at Roanoke Island, would stop and attempt to subdue the guns on Cobb's Point before they would advance on the Mosquito Fleet. Events would prove that he was sadly mistaken.[33]

Lynch had his exhausted crews up long before daylight on Monday, February 10, 1862. Quietly, on each boat, the men shuffled off to breakfast. As the eastern sky began to grow lighter, the galley fires were extinguished, shot lockers opened, and preparations made to man the guns. Down below, coal heavers swung chunks of green wood into the furnaces (coal being unavailable), while in the engine rooms, steam hissed and banged through the pipes and valves. Engineers watched their gauges with a practiced eye as the pressure began to rise in the boilers. Other sailors squeezed by their engine rooms to take up stations in the cramped passageways where they could pass the few remaining shells and bags of powder up to the gun deck.

As daylight broke over the river, the men standing by their guns could see that the Federal vessels were under way and headed upstream toward them. *The enemy was coming up at full speed,* wrote Parker, *and our vessels were under way ready to abide the shock, when a boat came off from the shore with a bearer of a dispatch for me; it read: "Captain Parker with the crew of the Beaufort will at once take charge of the fort—Lynch" "Where the devil," I asked, "are the men who were in the fort?" "All run away," said the messenger. And so it was. The enemy vessels were by this time nearly in range, and we were ready to open fire. I did not fancy this taking charge at the last minute, but there was no help for it, so I put the men in the boats with their arms and left the Beaufort with the pilot, engineer and two men on board.* (Parker also took all of the *Beaufort's* ammunition.) *I directed the pilot to slip the chain and escape through the canal to Norfolk if possible, otherwise to blow the steamer up rather than be captured. He "cut out," as Davy Crockett says, accordingly.*[34]

When Parker and the men from the *Beaufort* reached the battery, they found only the army engineer standing by the guns. The militiamen had indeed all fled. Ramming the charges down the smoothbores, the 32-pounders, one by one, roared to life. With no time to organize themselves, and finding the pieces difficult to train, the resultant shots were wild and missed their targets. By now the guns of the Mosquito Fleet had also opened fire, and the Federals, who were still plowing upriver at full speed, returned the fire. Four Union vessels in line abreast led the charge, the river being too narrow for the others who followed behind. Confederate fire from the gunboats, while it lasted, was thick and sometimes deadly, several hits being made, causing numerous Federal casualties. The report of the thundering guns reverberated in the still morning air, while smoke and flames covered the river making visibility difficult. Shells whizzed through the air, crisscrossing one another as they sped toward their intended targets. Lynch's gig had been cut in half by a shell and he was stranded at the guns with Parker. The Confederate commander stood on the parapet of the Cobb's Point battery and watched with dismay as the Federal warships sped past, paying no attention to Parker's hammering fire. Lynch watched in helpless disbelief as the Union boats headed straight for his Mosquito Fleet.[35]

The Union vessels never slackened their pace, and with engines belching fire and smoke, they stood directly for the Confederate squadron. Southern gunners fired their last remaining charges and began abandoning their boats in the face of such overwhelming forces. Harris set fire to the *Black Warrior* and ordered his crew to escape to shore. Amid a scattering of musket and pistol fire, a Federal vessel slammed hard into the side of the *Seabird*. Union sailors tumbled aboard, and 42 Confederates were made to surrender as the *Seabird* began to sink. The *Ellis* was boarded, and with most of his crew escaping over the side, Lieutenant Cooke stood bravely with cutlass and pistol in hand and refused to surrender. He was finally knocked down and subdued after being severely wounded. Midshipman William C. Jackson had leaped overboard and was swimming toward shore when a pistol ball caught him in the back. Taken on board a Federal steamer, he was well cared for, but the seventeen-year-old officer died at 10:00 p.m. that evening.

Suddenly, a tremendous explosion rocked the area. Having been set ablaze, the *Fanny* had been run ashore where her magazine exploded. The *Forrest*, drawn up on the way to repair her damaged propeller shaft, was set on fire and abandoned. His ammunition gone, Simms turned the *Appomattox* upstream and ran for the Dismal Swamp Canal. A Federal gunboat gave chase, and Simms banged away at him with a little howitzer on his stern, until finally leaving the Union boat behind. Arriving at the lock to the canal, the men of the *Appomattox* stared in disbelief—the boat was two inches too wide! Simms torched her, and the disheartened men trudged along the canal on a painful trek toward Norfolk.

Parker, not being able to train his guns on the Union vessels now milling about above his battery, and seeing that all was lost, ordered the guns spiked, the flag taken down, and the men to retreat to a body of woods to their rear. From there it was hoped that they could elude the victorious Federals by slipping around Elizabeth City to the west and then continuing on toward Norfolk. The Union gunners were now turning their attention to the exposed side of Parker's battery, and grape and canister began to whistle around the men. Quickly they raced for the wood line. Parker turned to leave, but something caught his eye. Captain Lynch was still standing quietly, gazing upon his shattered Mosquito Fleet which had just been destroyed before his eyes. *I knew pretty well what his feeling was,* Parker sadly remembered. *Turning to him I said, "Commodore, I have ordered the fort evacuated." "Why so, sir?" he demanded. I pointed out the condition of affairs,...and he acquiesced. Arm in arm, we followed the retreating men.*

The *Seabird* goes down as Lynch's "Mosquito Fleet" is destroyed by Union forces at Elizabeth City, North Carolina, February 10, 1862.

Chapter Four

The Behemoths of New Orleans

They were perhaps the most formidable ironclads ever constructed within the borders of the Confederacy. If they could have been completed, and become fully operational, their innovative design and powerful guns would have been far superior to anything the Federal Navy would have had to offer. Their fates were sealed, however, when the enemy succeeded in passing the forts below New Orleans, on April 24, 1862. To keep her from falling into the hands of the enemy, the mighty CSS *Mississippi*, only weeks from final completion, was set ablaze and cast loose into the swirling and turbulent waters of the Mississippi River. The CSS *Louisiana*, her steering propellers still not connected, could serve only as a stationary battery, firing devastatingly into the Union ships as they passed, but unable to pursue and destroy them. Later, she too, would be destroyed by her own crew to keep her from falling into the hands of the enemy. Most historians agree that if the *Louisiana* and the *Mississippi* had been completely operational, they most likely could have defeated Farragut's fleet and saved the Crescent City.

This destruction of the two most formidable ironclads ever built in the Confederacy was still in the unforeseen future, however, when Nelson Tift and his brother, Asa, arrived in the new nation's capital at

Richmond, Virginia. Nelson Tift, who had recently been joined by his brother after the latter's shipyard repair facility in Key West, Florida, had been seized by Federal authorities, had come from his home in Albany, Georgia. The Tifts carried a small wooden model of a radically new design for an armored warship. On their way to Richmond, they had stopped en route at Savannah and Charleston, and displayed their model to the various naval commanders of the area. Most of the navy men offered encouragement and advised the Tifts to hasten on to the Navy Department to lay their plans before Secretary Mallory.[1]

Mallory and a board of naval officers were very impressed with the proposal, and after the meeting, the Tifts penned a letter to the Secretary:

August 26, 1861

The undersigned having submitted the plan of a war vessel, for the defense of our harbors and coast, ...we propose to give to the Government the use of the invention and to superintend and direct, as your agents, the construction and completion of one or more vessels without pecuniary compensation from the Government for our services, or any reward other than that which every citizen must feel who can, in any way, contribute to the defense of our country.

Should you accept this offer, we would ask the appointment by you of such officers as may be found necessary to cooperate with us in the early and economical construction of the vessel.

Very respectfully, your obedient servants,

Nelson Tift, of Georgia
Asa F. Tift, of Florida.

Hon. S. R. Mallory, Secretary of the Navy.[2]

The Tifts' idea was unusual in that their vessel was designed to be constructed out of ordinary pine timber with all straight lines except for the four corners of the casemate. There was no framing or curved ribs that were common to most wooden hulls. This meant that ordinary house carpenters could be utilized instead of skilled ship carpenters.

On September 1, Mallory confided to his diary, "I have concluded to build a large warship at N. Orleans upon Nelson Tift's plan, & I will push it." On the following day, Mallory wired Captain George N. Hollins, Confederate naval commandant at New Orleans, to begin researching the cost and time required to manufacture three large high-pressure engines, three eleven-foot propellers, and ten boilers. On September 5, Mallory informed the Tift brothers that their plans were approved, and called upon Constructor John L. Porter, who was busy working on the CSS *Virginia*, to devote a portion of his time to drawing the construction plans for the *Mississippi*.

Captain George N. Hollins, commandant of the naval station at New Orleans, was recalled to Richmond prior to Farragut's attack.

Scharf, *History of the Confederate States Navy*

After visiting Gosport Navy Yard at Norfolk, where he witnessed John Brooke's experiments on inclined iron plates, Nelson Tift rejoined his brother in Richmond, and they left by train for New Orleans. Stopping in Albany, Georgia, to put certain family matters in order, Asa journeyed on to Savannah in search of a manufacturer who could build the three giant engines. Finding no one who could handle such large pieces of machinery, Asa went to Charleston where he found every shipyard and machine shop already overburdened with government contracts. Disappointed, but still confident that they could find some facility to build the power plants, Asa rejoined Nelson in Albany, and the two continued on to New Orleans where they arrived on the 18th.[3]

The brothers wasted no time. Not wanting to transport timber and other materials across the river to Algiers, where most of the shipyards were located, the Tifts accepted an offer to lease from Laurent Millaudon, a wealthy land owner, approximately four acres of ground at Jefferson City just north of the New Orleans city limits. Meanwhile, the search continued for a machine shop that could build the ironclad's engines. Leeds & Co. of New Orleans reported that they could accomplish the task, but because of their workload, could offer no reasonable timetable. The Tifts finally negotiated a contract with Jackson and Co. of the Patterson Iron Works to build the steam machinery in ninety days for $45,000.[4] Later, in testimony before a Congressional investigating committee in September of 1862, Nelson Tift reflected on how they began their work: *We commenced at once making preparations to build the Mississippi. We made contracts for timber, purchased bolt iron—such iron, at least, as we could get—selected a place for building the vessel; had a sawmill and blacksmith's shops and sheds for the workmen built, and also a foundation for the vessel. We commenced laying the first plank on the 14th day of October.*[5]

After consultations with government engineers and representatives of the various workshops, it was determined that the boiler capacity was insufficient, and a new design was drawn which incorporated sixteen double-flued boilers in two different sets, each thirty feet long. The three engines, developing a combined 1,500 horsepower, would be 36 inches in diameter, and drive their pistons with a two and one-half foot stroke. Power to the three 11-foot propellers was to be transmitted by a 50-foot center shaft and two smaller 33-foot outboard shafts. Two smaller engines were included to run pumps and blowers. When completed, the 280-foot *Mississippi* would weigh over 4,000 tons, and draw 14 feet of water. She was designed to carry twenty heavy guns on her main gun deck and incorporated a gallery above for the placement of sharpshooters. Her iron plates, which were rolled by Schofield & Markham of Atlanta, later known as the Atlanta Rolling Mill, were delivered before her final destruction. These plates, when installed, would have provided four inches of armor on her 30 degree inclined casemate. Her estimated speed was 14 knots.[6]

As the Tift brothers were arriving in New Orleans on September 18, 1861, Secretary Mallory was concluding a contract for another large ironclad. The contractor was E. C. Murray, a steamboat builder from Kentucky, who had more than twenty years' experience. Murray had traveled to Montgomery, Alabama, in April of 1861, and had submitted a proposal to build an ironclad warship for $126,000. It was August before funds were finally appropriated and the construction location leased by the Navy Department. The site that was chosen was a portion of the land already being developed at Jefferson City by the Tift brothers to build the *Mississippi*. A simple board fence was erected to separate the two shipyards. Murray's contract stipulated that the *Louisiana*, as the ironclad was to be named, should be completed by January 25, 1862.

The *Louisiana*, not quite as large as the mammoth *Mississippi*, was a unique design, being the only one of its kind ever built. Designed by Joseph Pierce, a naval constructor who had no experience with ironclads, his plans called for a vessel 264 feet in length, 64 feet abeam, and weighing approximately 2,118 tons when completed and fully provisioned. Her calculated draft was to be only six feet, enabling her to operate in extremely shallow water. She drew considerably more than this, however, once all her heavy armor was in place. Her casemate was to be slanted forty-five degrees on sides and ends and covered with two layers of railroad T-rails, there being no facility in New Orleans to roll the required iron plates. Murray purchased 500 tons of rails from the Vicksburg and Shreveport Railroad, and these were interlocked together to give the shield a relatively smooth surface. Although intended to carry up to twenty-two guns, her eventual battery would consist of only sixteen.

Situated in a well in the center line of the vessel were two 27-foot paddle wheels, one abaft the other. These wheels were driven by two 9-foot stroke engines, which were designed to provide the principal means of propulsion, while two 4-foot propellers at each corner of the stern, driven by two smaller engines, were intended, in conjunction with the twin rudders, to act primarily as steering devices. It was hoped, however, that the propellers would also aid in the propulsion of the vessel.[7]

At about the same time that the Tifts "commenced laying the first plank" for the *Mississippi*, the keel was laid in the adjoining shipyard for the *Louisiana*. While enough skilled workmen were available and were hired by each shipyard, inevitable obstacles soon manifested themselves. Murray purchased 1,700,000 feet of timber, which had to be cut and transported from the far side of Lake Pontchartrain, causing agonizing delays. Most of the *Mississippi's* timber came from the area around Ponchatoula, Louisiana and Summit, Mississippi, although some came from as far away as 700 miles. As winter approached, the wooden hulls of the two warships began to slowly take shape.[8]

While the Patterson Iron Works labored to build the engines for the *Mississippi*, the Tift brothers searched for someone who could turn the three large shafts that would power her propellers. The two side shafts were finally forged by a local foundry and turned to size on a lathe of the Leeds & Co. in New Orleans. The center shaft was fabricated by the Tredegar Iron Works at Richmond by removing two smaller shafts from the burned-out steamer *Glen Cove* and welding the two sections together to produce the required length. A special railroad flatcar had to be built to convey the shaft to New Orleans where it arrived in mid April. Testifying before the Congressional Investigating Committee,

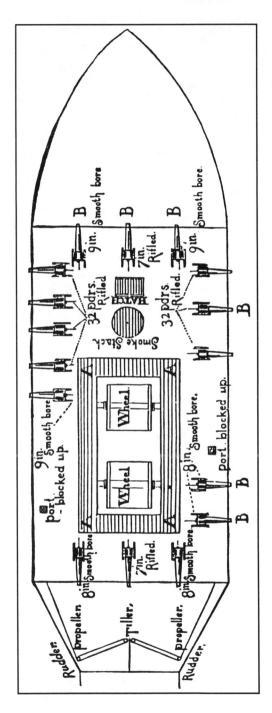

The gun deck of the CSS *Louisiana*, from a sketch made by Commander John K. Mitchell. Note "AA," bulkhead around center wheels, and "BB," guns used in the engagement.

Battles and Leaders

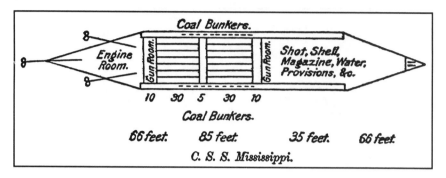

A drawing of the boiler arrangement on the *Mississippi* provided by the Tifts in a letter to Secretary Mallory dated October 9, 1861.

Official Records, Navy

Nelson Tift related in a few stark words, the sad tale of just how close they had come to being able to power the *Mississippi* with all this massive machinery: *We put the center shaft and propeller on board before the vessel was launched, but it was not connected with the engines. Some of the machinery was not completed at that time. The two side propellers were on the wharf at New Orleans when the vessel was burned, and the two side shafts had been put on board. I think the last of the side shafts had been put on board on the 22nd of April.*[9]

The machinery for the *Louisiana* was not as difficult to acquire, as most of it—engines and wheels—was transferred from the steamer *Ingomar*. But here, too, the fabrication of her two drive-wheel shafts and two propeller shafts proved troublesome. Two were eventually forged and finished by Roach & Long of Louisville, Kentucky, and two by Robert Kirk of New Orleans. All of the *Louisiana's* machinery, in a sad example of "what might have been," was finally installed and ready for testing the night before she had to be destroyed.[10]

As though the difficulty of acquiring building materials, engines, shafts, propellers, and various other machinery was not enough, labor problems now added to the delay. On November 6, all naval construction in the city of New Orleans was halted by the workers who demanded a dollar per day increase in their wages. Local workers were angered by carpenters who had been brought from Richmond by the government, and who were paid higher amounts. Most shipbuilders were adamant that they would not concede to the strikers, but Murray and the Tifts wanted their ships finished. Finally, after a delay of six days, the Tifts consented to the pay increase and the workers returned to the yards. Although the strike had been settled, it further antagonized the builders who were already resentful of the government practice of utilizing non-local labor.

Commander Charles F. McIntosh. Mortally wounded while commanding the *Louisiana*, McIntosh died May 17, 1862.

Additional delays were caused by frequent militia drills called by army commanders. Murray and the Tifts complained to the Navy Department, and orders were issued to exempt the crucial *Louisiana* and *Mississippi* workers, but local commanders tended to ignore the orders.[11] An additional delay of four to five days was incurred on the *Louisiana* when her future commander, Charles F. McIntosh, visited the yard and insisted that the gun ports be reshaped as ovals instead of squares.[12]

On the day after Christmas, they began laying the gun deck of the *Mississippi*. Hollins had suggested to the Tifts that they should acquire guns cast in New Orleans, rather than at Tredegar in Richmond, in order to save time and the expense and delay of shipping. The Tifts reported to Mallory, however, that when tested, the locally cast guns were a failure. Not only did the bores have numerous pits and cracks, but the rifling was too short and the grooves cut too deeply, resulting in a failure of the projectile to spin, thus giving a range less than a smoothbore. Consequently, the Tifts were forced to order the guns from Tredegar. The *Mississippi* was to be armed with four 7-inch Brooke rifles for bow and stern chasers, each weighing six tons, while the remaining broadside pieces were to be heavy shell guns.[13]

Eight guns had been sent from Richmond to Memphis to be used on the *Arkansas* and *Tennessee* which were being built there, but since these vessels were far from complete, Murray requested—and Hollins approved—their transfer to the *Louisiana*. When these guns reached New Orleans by steamer, they were promptly seized by the army for use in the forts. Hollins protested vehemently to Mallory who wrote to Secretary of War Randolph, who ordered the guns returned. The incident did little to improve the already strained relationship between the army and navy at New Orleans. The returned guns, along with others acquired, brought the *Louisiana's* armament eventually to include seven 32-pounder rifles, three 9-inch smoothbores, four 8-inch smoothbores, and two 7-inch rifles.[14]

By January of 1862—the month stipulated for the *Louisiana's* completion—she was far from being finished. Late in the month, Mallory instructed Lieutenant Robert D. Minor, chief of the Naval Ordnance Laboratory in New Orleans, to inspect the *Louisiana* and report on her progress. On January 31, Minor wrote his chief: *The Louisiana will be launched on Monday or Wednesday the third or fifth of February—no machinery in—but all ready to be put on board ... no iron on the roof, but the two layers of T-rails are ready and will be put on after she is launched. Men are working on the launching ways to take advantage of the rise in the river. Roof work is progressing and will be complete (24 inches thick) in 8 or 9 days...pilothouses forward and aft to be built.... In three weeks she will be ready for her armament. The vessel has great capacity for fuel, water, and provisions.*[15]

Finally, on February 6, with a large cheering crowd lining the levee, the CSS *Louisiana* was launched and slid majestically broadside into the river. She was, however, far from being completed. On March 2, Mallory officially assigned McIntosh as her captain. The *Louisiana's* commander began working relentlessly with Murray to acquire the materials needed to turn the wooden vessel, that now felt the cold waters of the Mississippi flowing beneath her keel, into a formidable armored warship. The storm clouds of war were gathering at the mouth of the Mississippi, however, and it was now a frantic life-and-death race against time.[16]

While workers swarmed over the *Louisiana*, the Tifts were pushing the work forward on the *Mississippi* next door. From Richmond, Mallory continued to telegraph on the progress of the central shaft, and to urge haste in the ironclad's completion:

March 15, 1862

The Tredegar Works have disappointed us terribly. The shaft is not ready, and although promised from day to day, may not be ready for a week. If you can supply its place, do so immediately. Work night and day to get your ship done, without regard to expense.

March 17, 1862

The shaft will leave in two days. Can I do anything to expedite your ship? Work day and night if possible. How near is she done?

March 20, 1852

Nothing from you. Please advise me of progress and push on your ship...day and night. Shaft leaves here in two days. Advise me fully.

March 22, 1862

The shaft leaves on Monday morning, the 25th, complete; a beautiful piece of work. Strained every nerve to finish ship. Expend money to encourage mechanics if essential to speedy completion. Work day and night.[17]

Prior to the end of the year, Mallory had dispatched another exceptionally capable officer, Captain John K. Mitchell, to take command of

Commander John K. Mitchell, in charge of all Confederate naval forces at the time of Farragut's attack on New Orleans.

the Confederate forces around Columbus, Kentucky. By the beginning of 1862, however, the Federal Navy, equipped with ironclads, was forcing its way down the upper Mississippi and Hollins led his New Orleans squadron northward to meet them. Mitchell was left in command of the naval forces at the Crescent City, which was now comprised of only the two unfinished ironclads. On March 21, Mallory directed Commander Arthur Sinclair to report to Mitchell, and assume command of the *Mississippi* as soon as she was finished.[18]

In his instructions to the commander, Mallory stressed the urgency of completing the ironclad: *This will, it is expected, prove a very formidable vessel, and every possible exertion must be made to complete her at the earliest moment. You will at once take such measures, in conjunction with Commander Mitchell and the Messrs Tift, as your judgment may approve, for having her battery, ordnance stores, coal, and provisions, etc., ready, so that she may not be detained from active service a day. You will please advise me fully, and the Department relies upon your energy to expedite the work in every possible way.*[19]

Midshipman William W. Wilkinson served on the CSS *Louisiana*.

On April 3, the center shaft, "a beautiful piece of work," as Mallory described it, finally arrived from Richmond. It was immediately sent to the machine shop where workers began fitting the couplings and propeller.

Meanwhile, workers toiled night and day on the *Louisiana* which was moored alongside the levee. In early April, Farragut's powerful fleet had crossed the bar at the mouth of the Mississippi, and now occupied the lower portion of the river. Most Confederate naval experts held little hope that the guns of Forts Jackson and St. Philip would be able to stop a determined enemy advance. On April 5, Secretary Mallory telegraphed Captain William C. Whittle, commander of the navy yard at New Orleans: *Work day and night to get the Louisiana and the Mississippi ready for action. The preparation of ordnance stores and the drilling of the crew should all progress simultaneously. Not an hour must be lost. Spare neither men nor money.*[20]

On April 18, Commander David Porter's mortar schooners opened fire on Fort Jackson with their huge 13-inch mortars. Anchored behind a neck of wooded land below the fort and out of sight of the Confederates, they directed their fire aided by lookouts perched in their mastheads. With Union mortar shells now pounding Fort Jackson, it was determined that the *Mississippi* had to be launched as soon as possible. The Tifts had delayed her launching for as long as possible in order to install the center shaft and propeller. Now, however, it was imperative to get her in the water where she might be towed to a place of safety should the enemy succeed in passing the forts.

On the same day that Porter's boats opened fire, several steamers tied on to the unfinished *Mississippi* and attempted to pull her into the river. The more they strained, however, the more the ways sank into the soft ground beneath her, and the heavy warship refused to budge. That night, a report reached the Tifts that a foreman and two

Major General Mansfield Lovell, Confederate army commander at New Orleans.

The Library of Congress

workmen, on inspecting the ways, had discovered a locust pin which had been driven through the ship's hull and into the way, holding her fast. By the light of a lantern, the pin was drilled out. The Tifts suspected sabotage, but Pierce later scoffed at the report, claiming that he had inspected the ways that night and had found nothing amiss. Nevertheless, the following morning, hydraulic rams were added to the power of the steamers and the *Mississippi* slid smoothly into the river.[21]

On Easter Sunday morning, April 20, the still unfinished *Mississippi* floated alongside the levee, while nearby, steam could be heard hissing in the *Louisiana's* cavernous engine room. Major General Mansfield Lovell, Confederate military commander at New Orleans, at the request of Brigadier General Johnson J. Duncan at Fort Jackson, had ordered Whittle to move the *Louisiana* the seventy miles down river to help defend the forts. While protesting that the ironclad was still far from finished, Whittle had given instructions to Mitchell to move the *Louisiana* at once. The first test, therefore, of the ironclad's engines and paddle wheels would be on her maiden voyage. Even as engineers prepared to start the engines, the ringing of hammers and other tools echoed throughout the vessel as mechanics continued to work on her complicated machinery. Only her center wheels were connected, but when sufficient steam was raised, Commander McIntosh ordered the lines cast off. His intent was to steam upriver a few hundred yards before making a wide turn, and then heading downstream.[22]

Lieutenant John Wilkinson, later to become famous as a captain of blockade runners, had been assigned to the *Louisiana* as her executive officer. Writing after the war, he described the condition of the uncompleted ironclad: *After a few days' service on board the Jackson, I was ordered on board the Louisiana then lying alongside the levee at New Orleans. Her battery was not mounted, and the mechanics were at work upon her unfinished armor and machinery. Much was to be done, and with the most limited facilities; but many obstacles had been surmounted and affairs were progressing favorably, when we received orders from Commodore Whittle to proceed down the river as far as the forts. Our wheels were in working order, but a great deal was to be done to the propellers, and the crew were still engaged in mounting the guns. But Commodore Whittle, though cognizant of our condition, was compelled against his judgment, to yield to the urgent telegrams of General Duncan to send the Louisiana down the river. We had been unable to man the ship with sailors, for although many of this class belonged to the various volunteer companies around New Orleans, their commanding officers were not disposed to part with them.... Our regular crew being too small to man the battery, we gladly accepted the services of the "Crescent Artillery," (Captain T. H. Hutton, commanding) a fine volunteer company raised in New Orleans. Two river steamboats were assigned to the Louisiana for the purpose of towage if necessary, and for the accommodation of the mechanics who were still at work on board.*[23]

With the heavy ironclad now floating free from the levee, McIntosh signaled the engine room to start the engines. Slowly, as the steam valves were opened, the two large center wheels began to turn. With the aid of the two steamers, the massive vessel was nudged toward the center of the river which was running at about six knots due to the heavy spring rains. McIntosh ordered full power. The wheels picked up speed, and as they did, sent water cascading between the uncaulked planks of the wheel housing, deluging the gun deck.

First Lieutenant John Wilkinson, executive officer on the CSS *Louisiana.*
Scharf, *History of the Confederate States Navy*

Water ran down the hatches, whose coamings had not yet been installed, and threatened to flood the magazine. With the paddle wheels churning at full power, and anxious crewmen watching as water rose over their shoe tops on the gun deck, another more serious problem presented itself. The two engines that should have turned the propellers were not installed, and without their steering effect, the *Louisiana* would not answer to the helm. In addition, much to McIntosh's disgust, the ironclad could not even stem the current and was being pushed slowly downstream. The *Louisiana* was uncontrollable. McIntosh ordered the engines shut down and called for assistance from the steamers.[24]

On the morning of April 21, the *Louisiana*, under tow, finally reached a spot on the right (east) side of the river just above Fort St. Philip and was secured to the bank by hawsers. Here carpenters and mechanics continued to swarm over her trying feverishly to rush her completion. That night, in the glare of lanterns and pine torches, the ironclad's guns were laboriously mounted. The gunners of the Crescent Artillery were perplexed, however, when they discovered that, due to the narrowness of the gun ports, the pieces could be elevated only approximately five degrees and had limited traverse. Nevertheless, they proceeded at a hectic pace. Caulkers and carpenters finally stopped the leaks in the wheel housing, and the machinists began to install the engines that would power the propellers. The crew worked incessantly, night and day, and was aided by men from the gunboat *McRae*. With mortar shells

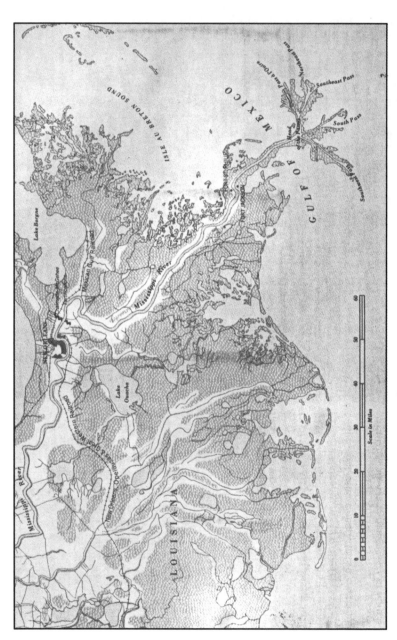

Map of the lower delta region of the Mississippi showing New Orleans, Fort Jackson, Fort St. Philip, and the Head of the Passes.

Official Records Navy

raining on Fort Jackson, and Farragut's immense fleet concentrated below the forts, the question remained: would there be enough time?[25]

Meanwhile, General Duncan had been pleading with Commander Mitchell to move the *Louisiana* to a spot below Fort St. Philip, and from here to open fire on the mortar boats that were pounding Fort Jackson. Mitchell refused, pointing out the immobility of the ironclad with her propellers still not connected, and the fact that her guns could not be elevated enough to reach Porter's mortar boats. By the 23rd, after exhausting and superhuman work, the mechanics had succeeded in installing the remaining engines, and even though they were still not connected to the propellers, Mitchell notified Duncan that he would move the *Louisiana* below the fort on the morrow. It would prove, however, to be too late.

At 3:30 a.m., on the early morning of April 24, 1862, the dark but starlit night was shattered by the guns of Fort Jackson which opened fire on obscure shapes moving up the river. (The intent here is not to render a detailed account of the Battle of New Orleans, but rather to chronicle only the part played by the *Louisiana*.) Within seconds, Fort St. Philip, just below where the *Louisiana* was moored, opened fire. Alarm bells rang on the Southern vessel; orders were shouted by startled officers as lanterns were lit on the ironclad's gun deck. Confederate sailors and artillerymen, who had been sleeping by their guns, fumbled in the flickering light to load their giant pieces. Once accomplished, willing hands of the gun crew heaved on the heavy tackle to run the guns out through the narrow ports. Within a few short minutes, two 8-inch smoothbores and a rifled 32-pounder were ready to fire on the starboard side. Simultaneously, the two 9-inch smoothbores and the 7-inch rifle at the bow were reported ready. Because the *Louisiana* was tied to the riverbank on her port beam, her starboard and bow guns

The CSS *Louisiana*, with the help of tugs, on the way to Fort St. Philip.
Battles and Leaders

would be the only ones that she could bring to bear on the approaching enemy.

Farragut's warships and Porter's mortar boats (downstream) returned the fire of the forts, and the darkness turned to orange and crimson as streaks of flame stabbed across the water toward the Southern positions. A Confederate captain, stationed in the water battery at Fort Jackson, later wrote: *The mortar shells shot upward from the mortar boats, rushed to the apexes of their flight, flashing the lights of their fuses as they revolved, paused an instant, and then descended upon our works like hundreds of meteors, or burst in mid-air, hurling their jagged fragments in every direction. The guns on both sides kept up a continual roar for nearly an hour, without a moment's intermission and produced a shimmering illumination, which though beautiful and grand, was illusive in its effect upon the eye, and made it impossible to judge accurately the distance of the moving vessels from us.* [26]

On the *Louisiana*, the Crescent City gunners stood anxiously by their guns with firing lanyards in hand. Approximately ten minutes after the commencement of the firing from the forts, they discerned the ghostly shape of a Federal warship moving through the smoke. She was coming upriver fast, and when she crossed the muzzles of their bow guns, they fired. Shafts of orange-white flame flashed across the *Louisiana's* bow, and three shells streaked toward the enemy vessel. The ironclad shuttered from the recoil, and bluish-white smoke swirled about the swaying lanterns on the gun deck. Nervously trying to recall

Mortar boats attacking the water-battery at Fort Jackson.
Battles and Leaders

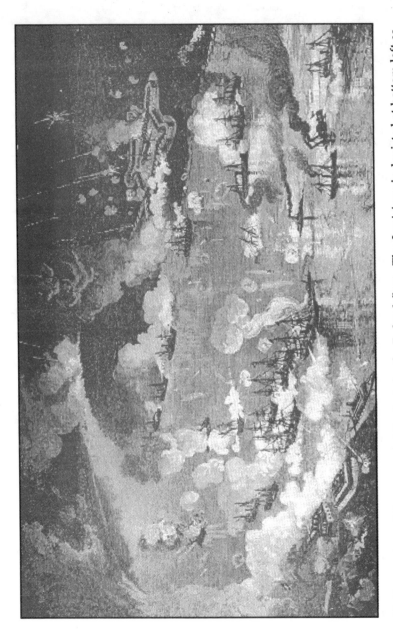

Bird's-eye view of the passage of the forts by the Federal fleet. The *Louisiana* is depicted at bottom left as she fires into Farragut's ships.

Battles and Leaders

the steps that they had learned only recently, the gun crews quickly began to reload. At that moment, another thunderous roar resounded through the casemate. The starboard battery had opened fire!

The Federal vessels came quickly now, and as each one passed, they sent their broadsides thundering into the side of the *Louisiana*. Shell and canister exploded and crashed against her iron casemate. Sharpshooters, posted above the gun deck, were cut and wounded by flying splinters of iron as the heavy canister rounds punched through the thin sheet-iron bulwark. The green Confederate gunners responded in kind, and their explosive rounds tore into the wooden Union vessels where they exploded, causing numerous Federal casualties. One heavy sloop-of-war, possibly the *Hartford*, swung drunkenly toward the *Louisiana*. At point-blank range she fired two 11-inch shells, striking the ironclad on the forward portion of the roof, crushing the railroad iron plating and then exploding into a thousand fiery fragments. The *Louisiana* rocked from the concussion, and men were thrown to the deck. Before the enemy vessel could move away, however, the *Louisiana's* three bow guns sent roaring charges exploding deep into her interior.[27]

When the Federal warship swung in close to the *Louisiana*, McIntosh believed that they were about to be boarded, and he led an armed party topside to repel them. The men had just reached the grating above the gun deck when suddenly a blast of canister swept across the casemate hitting several men, including Commander McIntosh. The *Louisiana's* captain was gravely hurt and was hurriedly carried below. There in the dimly-lit wardroom, surgeons found that both arms and the right knee had been badly shattered. McIntosh's right arm was amputated above the elbow, and he was made as comfortable as circumstances would permit. His wounds proved mortal, unfortunately, for the gallant Confederate commander died four days later.[28]

Lieutenant Wilkinson now assumed command of the ironclad, and her guns continued to hammer the darkened Federal ships as they passed by. Soon, however, the last shadowy image had steamed past, and the thundering guns of the *Louisiana* fell silent. While she had inflicted terrible punishment on those Federal vessels that had come within range of her guns, she could not pursue or destroy them because of her uncompleted machinery. By daylight, all of Farragut's fleet of fourteen warships—except the *Varuna* which had been sunk by the Louisiana state gunboat *Governor Moore*—had successfully passed the forts and was steaming upriver toward New Orleans. Except for the *Louisiana*, the Confederate flotilla had been smashed to pieces.[29]

Seventy miles upstream, Commander Sinclair was determined to try to save the *Mississippi*. Testifying later before the Congressional Investigating Committee, the Confederate officer described his efforts: *On the morning of the 24th, I employed, through the Messrs. Tift, the only two steamers then available—the St. Charles and the Peytona—to come immediately to the ship and endeavor to get her up the river. They did not come, however, until a late hour. During the day I was employed getting everything I could on board the ship, with a view to finishing her up the river, if possible. The steamers came about 8 o'clock at night, and made as an excuse for their failure to come earlier the want of engineers and hands. There was a great deal of confusion in the city at the time. I furnished the steamers with hands and an engineer, and after some difficulty we started. But we found it impossible to do anything with the vessel on account of the strong current. There was a freshet at the time, and this rendered the current much stronger than usual.*

Photographed as a first lieutenant while serving on the *Alabama*, Arthur Sinclair, Jr. earlier served as a captain's clerk for his father who commanded the unfinished *Mississippi*.

We tugged at her the whole of the night unsuccessfully, for, instead of making any headway, we lost ground considerably. Before 4 o'clock the following morning Colonel Beggs, one of the vigilance committee, came on board and offered me assistance in the shape of additional steam power, which he said would be ready at 4 o'clock, and which I willingly accepted; but they never came.[30]

There were other steamers at New Orleans which were considerably more powerful than the *St. Charles* or the *Peytona*, but they had either fled up the river or had been destroyed by their crews. By easing the *Mississippi* over to the east bank of the river and out of the strong current, the tugs were finally able to regain her original mooring along the levee.

Lieutenant James I. Waddell, the officer on the *Mississippi* who was charged with her destruction.

I then made fast the vessel and went up to the city myself in the Peytona for the purpose of getting additional steam power, continued Sinclair with his testimony. *I left an officer on board, Lieutenant (James I.) Waddell, and the naval constructor, Pierce, with orders if the enemy hove in sight during my absence, not to wait for me but to fire the ship. I went to the city and endeavored to get additional steam power. I found on getting there that the crews of the vessels had left them. The captains of some of them informed me that they went to look after their own private concerns. While there I saw the enemy coming up, and I regarded the case as hopeless. I started back to the Peytona for the purpose of returning to the ship and setting her on fire. As I got round the point I saw the flames issuing from her, and was satisfied that all was right. I saw it was impossible to get the ship up, and I fired her according to my orders from Captain Whittle, to prevent her falling into the hands of the enemy.*[31]

The vessel that could have smashed Farragut's wooden ships, and even perhaps broken the blockade along the Gulf coast, now drifted with the rapid current of the river from which she was named. Yellow flames crackled from her gun ports and hatches, while her iron plates lay upon the shield still unfastened, glowing a molten red. Even in her dying agony, she appeared formidable. Admiral Farragut in his official report stated that she was *to be the terror of the seas, and no doubt would have been so to a great extent, but she soon came floating by us all in flames, and passed down the river.*[32]

Even though the Federals had passed up the river, the forts still remained in Confederate hands, and the Stars and Bars still waved defiantly from the *Louisiana*. The workers and machinists had fled at the commencement of the battle, but the naval crew members continued to labor in her engine room connecting the two side shafts to her propellers. Just exactly what Mitchell intended on accomplishing is shrouded in mystery. Some reports indicate he was planning on steaming up the river and attacking the Union warships, much as Franklin Buchanan would do over two years later with the CSS *Tennessee* at Mobile Bay. Others contended that he had planned on taking the ironclad to Mobile, but she was already short of coal and provisions, therefore this seems unlikely.

By extreme exertions, the propellers were finally connected, although Mitchell and his officers harbored little confidence that the *Louisiana* would have sufficient motive power to stem the rushing current of the Mississippi. But her test, and perhaps an attack on the enemy upriver was not to be, as Mitchell later explained: *During the night of Sunday, the 27th, we had so far exceeded in operating the propellers that we expected early the next day to make a fair trial of them in connection with the paddle wheels, when at daylight, an officer, sent by General Duncan, came on board to inform me that many of the garrison of Fort Jackson had deserted during the night, that serious disturbances had occurred, and that the disaffection of the men was believed to be general, on account of what appeared to them to have become the desperate character of the defense of the forts. In consequence of this condition of affairs he, General Duncan, had dispatched a flag of truce to Commander Porter, commanding United States naval forces below, offering to surrender the two forts to him on the terms tendered by him the day before, but rejected by General Duncan.*[33]

Needless to recount, Mitchell was dumbfounded by the news. *I at once waited on General Duncan in Fort Jackson to learn from himself the particulars of his course,* he continued. *He informed me that in his offer to surrender the forts he had disclaimed all control over the forces afloat. This unexpected surrender of these important land defenses, seriously compromising the position and very safety of my own command, I expressed to General Duncan my deep regret that a previous knowledge of his intentions to surrender had not been communicated to me, particularly as I expected early in the day to test the full power of the Louisiana under propellers and wheels, and that if successful I might achieve something against the enemy. It was, however, too late; the flag of truce had been dispatched and could not be recalled; but I informed General Duncan that in no event would the enemy be allowed to obtain possession of the Louisiana.*[34]

Mitchell returned to the ironclad and called a meeting of his officers. With the enemy in possession of the river above and below the forts, and with the imminent surrender of these fortifications, the *Louisiana* was essentially isolated and cut off from all supplies or assistance. It would be only a matter of time until she, too, would be captured by the Federals. In addition, with white flags now flying from the ramparts of Forts Jackson and St. Philip, it was questionable whether any attempted offensive action might be regarded as a breach of the

Brigadier General Johnson K. Duncan, commander of Forts
Jackson and St. Philip.

Battles and Leaders

laws of war. With a heavy heart, Mitchell acceded to the recommendations of his officers and ordered Wilkinson to make preparations to
destroy the *Louisiana*.

The white flags of the two Confederate forts sparkled in the morning sunlight of April 28. Down river, two federal steamers, also with
white flags streaming from their mastheads, slowly made their way
up the river to accept the surrender of the gray-clad army garrisons.
Onboard the *Louisiana*, wisps of smoke began to filter from her gun
ports. Soon ugly and thicker black smoke was forcing its way out of
every hatch and crevice. The dull glow of flames could be seen through
the open ports, and now the smoke was billowing to enormous heights.
Her lines securing her to the riverbank caught fire and burned through,
setting her adrift in the swirling waters of the river. She drifted downstream toward the Federal squadron, and at 10:45 a.m., her 10,000
pounds of powder exploded with a horrendous roar. Pieces of the

mighty ironclad flew hundreds of feet in the air, some landing on Fort St. Philip where many were injured and one man was killed. When the smoke, debris, and water spray had abated, the CSS *Louisiana* was gone.[35]

The hopes and aspirations of the infant Confederate Navy to be able to protect the largest city of their country was shattered with the destruction of the *Mississippi* and the *Louisiana*. The Battle of New Orleans, and the loss of the two Southern ironclads, as one author has contended, was truly "The Night the War was Lost."

The destruction of the CSS *Louisiana.*

Battles and Leaders

Chapter Five

Victory at Galveston

When the Lone-star state of Texas seceded from the Union on February 1, 1861, it did not take long before it became painfully apparent that the state's 385 miles of coastline was extremely vulnerable to enemy assaults. With most of the troops from the state shipped off to Virginia, where it appeared the war would be fought, there were precious few Texans left to guard against a Federal attack. To add to the state's anxiety, the Lincoln government in April of 1861, declared a blockade of the entire Southern coast from Virginia to the Rio Grande. Proclaiming a blockade was one thing; having a sufficient number of warships to enforce it, however, was another. With most of the Federal attention focused on the harbors of Charleston, Mobile, and New Orleans, and with few vessels available to guard the approaches to Galveston, the port became a haven for blockade runners where the profits were high and the risks were low. Even before the war, the city had established itself as the busiest anchorage on the Texas coast. Of the 300,000 bales of cotton produced in Texas in 1860, 200,000 were shipped from Galveston.

On August 14, 1861, an order was issued from the adjutant and inspector general's office in Richmond, directing Commander William Wallace Hunter of the Confederate Navy to proceed to Galveston and to report to General Earl Van Dorn, commander of what few army troops there were in the district. Hunter's responsibilities included the overall command of all naval forces in the area. The naval commander was subject to the orders of the military chief of the district, but his orders directed him *to employ such boats propelled by steam or otherwise, as the service, in his judgment, rendered necessary.* He was to *take measures to guard against any surprise by the enemy in the harbor and bay of Galveston.* Hunter was also instructed to fortify Virginia Point, across the bay from Galveston Island, and to protect the long two and one-half mile railroad bridge that connected the island with the mainland.[1]

J. Thomas Scharf, in his *History of the Confederate Navy*, relates that: *Commander Hunter was exceedingly active, and directed all his energies and talents to fortifying Galveston, Brownsville, Pass Cavailo, and Sabine Pass. There were no vessels under his command, except a few improvised "cotton-clad" river steamers and with those he rendered efficient service to the army in transporting troops and munitions of war, and guarding the coast from the marauding expeditions of the enemy. The "mosquito fleets" of Texas cotton-clad steamers had many severe engagements with the enemy during the war, and their brave actions form a noteworthy series of episodes.*[2]

Both Brigadier General Paul O. Hébert, who had assumed command of the army forces when Van Dorn was transferred east, and Commander Hunter believed that Galveston was indefensible. Accordingly, they concentrated what few forces they had on Virginia Point and began fortifying the mouth of the Trinity River where it empties into the bay. All guns, except one 10-inch Columbiad which had to be left at Fort Point, were removed to the mainland, and all stores and ammunition were likewise salvaged. By the fall of 1862, with a Federal fleet threatening the city from out in the Gulf, Galveston had become a ghost town, with most of its inhabitants having fled.[3]

At daylight on October 4, 1862, eight Federal vessels were visible off the bar of Galveston Bay. They included: the *Westfield*, a side-wheel steamer with six guns; the *Harriet Lane*, another side-wheeler carrying five guns; the *Owasco* with five guns; the *Clifton* carrying eight guns, and the mortar schooner *Henry James*. Three schooners loaded with supplies accompanied the Union flotilla. The Federal armada was under the command of Commodore William B. Renshaw who flew his pennant from the *Westfield*. At 7:00 a.m., the *Harriet Lane*, flying a white flag, crossed the bar and steamed for the entrance to the bay. Confederate soldiers watched apprehensively until she came opposite their position on Fort Point, at which time they opened fire with their lone 10-inch Columbiad, sending its shot whistling across the *Lane's* bow as a signal to stop. Her commander, Lieutenant Jonathan M. Wainwright, immediately complied and the Federal warship came to anchor.[4]

Wainwright sent an officer in a small boat ashore who asked for an immediate interview with the Confederate commander. Colonel Joseph

J. Cook hurried to Fort Point and was told by the Federal naval officer that Wainwright desired a messenger to be dispatched by boat to Renshaw's flagship in order to receive a message from the fleet's commander. Not having a boat at the Point, Cook returned to Galveston to make the arrangements. After much difficulty, the Confederate colonel finally located a small skiff and dispatched two officers on their mission. By this time, however, Lieutenant Wainwright had grown impatient. Turning the *Harriet Lane* around, he steamed back over the bar to communicate with Commodore Renshaw. Soon Southern soldiers at the Point were aghast to see the entire Federal fleet, white flags flying from their peaks, cross the bar and head for the harbor. Cook's messenger boat was making slow progress toward the oncoming Union warships, when suddenly the big Columbiad on Fort Point thundered again, sending its shell streaking across the lead Federal's bow.

This time the enemy vessels refused to stop, and ignoring the white flags still flying from their own masts, opened fire on the lone gun in Fort Point and the positions on the narrow neck of land stretching between the fort and the city. The green Texas troops manning the Columbiad had never before been under fire, and with shells from twenty heavy guns bursting around them, quickly spiked their piece and fled toward the city. By this time Renshaw's fleet had come up with the Confederate flag-of-truce boat carrying the two Southern officers, and he ordered his flotilla to drop anchor and cease firing.

An uneasy silence now prevailed, as the two Confederate officers conferred with Commander Renshaw on board the *Westfield*. In his report, Colonel Cook described the results of the meeting: *At about 3:00 p.m. our flag-of-truce messenger returned to the city, bearing a demand from the enemy for the surrender of the city and demanding an immediate answer. I sent a messenger with the answer that I should not surrender the city, directing the messenger also to say to the commander of the fleet that there were many women and children, and to demand time to remove them. After some negotiation it was agreed that no attack should be made upon the city for four days; that during that time we should not construct any new or strengthen any old defenses within the city, and the fleet not to be brought any nearer the city. This arrangement gave us ample time for the removal of all who desired to leave the island, and also for the removal of our troops and material of every kind.*[5]

Renshaw had no troops with which to take possession of the city, but he effectively controlled every part of the town and island that was within reach of his guns. At the end of the agreed four-day truce, the Federal commander was left with a stalemate. As a token gesture by Colonel Cook to avoid a useless bombardment, Renshaw was given permission to dispatch a detail to raise the American flag over the

Major General John B. Magruder, commander of Confederate
forces at the Battle of Galveston, January 1, 1863.

Customs House for a period of a few hours. With this done, the Union
fleet settled down into an occupying force, closing the port and making access to the mainland over the railroad bridge a hazardous journey for the few Confederate troops still remaining in the city. Heavy
planking was laid down on the bridge, and Confederate cavalry pa-
trols frequently crossed over and visited the city, but for all intents
and purposes, Galveston was now in Union hands.[6]

On November 29, 1862, Major General John Bankhead Magruder,
fresh from his stubborn defense of the Peninsula in Virginia, arrived
to assume command of the Department of Texas. *On my arrival in Texas,*
he wrote, *I found the harbors of this coast in the possession of the enemy from
the Sabine River to Corpus Christi; the line of the Rio Grande virtually
abandoned, most of the guns having been removed from that frontier to San*

Antonio, only about 300 or 400 men remaining at Brownsville. I resolved to regain the harbors if possible and to occupy the valley of the Rio Grande in force....

I remained a day or two in Houston, and then proceeding to Virginia Point, on the mainland, opposite Galveston Island, I took with me a party of 80 men, supported by 300 more, and passing through the city of Galveston at night, I inspected the forts abandoned by our troops when the city was given up. I found the forts open in the rear, and taken in reverse by every one of the enemy's ships in the harbor. They were therefore utterly useless for my purposes. The railway track had been permitted to remain from Virginia Point to Galveston, and by its means I purposed to transport to a position near the enemy's fleet the heavy gun hereinafter mentioned, and by assembling all the movable artillery that could be collected together in the neighborhood, I hoped to acquire sufficient force to be able to expel the enemy's vessels from the harbor.[7]

Meanwhile, acting on Magruder's orders, Commander Hunter was making every effort to arm several of the boats, which had been purchased by the Confederate government, on the Trinity River. Two iron-strapped river steamers, which were being operated by the Texas Marine Department, were reasonably large and could carry a sizable boarding party. These two boats, the CSS *Bayou City* and the CSS *Neptune* were moved to Harrisburg, Texas, on the Buffalo Bayou where workers began building bulwarks of lumber and cotton bales. Two smaller vessels, the CSS *John F. Carr* and the CSS *Lucy Gwin*, were fitted out at Houston as transports.

Workers first stripped off the upper cabins and pilothouse of the *Bayou City*, and cotton bales were placed on their sides and stacked three tiers high. Another row, two bales high, backed these and provided a protected firing platform for sharpshooters. Boarding planks were constructed on each side of the boat and hoisted beside the smokestacks where they could be dropped instantly on an enemy vessel. Mounted on a pivot, and protruding ominously from among the cotton bales on the bow, was an old 32-pounder which had been reworked into a rifle. A company of cavalry, Colonel Tom Green's 5th Texas, and a number of volunteers from Colonel Arthur Bagby's 7th Texas Cavalry, all went aboard as sharpshooters. These troopers had fought well as part of the Sibley Brigade during the New Mexico campaign. From a distance the 165 foot *Bayou City*, under the command of Captain Henry S. Lubbock, who held the rank of master in the Confederate Navy, now resembled an ironclad ram.[8]

The *Neptune* sported two small 24-pounder howitzers, and she, too, was "armored" with cotton bales. Commanded by Captain William H. Sangster, the *Neptune* also carried her complement of sharpshooters, these being under the charge of Colonel Bayley of the 7th Texas Cavalry. The *Lucy Gwinn* and the *John F. Carr* had cotton bales protecting their engines and machinery, but being designed to act as tenders, were otherwise unarmed. All the "Horse-Marines," as the men described themselves, were armed with Enfield rifles and double-barreled shotguns. The Confederate naval force of approximately 250 men was under the command of one-time riverboat captain, Major Leon Smith, who, records indicate, had also served in the Texas Navy during that republic's struggle for independence. Magruder had met Smith while in California, and being impressed with his knowledge of steam boating, offered him a position on his staff.[9]

Meanwhile, Magruder was gathering his land forces. Again drawing upon the Sibley Brigade, the Confederate commander tapped the untried 20th Texas Infantry, the 21st Texas Infantry Battalion, and detachments of the 2nd and 26th Texas Cavalry for the land attack. All of these units were preparing to leave for Louisiana, but had been delayed for lack of transportation. Magruder scraped together all the artillery pieces he could find, and by December, he had accumulated fourteen field pieces, six larger siege guns, and one 13-inch Dahlgren which he had mounted on a railroad flatcar.

Magruder's haste in preparing his forces was well-founded, for on Christmas morning, 240 members of Companies D, G, and I of the 42nd Massachusetts Infantry Regiment, under the command of Colonel Isaac S. Burrell, landed on Kuhn's Wharf at the end of 18th Street. Working feverishly, the New England troops ripped out the planking leading from the wharf to the main dock area, which was named "The Strand," and proceeded to erect barricades and firing positions on the wharf itself. With the heavy naval guns at their backs, Colonel Burrell was confident that his men could successfully resist any determined Southern attack. Having learned through informants that more troops were on their way as reinforcements, Magruder realized he had to act quickly.[10]

Wednesday evening, December 31, 1862, was a cold and clear night in Texas. A brilliant full moon cast its soft rays over the placid waters of Galveston Bay where the Federal warships swung gently at their anchors. On board each vessel, deck watches began their usual rounds. Hammocks were lowered by tired Union sailors, who hoped the persistant rumors of a "rebel" attack would prove untrue for at least one more night. On Virginia Point, however, Confederate Army forces were on the move. Horses and mules strained at their harnesses as they pulled the six heavy siege guns across the wooden planking laid down on the long railroad bridge. Gray-clad troops trudged along beside, while other willing hands pushed the old railroad flatcar ahead of them carrying the 13-inch Dahlgren. Captain S. T. Fontaine and the men of the 1st Texas Heavy Artillery had the farthest to go. Their objective was to occupy Fort Point at the mouth of the harbor, and from that position, direct the fire of their heavy guns on the Federal fleet in the bay. Captain George R. Wilson's six siege guns would engage the Massachusetts troops on Kuhn's Wharf, while the big Dahlgren was stealthily run up to a point only 300 yards from the *Harriet Lane* which was anchored off the end of 29th Street. The remaining artillery was positioned within the town where they could bring their fire to bear on the other Federal vessels in the bay. In all, five formidable warships lay off the town, their 30 heavy guns covering the Northern troops on the wharf. Meanwhile, Colonel Cook had assembled a determined attack force of 500 men whose mission was to storm the Union troops barricaded on the wharf. Magruder's plans were to have everyone in place by midnight, at which time he would give the signal to open fire.[11]

Leon Smith, commander of the Confederate naval forces at the Battle of Galveston, Texas. Although never holding an official commission from the Confederate Navy, Smith was most often referred to in official reports as a navy captain or an army major. To confuse the reader even further, he is pictured here in the regulation uniform of a Confederate Navy lieutenant.
Courtesy of Rosenberg Library, Galveston, Texas

By the appointed hour, Major Smith and his cotton-clad flotilla had reached a point just north of Pelican Island. Fearful that he would be spotted in the bright moonlight—he was, for the *Harriet Lane* had flashed the alarm—Smith ordered his forces to withdraw northward several miles up the bay. With the faint sound of hissing steam audible from the engine rooms, the weary Confederate Horse Marines dropped down behind their cotton bales for a short period of rest, while Smith and his commanders waited anxiously for the opening sound of the land attack.

Midnight came and went, and all was still quiet in Galveston. Confederate soldiers, careful to stay out of the bright moonlight, huddled in the shadows of the buildings and in the alleyways along the waterfront. Weapons were checked and double checked. Some men, aided by the moonlight, wrote letters to their families and sweethearts. Waiting was always the most difficult, and it was now well past the appointed time and the order still had not come. Unknown to those anxiously awaiting the signal, was the fact that Magruder had decided to delay the assault in order to be certain that Captain Fontaine had reached his position at Fort Point. By 4:00 a.m., the moon finally slipped below the horizon, and a thin mist spread its veil over the darkened bay. While their horses were hurried behind some of the brick buildings, Texas gunners jostled their pieces to more advantageous firing positions and squinted across their sights at the enemy vessels still faintly visible by the light of the stars. A little after 4:00 a.m., General Magruder walked to the center siege cannon located at the end of 20th Street and pulled the lanyard. The heavy gun responded with a thunderous roar, and almost immediately, the whole Confederate line exploded in a sheet of flame as every Southern gun opened up. The Battle of Galveston had begun.[12]

It did not take the Federals long to reply. Within minutes every gun that had the range was sending charges of grape and canister whistling through the midst of the Confederates on The Strand. The deadly iron balls tore into buildings, and flesh alike. Cries of the wounded mixed with the dust and smoke as Texas gunners struggled to return the fire. The Union gunners began to alternate between shells and canister, and the streets and alleys leading to The Strand became a fiery death trap of massive explosions and streaking canister.

Four miles to the north, the thunderous discharges were distinctly heard. Smith, shouting into the *Bayou City's* speaking tube, yelled for the engine room to, "Give me all the steam you can crack on!" The *Neptune* was signaled and together, the two cottonclad's paddle wheels churned the water to foam as they began to pick up speed. Black smoke poured from their stacks as engines puffed and throbbed, while high pressure steam screamed from escape valves. The sleepy Horse Marines were now wide awake, and with dry mouths and pounding hearts, they scrambled for their positions behind the cotton bales.[13]

On The Strand things were not going well for Magruder's Texans. Other Federal warships had edged in closer to the wharves and now at less than 300 yards were sending their charges tearing into the Southern positions. Some Confederate gun crews had abandoned their pieces, while others struggled bravely to maintain their fire. Even the heavy Dahlgren on the flatcar had been abandoned. Some damage had been inflicted on the enemy vessels, but not enough to drive them off.

At about this time Colonel Cook led his 500-man storming party on a desperate bid to dislodge the Massachusetts troops barricaded on Kuhn's Wharf. The green troops of the 20th Texas immediately ran into trouble. Wading through the cold water from The Strand to the wharf, they attempted to raise their scaling ladders only to find that they had miscalculated the depth of the water and the ladders were too short. Fire from the Union ships combined with the musket fire from the 42nd Massachusetts spread panic among the floundering Texans, and they scrambled for any cover they could find.

Magruder knew it would be suicide to try to keep his troops and gunners in position at daylight, and so sent orders for his men to begin falling back. Exhausted and dazed Confederate troops, many encrusted with blood, dust, and powder stumbled through the town, some not stopping until they reached the Gulf shore. The decision to shield the horses behind the buildings proved fortuitous, for most gun crews were able to retrieve their pieces. Captain Fontaine's guns, however, which had been severely exposed at Fort Point, were spiked and abandoned.[14]

Suddenly, as daylight began to reveal the carnage and destruction around them, a feeble cheer arose among the Southern troops. Off to the north, through the smoke and early morning haze, came the Horse Marines!

"Puffing and snorting from their high-pressure steam," the Confederate cotton-clads drove straight for the Union vessels. Rosin and turpentine had been thrown into the furnaces of the two vessels to increase their speed. When the *Bayou City* and the *Neptune* drew within range, their bows suddenly were enveloped in smoke and flame as the 32-pounder and the howitzers let fly at the Federals. While the Union gunners on board the *Harriet Lane* hurried to pivot their pieces to meet this new threat, Texas cavalrymen on the *Bayou City* had another round loaded, and with a jerk of the lanyard, Captain Wier sent it streaking toward the *Harriet Lane*. His aim was true, the shell tore through the side of the Union gunboat knocking a hole in her big enough for a man to crawl through. Someone shouted for Captain Wier

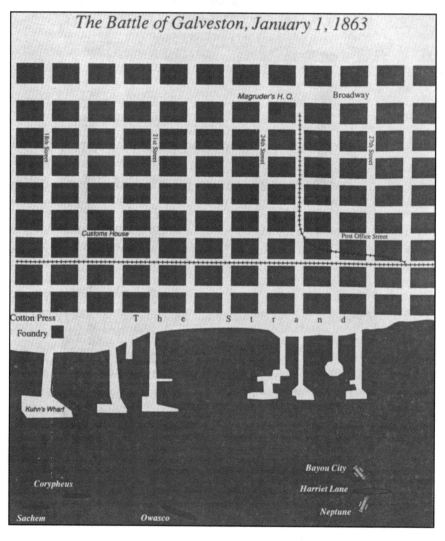

Map of the Galveston waterfront showing Kuhn's Wharf and the position of the opposing vessels.

to give them another New Year's present, and with a reply, "Well here goes your New Year's present!" the old 32-pounder exploded in a mass of flames, sparks, and spinning pieces of jagged iron. When the smoke cleared, Captain Wier and several others lay lifeless on the deck, their bodies torn to pieces by the exploding gun.[15]

On they came like infuriated beasts, the *Bayou City* slightly in the lead. By now they were within range of the Enfield rifles of the "Horse Marines," and they opened a blistering fire upon the Federal warship. Blue-clad sailors scurried for cover, abandoning any attempt to return the fire. Captain Lubbock shouted for the pilot, Captain Michael McCormick, to ram the Union vessel. *The Harriet Lane was lying at anchor with steam on, swinging with a strong ebb tide, bow to the west,* McCormick later reported. *I was instructed to endeavor to so hit her as to allow the men a chance to board. Going with a strong ebb tide I dared not run against her bow, so I endeavored to strike forward of the larboard wheelhouse. Owing to the position of the Lane and the strength of the ebb tide, I missed my aim, struck a glancing blow and passed by. The wheelhouse and upper works of the Harriet Lane, being very strong, tore off the outside planking of the Bayou City's larboard wheelhouse and side.*[16]

Blasts from double-barreled shotguns now mixed with the Enfields, as crewmen swung axes to cut the lines holding the port boarding ramp. The interval proved too great, and the ramp splashed into the water where it swung to the rear and was smashed to pieces by the *Bayou City's* revolving wheel.

While the *Bayou City* made a slow turn to port, and crewmen tore frantically at the wreckage in an effort to free the port wheel, the *Neptune* bore down on the beleaguered *Harriet Lane*. Captain Sangster ordered his helmsman to bring the bow a little more to port for a better ramming angle, when without warning, enemy cannon fire struck the *Neptune*, sending cotton bales flying and deadly wooden splinters spinning across the deck. With a full head of steam, the charging *Neptune* slammed hard into the *Harriet Lane*, ten feet behind her starboard paddle wheel. Men of the 7th Texas Cavalry, having been thrown to the deck, struggled unsuccessfully to grapple and secure the enemy vessel. Other Union warships, notably the *Owasco*, approached in an attempt to aid their stricken comrade, and a devastating fire was poured into the *Neptune*. Sangster recognized immediately that his boat was in trouble, and passed orders to the engine room to reverse engines and back away. Water poured in through the shattered bow and several holes punched in her side by the shots from the *Owasco*. The *Neptune* was sinking, and Sangster ordered her steered for the shallow water off 32nd Street. There, as she settled into the mud, her Horse Marines, standing knee deep in water, continued to pour their musket fire into the *Harriet Lane*.[17]

By this time the crew of the *Bayou City* had cleared the debris from her port wheel, and Lubbock ordered full speed toward the *Harriet*

Lane which was trying desperately to go back down the channel. With the musket fire from the *Neptune* keeping the Federal bluejackets from their guns, the *Bayou City* was able to maintain her collision course without being fired upon. With a tremendous crash, the Confederate boat drove her pointed bow deep into the port paddle wheel of the *Harriet Lane*. The crash sent stunned men on both ships tumbling across the decks as iron and wooden pieces hurtled through the air. The Federal vessel heeled far over to starboard. Timbers buckled and broke as the iron wheel braces impaled the *Bayou City*, locking the two vessels together.

Major Smith scrambled to the shattered bow and began slashing at the netting with his cutlass. Cutting the ropes free, he called for his men to follow him and bounded onto the deck of the *Harriet Lane*. With a cheer, the Texas troops downed the rest of the netting, and with pistols in hand, they tumbled aboard. The scene on the Federal vessel was one of absolute carnage. Evidence of the deadly rifle and shotgun fire was everywhere. Several dead crew members lay sprawled across the deck, along with their captain, Commander Wainwright. The *Harriet Lane's* executive officer, Lieutenant Commander Edward Lea, lay dying with five bullets in his abdomen. As the excited Texans surveyed the scene of destruction, a Federal sailor stepped quietly out from behind a door, raised his hands, and surrendered the ship.

Once the commander of the *Owasco*, the closest Union warship to the *Harriet Lane*, realized what had happened, he ordered his ship under way in an effort to recapture her. Soon the *Owasco's* guns were delivering a hot fire at the *Harriet Lane*. From a distance of only a thousand yards, the *Owasco's* powerful 11-inch Dahlgren hurled round after round of shell and canister at the Confederate boats. Gray-clad troops scurried for cover. Several men attempted to train the *Lane's* guns on the *Owasco*, but the Federal warship was listing so badly from the collision that the guns could not be brought to bear. Confederate Enfields began to bark, their fire swelling in intensity as more and more Texans fought savagely to retain their prize. Union sailors on the *Owasco* were soon driven from their guns by the intense fusillade, and their commander wisely ordered his vessel to back away.[18]

An uneasy quiet now settled over the bay. A white flag fluttered from the stern of the *Harriet Lane* while the Horse Marines, fearful that the Federals would renew the attack, worked frantically to separate the two vessels. It was no use, for the bow of the *Bayou City* was jammed tightly into the wheel braces of the *Harriet Lane*. The *John F. Carr* was called, and passing a line, the tender attempted unsuccessfully to pull the two boats apart. Finally the *John F. Carr* began dragging the two antagonists slowly toward the 27th Street Wharf where Texas troops

The *Bayou City* crashes into the *Harriet Lane*.

Major Leon Smith's Texans fight their way aboard the *Harriet Lane.*

gathered on the bow and tried rocking them apart. The stem of the *Bayou City*, however, still would not budge. It would take the skill of several mechanics and carpenters to eventually separate the two vessels.

While the Confederates struggled to untangle the two warships, Captain Lubbock and Major Smith initiated a daring bluff which, if successful, would guarantee complete victory for Magruder's forces. Ordering a small boat lowered, Lubbock along with the *Harriet Lane's* acting master, J. A. Hannum, ordered the oarsmen to row him to the *Clifton*, the closest Union vessel. Clambering aboard the Union warship, Lubbock boldly demanded the surrender of the entire Federal fleet, and instructed the Federal commander to choose one ship which would be allowed to carry the surviving Union crews out of the harbor. Captain Law, the *Clifton's* commander explained that he did not have authority to surrender the entire Union flotilla, but would need to communicate with Commodore Renshaw. Lubbock agreed to this request and stipulated a period of three hours in which Law was to transmit the demand to Renshaw and return with the commander's answer.[19]

While the demand for surrender of all the Northern vessels was being carried to the *Westfield*, Magruder ordered the 130 prisoners from the *Harriet Lane* removed and marched through the town to safety in case the shelling should begin anew. Also removed were the dead and wounded, including the *Lane's* commander, Lieutenant Wainwright, and his executive office, Lieutenant Commander Lea. As the bodies were carried ashore, Texas cavalrymen watched in silence as the stretcher bearing the lifeless form of Lea passed by. Walking next to the litter, in a tragedy of tragedies, was the young Union officer's father, Major A. M. Lea of the Confederate Army, a member of General Magruder's staff. The following day, Wainwright and Lea were buried with full military honors. Confederate and Federal officers stood quietly together, while a grieving Major Lea read the solemn service of the Episcopal Church for the burial of the dead.[20]

Back on Kuhn's Wharf, Colonel Burrell's three companies of the 42nd Massachusetts were still holed up behind their barricades. Peering over the obstructions, Burrell observed a flag-of-truce team approaching headed by Brigadier General William R. Scurry, commander of the 2nd Texas Cavalry. Scurry demanded an immediate surrender of the 240 Union troops on the wharf. Seeing the white flags flying from all the Federal vessels in the bay, Burrell considered that he had little choice and so surrendered his entire command.

It was now after 7:00 a.m. The end of the three-hour truce period was approaching and still no word had come from Commodore

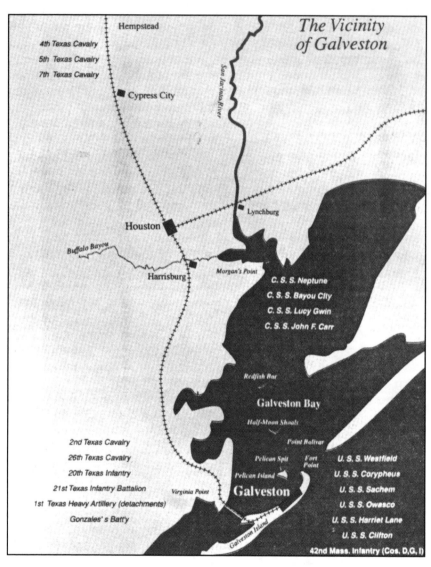

Galveston Bay at the time of the battle.

Renshaw. The Federal commander, whose flagship the *Westfield* had run hard aground near Pelican Island at the beginning of the engagement, was apparently somewhat panic-stricken. He refused to surrender his vessels, but rather than order continued resistance to the Southern forces, instructed Captain Law to inform the commanders of the remaining Union warships to attempt to escape as best they could. Against the remonstration of his own officers, Renshaw ordered his crew aboard the transports *Mary Boardman* and *Saxon* which were nearby and laid a fuse to the magazine intending to blow up the *Westfield*. Once the crew and their belongings were aboard the transports, Renshaw poured turpentine over the deck and lit the fuse. As he descended the ladder into his gig, the *Westfield* exploded in a thunderous blast, killing Renshaw, three other officers, and the entire crew of the waiting boat.[21]

While the Federal commander was destroying his flagship, Captain Law had proceeded down the channel and along the wharves informing the commanders of the four remaining warships, the schooners *Velocity* and *Corypheus* and the screw steamers *Sachem* and *Owasco*, that they must escape or destroy their vessels. Lubbock, still awaiting Renshaw's response to his demand of surrender, hurriedly rowed out to the *Clifton* to confer with Law and to ascertain why the *Westfield* had exploded. Even while the two men spoke, the *Clifton* was getting under way. Angrily Lubbock accused Law of a breach of faith and returned to his boat. Along the wharves, Confederate officers watched in growing astonishment as all the Federal vessels, white flags still flying from their mastheads, began running for the bar.

Southern artillery crews unlimbered their guns, and with some hesitation because of the white flags, opened fire on the fleeing vessels in an attempt to prevent their escape. Major Smith dashed aboard the *John F. Carr* at the 27th Street Wharf, and calling for volunteer sharpshooters, ordered the tender in pursuit. Even at full throttle, however, the little steamer was unable to catch the Union warships before they had crossed the bar. With the rough waves of the Gulf breaking over the fragile bow of the *John F. Carr*, Smith abandoned the chase and returned to the city. He was consoled somewhat by capturing and towing back with him the coal bark *Elias*. It had been six hours since General Magruder had jerked the lanyard of the center artillery piece to signal the beginning of the Confederate attack.[22]

The retaking of Galveston was not without a price. Confederate losses amounted to 27 killed and more than 100 wounded. The *Neptune* sank into the mud off 32nd Street as a result of her collision with the *Harriet Lane*, and the *Bayou City* was badly damaged. Federal forces

The explosion of the USS *Westfield*. The Federal vessel's commander, Commodore William B. Renshaw, was killed in the premature blast.

counted 5 fatalities and 12 wounded on board the *Harriet Lane*. The remaining crew members were taken prisoner. The *Owasco* sustained 16 casualties, and 12 crewmen had died in the premature explosion of the *Westfield*.[23]

The *Harriet Lane* would be repaired and later enter Confederate service as the CSS *Harriet Lane*, while the guns from the *Westfield* were salvaged and employed in the defenses of the city. Galveston, although blockaded, would remain in Southern hands until the very end, becoming the major port of supply for the beleaguered Confederate forces west of the Mississippi. In addition to becoming a safe haven for blockade runners, the recapture of Galveston denied the port to the Federals as a forward base of operations, and more importantly, protected the interior of the state from Northern invasion. Through the courage and determination of the naval force of Leon Smith, Henry Lubbock, William Sangster, and their Horse Marines, the largest port west of New Orleans had been restored to the Confederate cause.

Chapter Six

In March of 1864, two iron-hulled steamers slid gracefully into the Thames River from the Cubitt Town Yard near London, England. Incorporating the latest advances in marine technology, both vessels were destined to play a dramatic role in the last desperate months of the Confederate nation. Christened the *Atlanta* (some sources spell her name *Atalanta*) and the *Edith*, the twin vessels had been constructed by John and William Dudgeon Company, and were obviously intended to enter the risky business of running the blockade into the war-torn Southern states. Both ships were equipped with twin screws, each being driven by its own 100-horsepower steam engine. Driving the propeller shafts at 120 rpm, both engines could be operated together or individually, which by reversing one propeller, enabled the vessels to turn upon their own centers. Fast for their day, their top speeds would prove to be over seventeen knots.[1]

The *Atlanta* was 220 feet long, 24 feet wide, and drew only 9 feet of water when lightly loaded. Grossing 700 tons, her low silhouette displayed two smokestacks and two short, sparsely rigged masts. With the hull painted a light gray, she was almost invisible on a dark night and was ideally suited for her intended role as a blockade runner. (The *Edith* was similar in all respects, except, according to Lieutenant John Wilkinson, the *Atlanta's* last commander, the *Edith* was a "few feet"

110

shorter.) After her shakedown cruise, in which she raced the speedy packet *Empress* across the English Channel from Dover to Calais, winning by thirty minutes, the *Atlanta* steamed down the Thames and along the southern coast of England. On April 9, she headed across the Atlantic and eleven days later arrived at St. George, Bermuda.[2]

On May 3, the *Atlanta*, under the command of the bold Lieutenant Michael P. Usina, slipped into Wilmington through the tightening Federal blockade and delivered her load of dried beef and bacon for the Army of Northern Virginia. Within five days, her cargo was unloaded,

Lieutenant Michael P. Usina, courageous captain of the *Atlanta* before she was converted into the *Tallahassee.*

coal bunkers filled, a load of cotton shipped, and she was on her way to Bermuda. The *Atlanta* made three more inbound trips into Wilmington, arriving there on May 27, June 24, and July 13. Running down the Carolina coast from the north in broad daylight, the *Atlanta* was spotted on one of these trips by a Federal warship which opened fire and steered a converging course to cut the runner off. The unruffled Usina ordered the Confederate flag hoisted, swung the bow to port and charged directly toward the onrushing blockader. The Union commander became so rattled that he ceased firing, turned, and pursued by the unarmed blockade runner, fled out to sea.[3]

Secretary Mallory was well aware of the innovations incorporated in the two speedy vessels, and a few days after the *Atlanta's* arrival in July, he purchased the steamer for $125,000. Mallory's plan was to convert the blockade runner into a swift commerce raider. Little time was lost, and by July 23, the *Atlanta* had been commissioned as the CSS *Tallahassee*, ordnance had been mounted, and John Taylor Wood had been appointed her commander. Her three guns, all on pivots, included a rifled 32-pounder forward, a 100-pounder rifle amidships, and a heavy Parrott rifle aft. Cotton bales were placed on deck to protect her boilers, and after filling her coal bunkers, extra bags of coal were stacked on deck. As an ocean cruiser, however, the *Tallahassee* would leave much to be desired, as she was totally dependent upon her engines for motive power. With their alarmingly high rate of coal consumption

John Taylor Wood, commander of the CSS *Tallahassee.*

and her limited bunker capacity, the cruiser would be limited to a straight line range of only 1,000 miles or less.[4]

John Taylor Wood, the nephew of President Jefferson Davis, was one of the Confederacy's most daring commanders. Born at Fort Snelling, an army outpost in Iowa Territory on August 13, 1830, Wood had been graduated second in his class from the U.S. Naval Academy at Annapolis in 1853. The grandson of Zachary Taylor, twelfth president of the United States, Wood had resigned his commission in the "old navy" when war came, even though his father had remained loyal to the Union. Appointed a first lieutenant, and later a commander in Confederate service, Wood's first assignment was that of gunnery officer in charge of the aft pivot rifle on the CSS *Virginia* during her epic battles in Hampton Roads. Following this, he was active in leading many small boat actions on the Chesapeake Bay and later led a combined force of sailors and marines on an attack that resulted in the capture and destruction of the USS *Underwriter* off New Bern, North Carolina, on February 2, 1864. He was acting as an aide to his uncle, President Davis, when Mallory tapped him for the important task of commanding the *Tallahassee*.⁵ By the beginning of August, Wood had assembled an elite crew of 120 officers and men, most of whom were volunteers from the ironclads of the James River Squadron. First Lieutenant William H. Ward was detailed as executive officer; Chief Engineer John W. Tynan was delegated the important task of operating the engines; and Second Lieutenant Edward Crenshaw, CSMC, commanded the small marine detachment on board. The Confederate Marines were responsible for serving as sharpshooters, assisting in boarding operations, and repelling any enemy attempts to board the cruiser. Wood insisted on strict discipline from his officers and men, and as a consequence, spent ten days drilling his gun crews until he was satisfied with their performance. By Saturday, August 4, the Confederate commander felt his ship was ready, and the *Tallahassee* was cast off from her wharf in front of the city and steamed down the Cape Fear River to Smith's Island, coming to anchor near Fort Fisher. Here, where he could observe the positions of the Federal blockaders, Wood waited for darkness and an opportunity to make a dash for the open sea.⁶

Smith's Island divided the outlets of the river into New Inlet, guarded by Fort Fisher to the north and Old Inlet which was about six miles to the south and protected by Fort Caswell. Wood's plan was to depart through New Inlet, but the passage over the bar would be difficult, he knew, for the *Tallahassee's* draft had been increased to 13.5 feet because of the added weight of the crew, guns, and extra coal.⁷

Toward evening, as the hot August sun dropped slowly behind the western horizon, engineer Tynan ordered the grates shaken and the boiler fires stoked. Firemen swung shovels of soft bituminous coal into the furnaces, and soon the gentle hiss of steam announced that pressure was rising. Crewmen scurried about in the dim light below deck, stowing gear and completing final preparations for sailing. Above, additional crew members gathered by their guns where they checked, and checked again, to ensure that all was ready. Total darkness had now spread its veil over the river, and with a high tide and a moonless sky, it would be a good night to run the blockade. Quietly the anchor was raised, and with a signal from Wood on the bridge, Tynan opened the valves to start the engines. Noiselessly, the *Tallahassee* pushed out into the center of the river.

Everything was secured for sea, Wood wrote. *The lights were all carefully housed, except the binnacle, which was shaded; fires were cleaned and freshened, lookouts were stationed, and the men were at their quarters. The range lights were placed; these, in the absence of all buoys and lights, were necessary in crossing the bar, and were shown only when vessels were going in and out. The Mound, a huge earthwork (Confederate battery below Fort Fisher), loomed up ahead, looking in the darkness like a black cloud resting on the horizon.*[8]

The raider picked up speed as she headed for the bar. Her deck vibrated from the pulsating engines; thick black smoke, which spewed from her stacks, disappeared into the darkness. The anxious lookouts clutched their safety ropes and strained to pierce the gloom through their night glasses. Suddenly, without warning, the bow rose into the air and with a groaning of her iron hull, the cruiser lurched to a grinding halt. The *Tallahassee* had run aground. It took two hours before she could be pulled free, and with the tide falling, Wood canceled the departure attempt and ordered her back to her anchorage near Fort Fisher. The next night, the cruiser's commander tried again, and the *Tallahassee* ran aground so hard that it took three steamers to finally free her. It was now obvious that the heavily laden Confederate raider could never pass out to sea through New Inlet.[9]

The following morning, Wood steamed the *Tallahassee* down the river to a point opposite Smithville. Perhaps Old Inlet would have deeper water. During the remainder of the day, the cruiser's commander carefully studied the positions of the Federal blockaders through his telescope. Although he could not see them all, there were, at this late stage of the war, at least 50 Union warships patrolling the waters off the port of Wilmington. Those that were visible were the slower but heavily armed vessels that comprised what was known as the inner ring. Waiting beyond the horizon, 50 miles out to sea, was another ring of fast cruisers positioned so that the runners could be apprehended at daylight. Writing after the war, Wood described the qualities that were essential for a commander if he expected to survive these cordons of enemy warships: *The captain of a successful blockade runner needed to be a thorough seaman and a skilled navigator. His work required boldness, decision in emergencies, and the faculty of commanding and inspiring the confidence of his crew.... That absence of these qualities would invite loss was made apparent in a great number of instances, when the steamers were almost thrown away by bad landfalls, or by the captain or crew wilting at the first sight of a cruiser or the sound of a gun.*[10]

By 10:00 p.m. on August 6, 1864, the pale sliver of a moon had dropped below the horizon, and light mist rose from the surface of the sea. A scattering of low-hanging clouds blotted out most of the starlight, turning the night to a velvet black. Steam was once again hissing through the valves in the *Tallahassee's* engine room. Soon the signal gong rang, and Tynan opened the throttles to start the engines.

Within minutes the Confederate cruiser was rounding Fort Caswell and headed for the bar at Old Inlet. The engineer, his throttles wide open now, had the *Tallahassee* dashing toward the bar at a tremendous speed. Crew members braced themselves on deck and held their breath, while the leadsman softly chanted the depth of the increasingly shoal water: "By the mark three,—and a quarter less three,—and a half two,—and a quarter two." Suddenly, a pronounced shutter was felt throughout the ship. The hull had scraped the sandy bottom, but the expected rise of the bow did not come, and with only a tremor, the cruiser shot across the bar and into the deep water of the Atlantic Ocean. The leadsman confirmed the deeper sea, and Wood's thoughts now focused on the numerous and dangerous enemy warships that he knew must be lurking in the darkness.[11]

The *Tallahassee's* one advantage was her speed, and turning to Tynan who was standing on the bridge beside him, Wood ordered, "Open her out, sir, and let her go for all she is worth!" Tynan bounded below to the sweltering engine room where he shouted for resin and pine knots to be thrown into the roaring fires for quick heat. The reaction was almost instantaneous. Needles in the steam gauges quivered past the red line as pressure soared to dangerous levels in the boilers. As a result, the pounding engines spun the propellers at a rate that they had never reached before, and with dark spray breaking from her bow, the *Tallahassee* plowed through the sea at more than seventeen knots.

Unexpectedly, without warning, a sheet of flame shot out of the cruiser's stacks, the result of all the highly flammable combustibles that had been tossed into the fires. Immediately, Union signal rockets arced skyward alerting the fleet, and Wood instructed the lookouts to maintain a sharp eye. Soon a cry came from the forward watch: "A steamer on the starboard bow! A steamer ahead!" The two enemy vessels were barely visible in the inky blackness. Executive officer Ward ordered the helmsman to steer between them. Wood reported that the Confederate cruiser passed so closely to the stern of one that "a biscuit could have been tossed on board." The Federal vessels were signaling frantically to one another as the *Tallahassee* raced by, and Wood could distinctly hear the orders shouted by the Union gunnery officer: "Run out! Elevate! Steady! Stand clear!" Abruptly, the night exploded in flames as the aft pivot on the enemy warship opened fire, sending it's shell whistling between the *Tallahassee's* twin pipes, then trailing off into the night like a fiery comet. Other blockaders joined in, illuminating the sea with soaring rockets, blinding gun flashes, and the explosion of heavy shells. Wood was thankful for the low silhouette of the cruiser, for while most of the Federal shots were excellent line shots, all were aimed too high. Soon the tremendous speed of the

The *Tallahassee* escaping from Wilmington, North Carolina, August 6, 1864.

Tallahassee carried her off into the protective shrouds of darkness and the firing ceased. Three more blockaders were spotted; the *Tallahassee* steered around them, however, without being observed. Although his men were at their guns, Wood did not return the fire, leading the Federal commanders to believe that, instead of a dangerous Confederate cruiser, just another blockade runner had escaped.[12]

Tynan reduced his throttles and the *Tallahassee* steamed easily toward the southeast. Before daylight, Wood ordered her course changed to the east, for by now the cruiser was safely over Frying-Pan Shoals, an underwater ridge of sand that extended some eighteen miles out from Smith's Island. As the early Sunday morning light began to filter into the eastern sky, a shout came from the aft lookout. Barely visible against the gloom of the still darkened western horizon was an enemy steamer in rapid pursuit. The *Tallahassee*, silhouetted against the eastern light, had been spotted first, and the Federal vessel—black smoke pouring from her stacks—was closing rapidly. Once again Tynan's throttles were banged wide open, the *Tallahassee* picked up speed, and the chase was on. Soon another blockader was spotted dead ahead, and Wood instructed the helmsman to steer eight points to the north, which positioned both pursuers off his beam. Fortunately the wind was light, and the Federal vessels could gain little advantage from their sails.

For eight hours, under a hot blistering sun, the *Tallahassee* ran at full throttle. Wood wrote: *It was at times like these that the ship and engines proved themselves reliable; for had a screw loosened or a journal heated, we should have been lost.* When it became evident that the blockaders were not gaining on the speeding Confederate warship, Wood mustered the crew on deck for Sunday services. There, with the *Tallahassee's* engines throbbing below, and the red and white ensign of their struggling homeland snapping above, Wood and his men knelt on the quarterdeck and offered prayers of thanksgiving.

Finally the two Union warships gave up the chase and turned back, but later in the day a third vessel was spotted by the lookout from the cruiser's masthead. Wood kept a respectable distance, and the enemy ship pursued only briefly. Toward nightfall the speeding *Tallahassee* almost collided with another blockader before the Union vessel was spotted. As the Southern cruiser dashed by, the Federal ship opened fire, sending her shells screaming low overhead. Again the superior speed of the raider soon carried her out of danger, and she was quickly lost in the velvet folds of darkness. Wood had run a blockade of over fifty enemy warships that had extended more than 100 miles from the Confederate coast. And yet, as a result of Wood's courage and the great speed of the cruiser, the *Tallahassee* was at last unfettered upon the open sea, and her commander could now begin his deadly search for Northern commerce.[13]

The *Tallahassee* steamed northeastward for the next three days. Wood overhauled and stopped several vessels, but they all proved to be legitimately foreign owned. Finally at first light on August 11, while steaming only eighty miles off Sandy Hook, the *Tallahassee's* lookouts spotted what would become their first prize. The cruiser gave chase and soon a simple musket shot was all that was needed to bring the fleeing merchant ship to a stop. She was the coastal schooner *Sarah A. Boyce*, in ballast out of Boston bound for Philadelphia to pick up a load of coal.

Secretary Mallory had given Wood very broad instructions on how the *Tallahassee's* commander was to handle his mission. *Relying confidently upon your judgment and ability,* Mallory had written, *and believing that the untrammeled exercise of your own wise discretion will contribute to your success, it is deemed unnecessary to give instructions in detail for your cruise.* It was clear, however, that the Secretary expected Wood to attack and destroy all Northern vessels that he might encounter along the eastern coast of the United States.[14]

The *Tallahassee's* commander wasted little time. Removing the crew, chronometers, and a few provisions, Wood scuttled the schooner rather than set her on fire so as not to reveal his position. Lowering the Confederate flag, Wood ordered the Stars and Stripes hoisted to the cruiser's masthead. Shortly, around 9:00 a.m., a New York pilot boat approached the raider. The *James Funk* lowered a boat, and the *Tallahassee's* officers watched as a tall distinguished gentleman dressed in a black suit, top hat, and an enormous watch chain, was rowed to their side. Clambering aboard, the dignified pilot was no doubt anticipating a hefty fee for guiding the visiting steamer into New York harbor, when glancing above his head, he discovered that the American flag had been replaced by the Confederate banner. "My God! What is that? What ship is this?" *A more astonished man never stood on the deck of a vessel,* Wood wrote. *He turned deadly pale, and drops of perspiration broke from every pore.* The shaken pilot was politely informed that he was standing on the deck of a Confederate warship, and that his sleek pilot boat was about to be destroyed.[15]

Before applying the torch to the *James Funk*, however, Wood placed two officers and twenty men on board and instructed them to assume the role of a New York pilot boat and to escort their customers to the side of the *Tallahassee*. This ploy worked so well that by that afternoon, a bark and two brigs lay rolling with the swells next to the raider, and forty prisoners crowded the cruiser's deck. Hence, late in the afternoon when another schooner, the *Carroll*, was brought alongside, Wood bonded her for $10,000 and placed all of his prisoners on board.

Toward evening, another pilot boat approached the *Tallahassee* and her prizes, but becoming suspicious that all was not well, her master cracked on full sail and headed back toward New York. Bells rang in the cruiser's engine room, and within minutes the raider was bounding after the swift pilot boat. She was a fast one, and Wood ordered the cruiser's meager sails hoisted in an effort to increase her speed and close the gap. Finally the range closed sufficiently for Wood to order Lieutenant Ward to call the forward gun crew to quarters. Quickly the piece was sighted, and with a thunderous roar a shell streaked after the pilot boat, splashing some distance beyond. The master of the fleeing boat, so close to sanctuary, still refused to stop. Two more shots were required before the speedy boat's sails were luffed and her master finally surrendered.

She was a splendid craft, with the name *William Bell* emblazoned on her stern. When James Callahan, her captain, was brought on board the *Tallahassee*, he found Wood seated in an armchair on deck.

The *Tallahassee* chasing the pilot boat, *William Bell.*

Callahan pleaded passionately for the release of his pristine boat, even offering to bond her for $30,000 to secure her release, but to no avail. Wood did offer to consider the captain's proposal, however, providing he would guide the cruiser up the East River where the *Tallahassee* could shell the Federal Navy yard. To his credit, Callahan refused to betray his country, and the fate of his beautiful boat was sealed. As distasteful as it was for a sailor to destroy a ship, Wood had his orders. This was a pilot boat of the enemy, and knowing that his position could no longer be concealed once the paroled prisoners on the *Carroll* reached shore, he ordered a party of men to set fire to the *William Bell*. Wood also burned the two brigs and the bark, retaining the little *James Funk* as a tender and a scout. It had been a profitable day's work, and as the Confederate raider steamed silently away into the gathering darkness, the eastern horizon off New York City was illuminated by the distant and ominous orange glow of burning ships.[16]

The next day, August 12, proved equally successful for Wood and the *Tallahassee*. By the end of the day, six more Northern vessels had been burned or bonded. One of these was the 989-ton London to New York packet *Adriatic*, which was carrying 170 German emigrants, who, Wood was confident, were destined for forced enlistment into the Union armies. When word spread that their ship was to be burned, panic erupted among the Germans who assumed that they, too, were to be roasted by the Southern "pirates." With much difficulty, Wood's men succeeded in transferring the terrorized passengers to one of the bonded schooners that the raider had captured earlier, and the packet ship was then set ablaze. With darkness once again upon them, Wood directed his course for the New England coast, while in his wake the *Adriatic* illuminated the night sky as the roaring flames burned her to the water's edge.[17]

The following morning, while steaming slowly near Boston, Wood captured the 789-ton bark *Glenarvon*. Her registration revealed that she was from Thomaston, Maine, and was en route from Glasgow to New York with a cargo of iron. After taking some provisions, including chickens and pigs, and transferring the passengers and crew, Wood scuttled the vessel, writing later that: *We watched the bark as she slowly settled, strake by strake, until her deck was awash, and then her stern sank gradually out of sight until she was in an upright position, and one mast after another disappeared with all sail set, sinking as quietly as if human hands were lowering her into the depths. Hardly a ripple broke the quiet waters.*[18]

One of the *Glenarvon's* passengers taken on board the cruiser was the wife of a retired sea captain who, wrote Wood, *came on board scolding and left scolding. Her tongue was slung amidships, and never tired.* In a futile attempt to pacify the fiery lady and her sea captain husband, Wood offered his cabin as accommodations for them, but his offer was

The burning of the *Adriatic*.

The sinking of the *Glenarvon*.

scornfully refused. In desperation, the *Tallahassee's* commander hailed a passing Russian ship which agreed to take them on board. When the woman left the cruiser, Wood wrote, *as a final effort to show how she would serve us, she snatched her bonnet from her head, tore it into pieces, and threw it into the sea.*[19]

By now the alarm had spread up and down the east coast, and on the same day that Wood was scuttling the *Glenarvon*, and incurring the wrath of the sea captain's wife, a frantic telegram was handed to Gideon Wells, Federal Naval Secretary:

New York, August 13, 1864.
(Received at Washington 12:30 p.m.)

Confederate steamer Tallahassee is reported cruising within 60 miles of this port. She has already captured six vessels. Will you please have the necessary measures taken, if not already done, to secure her capture? If practicable, please answer by telegraph.

John D. Jones,
President Board Underwriters.

Hon. Gideon Welles.

The harried secretary took only 30 minutes to send off his reply:

Navy Department, August 13, 1864—1 p.m.

Three vessels left New York Navy Yard yesterday afternoon; more leave today. Vessels left Hampton Roads last night; more leave today. Several vessels leave Boston today and tomorrow. Every vessel available has been ordered to search for the pirate.

Gideon Welles,
Secretary of Navy.

Jno. D. Jones,
President Board of Underwriters, New York.[20]

Besides the numerous enemy warships that were now scouring the ocean for him, Wood had another problem. The constant steaming had dwindled his precious coal supply to a dangerous level. It was like a gift from heaven, therefore, when on August 14, off the coast of Maine, the 547-ton ship *James Littlefield* was captured. Her hold brimmed with a full load of anthracite coal. A heavy fog, however, began to roll out from the Maine coast; this, along with a rising sea, forced Wood to cancel the transfer of coal. Reluctantly the *James Littlefield* had to be scuttled.

The following day, August 15, a total of six small fishing schooners were captured, and all but one, which was bonded to carry the prisoners ashore, were scuttled. The next day brought more New England fishermen into the raiders net, with four schooners and one bark taken captive. Because of the fear along the New England coast, however, heavy merchant vessels were becoming rare, which forced Wood to operate much closer to the shoreline than he had anticipated. A few prizes were captured within sight of Matinicuss Island off Penobscot Bay, where horrified residents watched from shore as, one by one, the captive vessels were set on fire. On the 17th, four more schooners and one brig carrying coal were seized. The fishing boats were quickly destroyed, but the persistent fog and heavy seas prevented any transfer of coal, so the brig was bonded and the prisoners placed on board. On the morning of August 18, Engineer Tynan reported that only 40 tons of coal remained in the cruiser's bunkers. Fortunately, the *Tallahassee* stumbled upon a Nova Scotian pilot later in the day, who guided the raider through the fog and into the neutral port of Halifax.[21]

In seven days Wood had captured thirty-two Northern vessels, of which fifteen were burned, ten scuttled, five bonded, and two released. It was a remarkably prosperous seven days. All that was required was a bold and resourceful commander who was unafraid to carry the war to the enemy's shores. In John Taylor Wood, Secretary Mallory had found that man.

The war was not going well for the struggling Confederacy at this time, and as a consequence, Wood was destined to receive a cool reception in Halifax. British authorities, who still endeavored dutifully to maintain their stated positions of neutrality, realized that they soon might be called upon by a spiteful and victorious United States to answer for any courtesies extended to a visiting Confederate warship. The *Tallahassee* needed coal, however, which was a legitimate request under international law, and Wood called immediately upon the admiral of the port to present his request. In a letter to Mallory later, Wood bemoaned his treatment at the hands of the ranking English officer: *I found in the port of Halifax on my arrival, the H.M.S. Duncan, bearing the flag of Rear Admiral Sir James Hope. I called promptly upon him, though he took no notice of my presence by the customary boarding and offering the courtesies of the port. Neither on arriving nor leaving were the honors of the side extended. On being shown into his cabin he did not rise from his seat, nor shake hands, nor offer me a seat. His manner and tone were offensive.*[22]

Wood's next course of action was to call upon the Lieutenant Governor Richard G. MacDonnell at 11:00 a.m., and request that he be allowed to purchase the required fuel. MacDonnell was more amiable, but emphasized that he was bound by the Queen's Neutrality Proclamation, and that he could only permit the *Tallahassee* to load enough coal to take her to the nearest Confederate port. The lieutenant governor also emphasized that, according to the proclamation, unless the *Tallahassee* needed repairs to make her seaworthy, she must be gone within twenty-four hours. As soon as Wood had left the Government House, the American consul, Mortimer M. Jackson, called upon MacDonnell and demanded that British authorities detain the "rebel pirate" until he could furnish proof that Wood had violated international law, and that he intended to load munitions of war while in the neutral port. The lieutenant governor, knowing that the law had not been violated and that Wood harbored no such intent, dismissed the American demand.

The unofficial reception to the cruiser in the harbor at Halifax, however, was just the opposite to that of the government officers. Wood sent his paymaster Charles L. Jones ashore with instructions for contacting B. Wier and Company, Confederate agents in Halifax, to purchase the authorized amount of coal, a few provisions, and a new mast. An accidental collision with the *Adriatic* had carried away the aft mast, and Wood did not wish to put to sea without a new one. Jones was met at the dock by a swarm of at least a thousand cheering people. *As I stepped from the boat,* he wrote, *it was with great difficulty that I could get away from the crowd who showed in their manner the greatest interest in our cause.* Later that evening, Jones and several other officers from the *Tallahassee* attended a ball hosted by a local regiment. Amid the glare of the gaslights, faded Confederate gray mixed with exquisite red and white British uniforms in a scene that was soon never to be witnessed again.[23]

In order to ascertain the amount of coal that the cruiser would require to reach a Southern port, MacDonnell instructed Admiral Hope to dispatch a party of officers to the *Tallahassee* on the pretense of inspecting the twin-screw propulsion system. After the British officers had departed, Wood received a note from the lieutenant governor restricting his purchase to only 100 tons. To enforce this order, Hope

The CSS *Tallahassee* in the harbor of Halifax.

dispatched eleven boatloads of Royal Marines which surrounded the *Tallahassee*. Wood protested to the lieutenant governor, and the boats were withdrawn, cutting short the unpleasant scene of armed British sailors confronting armed Confederates. Hope's inspectors remained on board, however, to observe the coaling operation.[24]

On the following morning, August 19, Wood requested that MacDonnell grant him an additional twenty-four hours in order to finish the coaling operation and to replace the mast. The British official agreed to the extra time, but Wood expected Federal warships to appear off the mouth of the harbor at any moment, and had no intention of remaining that long. Contacting agent Weir, Wood asked that a trusted pilot be dispatched to him immediately. Soon Jock Fleming, a burley Halifax harbor pilot, was standing on the deck of the *Tallahassee*.

He was six feet in height, Wood wrote, *broad, deep chested, and with a stoop. His limbs were too long for his body. His head was pitched well forward, and covered, as was his neck, with a thick stubble of grayish hair. His eyes, small and bright, were almost hidden beneath overhanging eyebrows. His hands were as hard, rough, and scaly as the flipper of a green turtle. Bronzed by the exposure to sixty seasons of storm and sunshine, he could tell of many a narrow escape.... He knew the harbor as well as the fish that swam its waters. He was honest, bluff, and trusty.*[25]

Wary that an enemy warship might have already arrived and was secretly awaiting his departure, Wood requested Fleming to search for an obscure and little used channel; one that the cruiser with her twin screw system could safely navigate to make her escape. In the fading light of day, Fleming studied his charts. Meanwhile, agent Weir succeeded in having 40 more tons of coal delivered to the cruiser's bunkers, making a total of 140 tons on board. Even the new mast arrived, but not wanting to take the time to install it, Wood had it lashed to the deck.[26]

Fleming had now chosen a channel; a small obscure eastern inlet, with many sharp turns and numerous areas of shallow water. *"How much water do you draw Cap'?"* Fleming asked.

"Thirteen feet, allowing for a little drag," was Wood's response.

"There is a good tide tonight, and water enough;" Fleming explained, *"but you are too long to turn the corners."*

"But, Pilot, with our twin screws, I can turn her center, as I turn this ruler." Wood illustrated by spinning the ruler around on the chart table.

"Well, I never was shipmate with the likes of them;" said Fleming, *"but if you will steer her, I'll find the water."*

"Are you certain, pilot, there is water enough?" Wood questioned. *"It would never do to run ashore at this time."*

"You sha'n't touch anything but the eelgrass," assured Fleming. *"Better get ready about eleven."*

I hesitated; Wood wrote, *and divining from my face that I was not satisfied, he said as he rose: "Don't be 'feared; I'll take you out all right; you won't see any of those chaps off Chebucto Head!"* As he spoke, Wood continued, *he brought his hand down on my shoulder with a thud that I felt in my boots. His confidence, and my faith in the man, determined me to make the attempt.*[27]

The *Tallahassee's* commander waited patiently for the next high tide, and at 1:00 a.m., the order was quietly given to hoist the anchor. Soon the signal gong rang in the engine room with a request for "all ahead— slow." Silently, the Confederate warship stole toward the obscure eastern channel. Black clouds skirted across the darkened sky as all eyes strained to find the elusive passageway. *Once or twice,* Wood wrote, *Fleming appeared lost, but it was only for a moment. At the sharp twists in the channel I sent a boat ahead with a light to mark the turns. At one place, by the lead, there was hardly room between the keel and the bottom for your open hand. In an hour we opened the two lights on Devil's Island, and the channel broadened and deepened. Soon we felt the pulsating bosom of the old Atlantic and were safe outside.*[28]

Jock Fleming was as good as his word, for by utilizing the twin screws to navigate the sharp turns, Wood and the skillful pilot had kept the *Tallahassee* gliding smoothly through the underwater eelgrass toward the open sea. By 2:00 a.m., the ocean was reached, and not an enemy cruiser was in sight. As Fleming clambered into his boat to leave, he grasped Wood's hand and wished him an emotional "Godspeed." With heartfelt thanks to the departing pilot, Wood signaled Engineer Tynan to open the throttles wide and ordered Lieutenant Ward to set a homeward course. Four hours later, just after 6:00 a.m., the USS *Pontoosuc* steamed into Halifax harbor. Wood's caution in using the obscure channel had proved unnecessary, but his decision to leave when he did, was a good one.[29]

Without a full load of coal, Wood had determined that he would have to sail directly for Wilmington and would not be able to resume his hunt for Northern merchantmen. Still, the course to the North Carolina port would take them reasonably near the northeastern seaboard, so Wood ordered a sharp lookout to be kept. On the first day, August 20, the tiny 127-ton brig, *Roan*, was captured and burned. She became the *Tallahassee's* thirty-third, and final prize. Several other vessels were stopped and searched, but all proved to be of foreign registry.[30]

Nearing the North Carolina coast, the Confederate cruiser was spotted by two vessels of the blockading force. With her superior speed, however, the *Tallahassee* soon outdistanced them. Wood decided to wait until dark, and then by steaming closely along the shore and approaching from the north, he would make a run for New Inlet. This had become a favorite tactic of blockade runners inbound for Wilmington, because soundings could be taken easily in the shallow water, and it brought the runners under the protection of Fort Fisher and additional Confederate batteries along the beach. Soon after dark, Wood called his crew to general quarters. Ordering Tynan to bring the engines up to full power, he directed the helmsman to steer parallel to the white foam of the breakers. With the surf roaring off her starboard side, the *Tallahassee* plowed through the rolling swells just yards from the Carolina shore.

Suddenly a cry came from the forward lookout. An enemy warship, the USS *Monticello*, was dead ahead. For a few seconds, Wood contemplated passing to the inside of her, but the Federal vessel was almost in the surf and the speeding *Tallahassee* would most surely run aground. At the last instant, he veered the cruiser to port and passed outside of the *Monticello* as two other blockaders closed in. The Union ships wasted precious time signaling one another, giving Wood a few minutes to swing the *Tallahassee* back on course. Satisfied that the intruder was an enemy, the Federals opened fire. Shafts of flame lit up the surrounding area, as explosive shells shrieked over the *Tallahassee's* stacks, splashing in the sea beyond. There was no need for deception now, and Wood ordered his gunners to return the fire. Directing their aim at the Union muzzle flashes, the three pivot guns opened fire with a thunderous roar, sending their shells streaking toward their tormentors. Blockade runners did not normally return fire, and fearful that they had made a mistake and might be shooting at one of their own, the Federal commanders ceased firing, giving Wood a few more precious minutes.

Soon the *Tallahassee's* guns thundered again, and the Federals, satisfied that she was, indeed, an enemy, opened a brisk response. Black smoke poured from the raider's stacks as she pounded along at over fourteen knots, only yards from the roaring surf. Gun flashes, sputtering fuse, and exploding shells illuminated the speeding cruiser, blinding her gun crews and sending dense smoke blowing out to sea. The USS *Britannia* dropped a howitzer shell directly over the raider where it exploded, lighting up her deck yet doing no damage. Soon the welcome bark of field pieces could be heard, as Confederate artillery along the beach opened fire. A deep resonant boom announced that Fort Fisher's great guns had also opened up, their heavy shells whining over the *Tallahassee* and exploding with a jarring concussion in the midst of the pursuing blockaders. Wood signaled the fort, and the range lights were set. The *Tallahassee*, being lightly loaded, rounded Confederate Point and dashed easily across the bar. At 10:30 p.m., in a cloud of smoke and hissing steam, the cruiser came to anchor under the protective guns of the towering fortification. The *Tallahassee* was safely home. The officers and crew were wild with jubilation, but Wood knew where his duty lay. Calling his men on deck, he offered prayers of thanksgiving to almighty God for their safe return. At dawn the next morning, the Confederate ensign was raised, and the *Tallahassee* exchanged a twenty-one gun salute with the fort. Wood then steamed the cruiser up the Cape Fear River to a spirited and joyous welcome at Wilmington.[31]

In spite of the enthusiastic crowds that greeted Wood and his crew, not everyone was exhilarated by the raider's exploits. Governor Zebulon Vance of North Carolina asserted that the cruise of the *Tallahassee* had only irritated the enemy causing him to send extra warships to tighten the blockade off Wilmington. Vance claimed that the raider had appropriated the remaining stockpile of anthracite coal which forced blockade runners to burn soft coal. Several runners, including the state's own vessel, the *Advance*, were lost shortly after Wood's return. Mallory vehemently denied that the *Tallahassee* had confiscated all of the hard coal and pointed out that the raider had loaded fuel from a common heap of Welsh. General W. H. C. Whiting, military commander at Wilmington, contended that the *Tallahassee* was unsuitable as a warship, and that her crew could be better utilized by manning the naval batteries at the entrance of the Cape Fear River. Mallory, and more importantly, President Davis, disagreed, and the controversial Confederate cruiser was soon ready for another dash at the enemy.[32]

Wood was recalled to Richmond by President Davis, and Lieutenant Ward was given command of the raider. Ward hurried forward his preparations for going to sea, and in an attempt to deceive and confuse the blockading squadrons as to how many cruisers there actually were, the *Tallahassee* was re-commissioned as the CSS *Olustee*. Finally on the dark night of October 29, 1864, Ward drove the *Olustee*

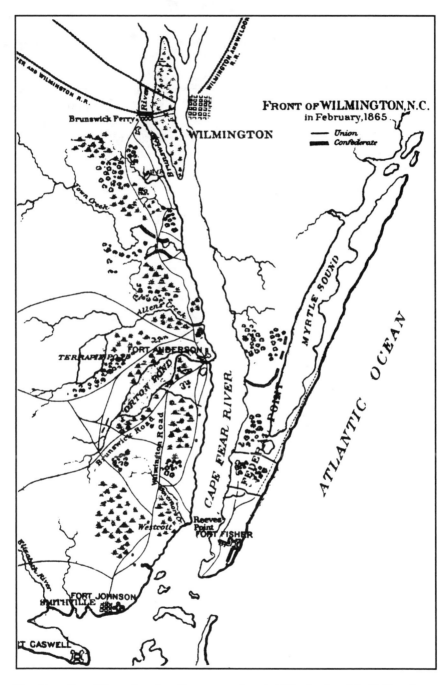

The Cape Fear River showing the approaches to Wilmington, North Carolina.
Confederate Military History, vol. 4

over the bar at New Inlet and was soon lost in the dark expanse of the Atlantic with no trouble from the enemy blockaders. Not much is known concerning Ward's cruise with the *Olustee*, because no Confederate report of his cruise has survived. From Federal dispatches, however, it can be ascertained that in his nine-day cruise, six enemy vessels along the Delaware coast, the *Empress Theresa*, the *A. J. Bird*, the *E. F. Lewis*, the *Vapor*, the *Arcole*, and the *T. D. Wagner*, were captured and destroyed.[33]

The *Olustee* returned to Wilmington in broad daylight on November 7, and exchanged gunfire with several of the blockade runners as she sped toward the bar. The USS *Montgomery* was one of the Union vessels that gave chase, and her commander, Lieutenant E. H. Faucon, reported that: *At 1:23, ...as soon as it was thought that we could reach the chase with our rifled gun, we began to fire, and although the gun was at extreme elevation, the shot fell short. Soon after, on getting a little nearer, we again opened our fire, the shot striking very near the chase. At 1:53 the chase displayed a large Confederate flag and a long pennant, and it was evident that she had a large number of men on board.... At 2:00, the chase fired at us from her stern gun, and continued his fire at intervals for about half an hour, the shot passing over us and falling very near.*[34]

The *Montgomery*, which had now been joined by additional blockaders, continued the chase all afternoon, firing forty-four times in a vain attempt to hit the *Olustee*. Late in the day, as they neared the North Carolina coast, it began to look a little more favorable to Lieutenant Faucon: *At 4:00 we made the land, and the chance seemed favorable of running him on the beach before dark. At 4:20 the chase was running about W. S. W., and bearing N. N. W. of us. At 5:30 the chase was close in to the beach, and barely visible. Before 5:00 it became very hazy and smoky over the land, and at dusk was quite cloudy, and soon after it became impossible to distinguish anything. From 6:50 to 7:20 lights were seen along the beach, and three heavy guns were fired.*[35] These were evidently the range lights that were set to guide the raider in while the big guns of Fort Fisher provided covering fire. Once again the speedy Confederate cruiser was safely anchored under the protective guns of the towering fortress.

By the time the *Olustee* had returned to Wilmington, the war situation was becoming extremely grave. Lee's army was pinned down in the muddy trenches around Petersburg by Grant's overwhelming hosts, and farther south, Atlanta had fallen, and Sherman was beginning his infamous "march to the sea." The area of the country remaining that could be depended upon to feed and sustain the gray armies was shrinking fast. Shortly after the *Olustee* arrived in the North Carolina port, the foremost blockade-runner captain, Lieutenant John Wilkinson of the Confederate Navy, was summoned to Richmond. Aware of the superior speed of the twin screw steamer, Wilkinson recommended that the *Olustee* be converted back to a blockade runner, with the express purpose of running food from Bermuda for Lee's starving troops. His plan was approved and Wilkinson returned immediately to Wilmington and set to work.

The cruiser's guns were removed, and her name changed, appropriately, to the *Chameleon*. Loaded with a cargo of cotton, Wilkinson sailed during the night of December 27, amid the confusion of the Federal's great bombardment of Fort Fisher. Not an enemy blockader was encountered as the *Chameleon* sped over the bar and headed for the open sea. Three days later she arrived at St. George, Bermuda. Encountering difficulties convincing the British authorities that the *Chameleon* was no longer a warship, it was not until January 19, 1865, that the Confederate vessel was finally loaded with provisions and steamed out of St. George. Wilkinson set a direct course for Wilmington and related later in his memoirs what they encountered when they reached the North Carolina coast:

Our voyage across was very rough, and the night of our approach to New Inlet was dark and rainy. Between one and two o'clock in the morning, as we were feeling our way with the lead, a light was discovered nearly ahead and a short distance from us. As we drew closer in and "sheered" the Chameleon, so as to bring the light abeam, I directed our signal officer to make the regular signal. No reply was made to it, although many lights now began to appear looming up through the drizzling rain. These were undoubtedly campfires of the United States troops outside Fort Fisher; but it never occurred to me as possible, that a second attack could have been made, and successfully in the brief period of time which had elapsed since our departure from Wilmington. Believing that I had made some error in my day's observations, the Chameleon was put to sea again, as the most prudent course in the emergency. Orders were therefore given to go at full speed, and by daylight we had made an offing of forty or fifty miles from the coast.

Clear and pleasant weather enabled me to establish our position accurately—it was my invariable custom, at sea, during the war, to take my own observations—and early in the night we made the Mound Light ahead, for which I shaped our course. The range lights were showing, and we crossed the bar without interference, but without a suspicion of anything wrong, as it would occasionally happen, that we would cross the bar without even seeing a blockader. We were under the guns of Fort Fisher in fact, and close to the fleet of United States vessels, which had crossed the bar after the fall of the fort, when I directed my signal officer to communicate with the shore station. His signal was promptly answered, but turning to me, he said, "No Confederate signal officer there, sir; he cannot reply to me!" The order to wear round was instantly obeyed; not a moment too soon, for the bow of the Chameleon was scarcely pointed for the bar before two of the light cruisers were plainly visible in pursuit, steaming with all speed to intercept us.

Nothing saved us from capture but the twin screws, which enabled our steamer to turn as upon a pivot in the narrow channel between the bar and the "rip." We reached the bar before our pursuers, and were soon lost to their sight in the darkness outside. Our supply of coal being limited, the course was shaped for Nassau as the nearer port, where we arrived without accident. A day or two after our arrival the news came of the fall of Fort Fisher.[36]

Wilkinson was still determined to try to deliver his load of food-stuffs to a Confederate port, and so departed Nassau for Charleston, along with the *Owl*, the *Carolina*, the *Dream*, and the *Chicora*, on February 1. Arriving off the South Carolina port several days later, Wilkinson found the harbor so tightly blockaded by the enemy that had been re-inforced by vessels no longer needed off Wilmington, that he was forced to return to Nassau. *As we turned away from the land,* he wrote, *our hearts sank within us, while the conviction forced itself upon us, that the cause for which so much blood had been shed, so many miseries bravely endured, and so many sacrifices cheerfully made, was about to perish at last.*[37]

Ordered to take the *Chameleon* to Liverpool, Wilkinson arrived there on April 9, 1865, the same day that the gallant Army of Northern Virginia was stacking arms at the tiny hamlet of Appomattox, Virginia. Wilkinson handed the former cruiser over to Commander Bullock, who offered the vessel for sale. With the war in America over, she was eventually seized by the British government and handed over to the United States, who later sold her to Japan.

The ship of many names—*Atlanta, Tallahassee, Olustee*, and finally *Chameleon*—had served her country well. An innovative design, far advanced for her time, her twin screws and powerful engines had carried her officers and crew many times through the Federal blockade without a scratch. She had delivered hundreds of tons of supplies to the struggling Confederacy and had taken the war to the enemy, not once, but twice, sailing from and returning to the same Southern port in spite of the best efforts of the Federal Navy to stop her. The exploits of this speedy Southern vessel, including her officers and men, were deeds of which the Confederate Navy, and in fact the whole Southern nation, could well be proud.

Chapter Seven

Havoc Off the East Coast – Part II

The *Edith*, sister ship to the *Atlanta*, or CSS *Tallahassee*, was of the same configuration but slightly shorter in overall dimensions. One hundred seventy-five feet from bow to stern and 25 feet abeam, she, too, was equipped with two powerful engines driving twin screws. Owned by Collie and Company of London, England, the *Edith* sailed to Bermuda almost a month in advance of her twin sister, and arrived at Wilmington, North Carolina on her maiden voyage to the Confederacy on April 12, 1864. Fourteen days later, with her hold and deck piled high with valuable Southern cotton, she ran out undetected and unmolested on or about April 26, and shaped her course for Nassau. For the next four months during the hot summer of 1864, the *Edith* plied back and forth between Wilmington and Nassau (sometimes alternating with Bermuda), her superior speed enabling her to easily outdistance the enemy blockaders.[1]

After making five round trips between the islands and the port of Wilmington, the *Edith* was purchased by the Confederate Navy Department in early September of 1864. In the same manner as the *Tallahassee*, the *Edith*, now commissioned the CSS *Chickamauga*, had three pivot guns mounted on her main deck. They included a rifled 12-pounder forward, a 64-pounder amidships, and a rifled 32-pounder

133

First Lieutenant John Wilkinson, commander of the CSS *Chickamauga*.

aft. Near the end of the month, First Lieutenant John Wilkinson was ordered to the *Chickamauga* as her commander.

Wilkinson was one of the more daring and innovative commanders in the Confederate Navy. Born in Norfolk, Virginia, in 1821, he entered the United States Navy as a midshipman in 1837, and later saw service in the Mexican War. When Virginia seceded, Wilkinson resigned his commission in the "old service," and offered his sword to his native state. On June 10, 1861, he was appointed a first lieutenant in the Confederate Navy, and ordered to the command of the CSS *Jackson* which was stationed at New Orleans. Later he was detailed to the newly built and unfinished ironclad, the CSS *Louisiana*, as her executive officer where he was taken prisoner upon the fall of New Orleans to Farragut's forces. Exchanged and sent to Europe to procure a fast steamer for blockade-running duties, Wilkinson purchased the *Giraffe*, later known as the *R. L. Lee*, and proceeded to become one of the most courageous and successful commanders of those speedy vessels. In Secretary Mallory's opinion, the lieutenant's experience in penetrating the blockade made him a wise choice to command the swift *Chickamauga*.[2]

Midshipman Daniel Murray Lee, an officer on the *Chickamauga*, and a nephew of Robert E. Lee.

Wilkinson, with the help of his executive officer, First Lieutenant William G. Dozier, hurried to prepare the newly commissioned cruiser for sea. The raider's commander did not consider the prospects for a lengthy cruise with the twin screw steamer very promising, for many of the same reasons that had hampered the *Tallahassee*, namely, her limited coal capacity. Writing in his memoirs after the war, Wilkinson, while acknowledging that the steamer was very fast under steam, described the *Chickamauga* and reiterated her limitations: *She was more substantially built than most of the blockade runners, but altogether unfit for a cruiser, as she could only keep the sea while her supply of coal lasted. She was schooner rigged, with very short masts, and her sails were chiefly serviceable to steady her in a sea-way. Under all sail and off the wind, without steam, she could not make more than three knots with a stiff breeze; by the wind under the same circumstances, she had not even steerage way.*[3]

Wilkinson seems overly critical of the *Chickamauga*, and fails to acknowledge that the steamer was not designed as a sailing craft, but rather depended on her twin screws and powerful engines for her principal means of propulsion. Nevertheless, by the end of September, a full complement of officers were on board; a "motley crew," as Wilkinson described them, was shipped, and the *Chickamauga* was ready. No official record of the *Chickamauga's* voyage has survived, but posterity is indebted to Midshipman Clarence Cary who kept a log during the cruise. His log covers the period from September 26, 1864, until the *Chickamauga's* return on November 19, and paints a striking portrait of the numerous difficulties encountered at Wilmington and at sea. To give the reader a broader understanding of the obstacles the Confederate Navy faced at this late stage of the war, Cary's log is reproduced here in its entirety.

September 2, 1864.—Made preparations for leaving the navy yard [Wilmington], and at 12 m. hauled across the river and made fast to the wharf above the *Tallahassee.*

September 29.—There is no encouraging prospect for us to get out, as the steamer *Lynx* was struck eight times while running out the other night, and had to be beached to save her from sinking.

September 30.—Last night was thought very favorable for running the blockade, and a steamer tried coming in, but was much cut up and had to be beached. I have not heard her name. The *Wild Rover* is supposed to have gone out without being hurt. The steamer *Lady Sterling,* which came in a night or two ago, has come up to the city.

October 1.—At 11:30 this morning we got under way and stood down the river. At 12:40 p.m. we anchored in Five Fathom Hole. The *Falcon* and *Owl* are lying near us; they will go out tonight. About 5 p.m. we got under way and stood down the river toward Smithville, which is about 5 miles off, but upon striking upon a bar about halfway we determined to wait for the next tide, and accordingly backed off and came to anchor. I went aloft this evening and saw seven blockading vessels off New Inlet.

October 2.—This morning in my watch we got under way and came down to Smithville and anchored. The steamer *Hattie* came in last night; she is from Halifax. The *Owl, Falcon,* and *Helen* did not attempt to go.

October 3.—The steamer *Talisman,* from Bermuda, came in last night without being fired at. The *Owl* went out and had nine shots fired at her. The Yankees know perfectly well that we are waiting to go out, as we are in sight from their mastheads, and then we fired a shot from each gun this morning.

October 4.—Last night at about half past 8 we got up steam and got under way and stood down to the Western Bar, or Old Inlet, with the intention of going out if possible; but the night was, unfortunately, too light, and we had to return. We went out about 5 or 6 miles, and when we were preparing to go over the outer bar we sighted three Yankees lying right in the channel where we had to go, and as going on was impossible we had to turn back. We would have gone on but for the brightness of the night. The steamer *Banshee II* came in New Inlet last night, and had but two shots fired at her; she was from Bermuda, and will be quarantined for thirty days.

October 5.—The *Falcon* and *Helen* both got up steam to go, but failed. During my watch last night there was some musketry firing down at Caswell, and the long roll was beaten all around. We immediately prepared to meet an attack, but it turned out to be a false alarm. There is but one way open for us now (as there is not enough [water] on the Rip at New Inlet), and that is this bar, which is well blockaded. There were eleven off here today.

October 6.—Last night was, as usual, very light, and of course we could not go. The steamer *Florie* ran out of New Inlet and had over sixty shots fired at her, besides innumerable rockets. This morning I went with some of our officers in the cutter to Bald Head for fish. I went to the top of the lighthouse and had a view of the blockade. I counted ten vessels off New Inlet.

October 7.—Last night being dark enough, the captain determined to go out if possible; so we got under way at 9:30 p.m. and proceeded down to the Rip, upon which we grounded; after some trouble we succeeded in backing off. We tried again and again, but with ill success, and finally we had to go back to our old anchorage.

October 8.—Last evening the pilot came on board and had a consultation with the captain. It turns out that we will not go out for three weeks (that is, until the 28th) from today. The moon is very bright now and the tides will not suit. The *Helen* went out clear last night and had no shots fired at her. She draws 10.5 feet water; we draw 11 feet 3 inches. At meridian we got under way and headed up toward Fort Fisher. Set the foresail and jib and made splendid time, considering the small amount of steam and bad trim of our ship. The explosion [heard] last night has turned out to be a Yankee gunboat, which had come in too close and got aground. She was set on fire by her own crew, who escaped in boats. The steamer *Annie* got aground outside of [Fort] Fisher last night, while running in. We arrived in Wilmington at about 5 p.m.

October 13.—There were three deaths from fever yesterday [in Wilmington]. All the population seems to be in a panic.

October 20.—At about 4 p.m. hauled out to our old anchorage. The vessels are commencing to run in and out now, and it will not be long before we go, I hope. The steamer *Virginia* came in last night from Bermuda. The steamers *Wando* and *Talisman* went down today to the forts.

October 21.—They anticipate an attack on Wilmington from the Yankee fleet under Porter.

October 23.—The steamers *Virginia* and *General Armstrong* came up to the city. The *Talisman* and *Wando* went out night before last. General Bragg arrived in Wilmington and has taken command of this department. No news of the meditated attack of the Yankees on this place. I believe the Yankee fleet is preparing for a fight on the James as soon as Butler's canal is finished.

October 24.—Steamer *Lucy* came in last night. C.S.S. *Tallahassee* hauled out in the stream and will probably go day after tomorrow.

October 27.—At 3:40 p.m. we hove up anchor and proceeded down the river in company with the C.S.S. *Tallahassee*. At 5:40 anchored; the *Tallahassee* anchored about half a mile above.

October 28.—At 8 a.m. stood down the river toward Smithville. The steamers *Virginia* and *General Armstrong* went out last night without a shot. We will go tonight if there is sufficient water on the Rip. Left the *Tallahassee* at New Inlet. At 5 p.m. got under way and proceeded down to the Rip, which, after one unsuccessful attempt, we crossed with little difficulty at 6 p.m. At 7 crossed the bar and passed through the Yankee fleet. We sighted ——— vessels, one of which threw up rockets and gave chase, also firing her guns. She fired twelve shots at us, all of which were too high, but were pretty good line shots. It was so rough on the bar that they could not fire with any accuracy. As soon as the Yankee gave chase we shifted some of the coal from the forehold and trimmed the ship in that way. The ship has been running very well. We dropped the Yankee about 8 p.m.

October 29.—After we got clear of the blockade we steered E. 1/2 N. for some hours.

October 30.—At 11 a.m. sighted a sail right ahead, which we chased and overhauled. She was the bark *Mark L. Potter*, of Bangor, Me., bound to Key West with a cargo of lime, bricks, and lumber. Took on board the officers and crew (thirteen in all) and set fire to her. At 4 p.m. stood off on our course. Got plenty of good provisions off the prize and many valuable articles for ship's use; also took five boats, three of which are very pretty little dinghies. Threw overboard one of our own old boats. Got under way and stood to the northward and westward.

October 31.—About 10 a.m. sighted a sail ahead and gave chase. About 10:30 came alongside of her and hove her to. She proved to be the bark *Emily L. Hall*, of New York. She was from Cardenas, Cuba, bound to New York with a cargo of sugar and molasses. This ship we burned, and stood on in chase of a ship which turned out to be the ship *Shooting Star*, of New York. She was from New York and bound to Havana with a cargo of coal (1,500 tons). While alongside of her another sail hove in sight. We stood for her and hove her to. She was the *Albion Lincoln*, of [Harpswell], Me., with a cargo of lumber, bound to ———. The former we burned and the latter we bonded for $18,000. To her we transferred all the prisoners (about thirty in number), after giving them their parole. A fine ship passed to windward of us, but we were too busy to notice her, and she got away.

November 1.—At 12 [meridian] sighted the lighthouse on Montauk Point—that is, on the end of Long Island. At 3:30 p.m. passed and spoke the schooner *Reliance*, of Annapolis, Nova Scotia. At 6 hove to the schooners *Goodspeed*, of Philadelphia, and *Otter Rock*, of Boston, both of which we scuttled. Got late Yankee papers, which say the enemy have discovered our exit from Wilmington, and have sent three steamers after us; so in a few days we are likely to have a lively time. An alarm was just now made that the Yankees were bearing down upon us in a steamer. All lights were put out and everybody ran on deck, when down came a large schooner with both lights set, which nearly ran us down.

November 2.—This morning about 8 a.m. caught up with the bark *Speedwell*, of Boston, bound to Philadelphia, in ballast. She was an old craft, and had ladies on board, and on this account we bonded her for $18,000, to be paid in gold. Paroled her crew and the crew of the schooner and sent them off. Got from her Boston papers of the 1st. We find from them that the Yankees "know we're out." They have sent steamers after us already; the *Vanderbilt* is out.

November 6.—Altered our course and stood for Bermuda. At 4 p.m. standing around S. W. end of Bermuda. Too late to take a pilot. All night we kept the ship steaming slowly between David's Head and Gibbs Island [Hill] light.

November 7.—At 7:25 a.m. took a Bermuda pilot. At 8 a.m. let go the port anchor with 25 fathoms chain in Five Fathom Hole, off St. George.

November 8.—Hove up anchor at 5 p.m. and came to St. George, and let go anchor at about 4:30.

November 13.—About sixty-five men, including the gunner have left without leave.

November 14.—Went to Hamilton early this morning, but was not successful in getting the men. The governor-general has decided that we, not being a recognized power, have no right to arrest our men.

November 15.—At 2:30 p.m. got under way and stood out of the harbor. Heard of Lincoln's election; am glad of it. Heard the *Tallahassee* had destroyed four vessels.

November 16.—About 8 a.m. sighted a sail; gave chase, and about 10 a.m. came up with it. Proved to be the ship *Christine*, of Kien, Norway. Showed her our true colors, upon which she saluted us. We continued on our course. At about 4 p.m. made a sail; proved to be the *Jacob Cappe*, of St. Thomas, a barkentine. As she was French, we passed on without further delay.

November 18.—Saw two sails during the day, one of which was a steamer. We changed our course twice to avoid the latter; he did not see us, fortunately, and we stood on for the land, hoping to reach the bar (New Inlet) before 10 p.m. — that is, before the moon rose. We did not calculate well, however, for at 10 we were not in soundings. About 11 we saw breakers ahead and had to back both engines to get clear of them; then we saw houses on the beach and two wrecks which everybody declared to be those at New Inlet. All hands were congratulating one another upon having run the blockade without seeing anything, but after signalizing and getting no answer the talk began to change. We sent a boat into the beach and the pilot soon came back and said he did not recognize the coast at all. The captain then took the ship himself and stood to the southward and eastward [westward].

November 19.—At 5:30 a.m. found ourselves really inside the blockade and just under the guns of Fort Fisher. We let go anchor to wait until the tide made sufficiently for us to cross the bar. Found the place where we had sent the boat on shore to be Masonboro Inlet, about 20 miles to the northward. About 7 a.m. the fog lifted and a small Yankee gunboat came in and opened fire. We answered from our large gun. The firing brought up three more, who all commenced firing as fast as they could, we replying and the forts firing occasionally. About 7:30 the Yankees drew off. At 8 a.m. they returned to the attack with five vessels, whereupon we got under way and crossed the bar in safety. At 10:45 crossed the Rip and proceeded in toward Wilmington. The forts opened fire as we came in and the Yankees hauled off again. Reached Wilmington about 11 a.m. Found the *Tallahassee* safe in port, she having destroyed six vessels, one of which was a brig that we chased the second day out.[4]

The *Chickamauga* captured only seven vessels in her abbreviated three-week cruise, but her presence contributed to the decline of the American merchant service by causing many shippers to transfer their vessels to foreign registry from which few ever returned. Her foray against the Northern merchant marine coincided with the second cruise of her sister ship, the *Tallahassee,* and added to the panic and consternation along the east coast. Insurance rates skyrocketed, and many merchants were forced into bankruptcy while their vessels rotted at the wharves. In spite of the criticism from such quarters as Governor Vance and General Whiting, the two twin screw cruisers caused a considerable amount of damage to the United States, and drew countless enemy vessels away from their duties as blockaders.

Unlike the *Tallahassee,* the *Chickamauga* was not converted back to a blockade runner, but was retained as a warship. The raider's commander, Lieutenant Wilkinson, was transferred to the re-christened *Chameleon,* and Lieutenant Ward was assigned as the *Chickamauga's* new commander. By December, it was plainly evident that an attack against Fort Fisher was imminent. Because some of the guns along the sea face of Fort Fisher, and in Battery Buchanan which guarded the entrance to New Inlet at the southern tip of Confederate Point, were Brooke rifles on naval carriages, part of the *Chickamauga's* crew was

The CSS *Chickamauga.*

dispatched to man them. Now, as the cold December winds whistled and howled around the sand dunes, Confederate sailors and marines, along with their army comrades, kept an anxious eye out for the expected Federal fleet.[5]

The storm broke on the morning of December 24, 1864. More than fifty-six Federal warships of Rear Admiral David Dixon Porter's fleet, carrying 619 heavy guns, opened fire on the Confederate positions at Fort Fisher, the Mound Battery, and at Battery Buchanan. During the next two days the Southern bastion was pounded by a most horrific bombardment, surpassing anything seen in naval warfare up to that time. The Confederate garrison responded sporadically, but most of their time was spent huddled in the bombproofs to escape the hurricane of exploding shells and whizzing shrapnel. Federal troops commanded by Major General Benjamin Butler, landed on the peninsula to the north, and advanced to within only yards of the fort, when, at the last moment, fearing that they lacked the strength to carry the fortification, their attack was canceled.

The sailors and marines at Battery Buchanan braved the storm and returned the enemy fire, keeping the Federals from gaining access to the channel over the bar at New Inlet. Two of the big Brooke rifles burst from the heat of firing, injuring scores, but fortunately causing no deaths. Midshipman Cary, the same officer who had kept the log on the *Chickamauga*, estimated that 100 shells per minute were

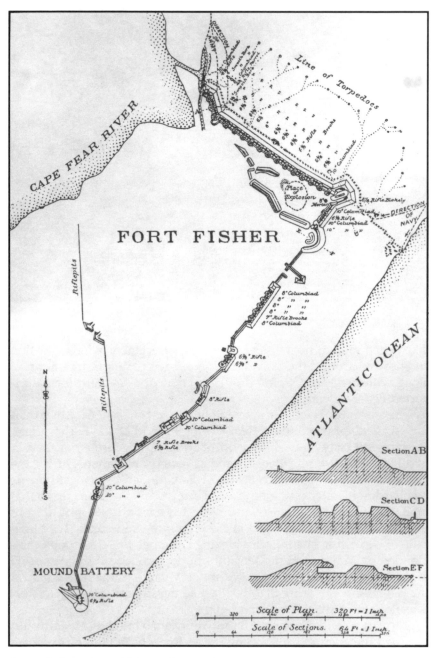

General plan of Fort Fisher. The 7-inch Brooke rifles on the sea face wall were
manned by sailors from the *Chickamauga*.

Battles and Leaders

exploding on their positions. Seaman P. A. Foster was killed outright by a piece of shrapnel, and Seaman J. F. Higgins, serving in an adjoining Brooke battery, was horribly wounded by an exploding shell that severed his leg. With most of her crew manning the guns on the extreme end of Confederate Point and along the sea face, the *Chickamauga* was extremely shorthanded, but in spite of this, Lieutenant Ward kept the cruiser plowing back and forth between Wilmington and the wharf at Battery Buchanan, delivering supplies and ammunition. By December 26, the Federals had started pulling out in order to regroup. Later in the day, the shaken *Chickamauga* survivors who had manned the Brooke rifles on the sea face wall, trudged over the sand to their comrades at Battery Buchanan. Creaking along behind them came a battered oxcart filled with the wounded. Observing their approach, their fellow crewmen at the battery formed a hollow square and received them with cheer after cheer. While many rejoiced, most Confederate commanders knew that it would be only a short matter of time until the armada of enemy warships returned.[6]

The gray-clad soldiers and sailors did not have long to wait. On January 13, 1865, Admiral Porter's fleet again appeared, this time accompanied by numberless troop transports carrying 10,000 Federal soldiers and marines. Once more the 1,500 Southern defenders took to their bombproofs as the entire Confederate Point became smothered in exploding shells and spinning shrapnel. The Union troops, now commanded by Brigadier General Alfred H. Terry, splashed ashore two miles above the fortress and quickly extended their lines across the peninsula to the Cape Fear River. Working their way down the riverbank, they soon captured Craig's Landing, Fort Fisher's supply wharf. Shortly after the capture of the landing, the fort's commander Colonel William Lamb, squinting through his telescope, watched helplessly as the Confederate supply ship *Isaac Wells* approached the dock. Lamb ordered a round fired across the

Colonel William Lamb, CSA, the ever vigilant commander of Fort Fisher.
Battles and Leaders

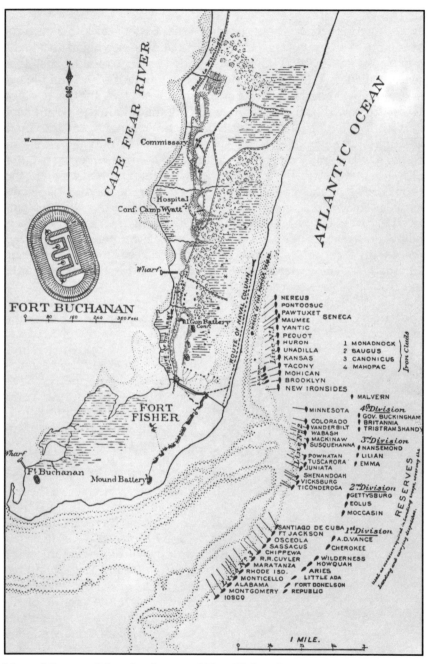

Map of the naval bombardment of Fort Fisher, January 15, 1865. Battery Buchanan was manned by crew members from the *Chickamauga*.

Battles and Leaders

Isaac Wells' bow as a warning, but with so many shells and shrapnel splashing in the river from the Federal barrage, the vessel's commander paid no heed. The supply ship had just been tied to the wharf when joyous blue-coated infantry swarmed all over her.

At that moment, as the Union infantry celebrated its capture of the Confederate supply ship, Lieutenant Ward and the *Chickamauga* hove into view. Ward had been keeping pace with the Federal advance down the Point, and had shelled them continuously, killing and wounding many. Quickly recognizing the situation at the landing, Ward shouted for his gunners to switch their fire to the Confederate supply ship. Quickly the *Chickamauga's* three large pivot rifles were swung in the direction of the landing. Almost in unison her guns roared, and rifled shells and rounds of canister streaked toward the wharf. Iron balls and exploding fragments whistled across the supply ship's deck as the celebrating Union troops tumbled onto the dock and scurried for cover. The *Chickamauga* fired again—and again, and within minutes the *Isaac Wells*, her hull riddled with holes, sank to the bottom, her lines still secured to the dock. [7]

On Sunday, January 15, the naval bombardment continued, and Terry's blue-clad troops inched closer to the north face of the fortification. Ward kept the *Chickamauga* out in the river and continued to shell the advancing Union troops with the cruiser's three pivot guns. About noon, however, the USS *Monticello* moved in close to shore and began lobbing her big 100-pounder shells across the peninsula, aiming them for the *Chickamauga*. The fire became so intense that Ward was forced to retire out of range. Late in the day, about 6,000 Federal infantry stormed the land face of the fortification, and after the most vicious hand-to-hand fighting ever witnessed on the American continent, the Southern defenders were forced to surrender. [8]

The *Chickamauga* was powerless to prevent the catastrophe that had happened at Fort Fisher. One lone Confederate warship was of no significance compared to the mighty fleet of warships that the United States had deployed against the fortification. As Ward and his depleted crew steamed the cruiser back up the river to Wilmington, it must have been despondently apparent that the cause for which they had struggled so long, was rapidly slipping away. Except for Galveston, on the far Texas coast, all Southern ports were now cut off, and no outside aid could reach the starving gray armies.

By February 21, Federal troops were poised on the southern outskirts of Wilmington itself. Confederate units were ordered out of the city and retreated northward to avoid being trapped by Sherman's forces which were advancing from the south. A pall of smoke hung over the city. Businesses were closed and most citizens had fled.

The bombardment of Fort Fisher, January 15, 1865.
Battles and Leaders

Military supplies, warehouses, cotton, tobacco, and even ships at the docks, were put to the torch. While Wilmington burned, and dusty Southern soldiers plodded northward, the *Chickamauga* steamed slowly up the winding and increasingly narrow northwest branch of the Cape Fear River on a disheartening journey. Ward had orders not to allow the cruiser to fall intact into the hands of the enemy. He was also instructed to do all in his power to impede the linkup between the enemy's troops advancing from Wilmington and those of General Sherman.[9]

Consequently, on February 25, 1865, just below the hamlet of Indian Wells, the *Chickamauga* was swung cross-wise to the river, then burned and scuttled. Ward and his crew gathered their sidearms, and with their few meager possessions, trudged onward over the frozen roads toward Fayetteville. From there the remnants of the *Chickamauga's* crew made their way to Lee's army, where, during the painful retreat to Appomattox, they fought savagely at the Battle of Sailor's (Sayler's) Creek, April 6, 1865, before being taken captive. Lieutenant Ward, taken prisoner with the others at Sailor's (Sayler's) Creek, was transported to the hell hole at Johnson Island, Lake Erie, where he remained until finally released on July 25, 1865.[10]

During the war, the *Chickamauga*, and her sister, the *Tallahassee*, were unique in that they were the only two Confederate cruisers that sailed from, and returned to, the same Confederate port. In addition, unlike the English-built cruisers, such as the *Alabama* and the *Florida*, the crews of the *Chickamauga* and *Tallahassee* were regular Confederate Navy long before they had volunteered to serve on the twin screw steamers. Some may argue that the two vessels could have been better utilized as blockade runners. Recent research has shown, however, that the scarcity of supplies and war materials for the Confederate armies was due more to the breakdown of rail transportation than to actual shortages. As cruisers, therefore, the two speedy warships had struck terror into the merchant service of the enemy and had lifted Southern morale at a time when despair hung like a suffocating cloud over the land. For Southerners, it was a way of striking back at the hated Northern enemy who was ravaging their beloved Southern homeland. If for no other reason than this, it was considered worth the effort.

Chapter Eight

The Last Blockade Runners

The years of 1864 and 1865 were ones of peak activity for the long, sleek vessels that stole into Confederate ports almost every night. In spite of the increasingly effective Federal blockade, more and more fast steamers plied the waters between the Confederacy and Nassau, St. George, and Havana, bringing supplies and munitions to the fighting Southern armies. It is an enlightening fact that surviving records indicate a total of 199 safe arrivals of blockade runners in Confederate ports for 1863. The year 1864, however, discloses an increase to 244 successful arrivals. There were another 30 safe arrivals recorded for 1865. This, even though the Federal blockade at this late stage of the war was at its most efficient level. To achieve this astounding record, required a special breed of steamer, one with high speed, large cargo capacity, and a low silhouette. Add to this, a brave and courageous commander, and success was usually—but not always—assured.[1]

The remarkable record compiled by these blockade runners encompasses an important and inspiring chapter in Confederate naval activity. As the Confederacy's fortunes began to wane in the winter of 1864–1865, successes for the even the fastest runners were becoming more and more difficult. Two vessels—two of the last blockade runners—can best serve to illustrate just how dangerous, and perhaps exciting, the game of blockade running had finally become. The two steamers, one civilian and one Confederate Navy owned, were the *Banshee II* and the *Owl*.

***

Tom Taylor was glad to see his new steamer pull into Wilmington. She was the 252-foot *Banshee II* and her arrival could not have come at a more fortuitous time. Taylor, "supercargo" for the Anglo-Confederate Trading Company of Liverpool, England, had been struggling to re-float another company runner which had been damaged by fire and was hung up on a sandbar in the Cape Fear River. With a tow from the powerful *Banshee II*, the damaged *Night Hawk* was at last free and able to steam under her own power up the river to Wilmington.

Taylor, an Englishman, managed the loading and the delivery of all payloads consigned to the Confederacy by his company. During the war his steamers compiled an astounding record, successfully completing forty-nine runs out of fifty-eight attempts. Throughout the conflict, Taylor supervised the operations of nine blockade runners, making twenty-eight trips himself to assure the safe delivery of his company's merchandise. Ardently sympathetic to the South's cause and her struggle for independence, he nevertheless, like most civilian runners, put his vessel's and his own life in harm's way, not only for patriotism, but for the enormous profits that could be accrued by successfully running the Federal blockade. Little did he realize, however, when the big *Banshee II* steamed majestically into the Cape Fear on that crisp fall morning of October 15, 1864, that she would be his very last.[2]

The *Banshee II* represented the state of the art in shipbuilding when she was launched at the Aitken and Mansel facility at Glasgow, Scotland in the summer of 1864. She was very advanced in concept, and constituted a class of vessel, developed by British builders, that helped catapult the design of steam-driven merchant vessels into the twentieth century. Grossing 439 tons, the *Banshee II* was 252 feet long with a beam of 31 feet. She drew only 11 feet of water when fully loaded, which permitted her to cross the bar easily at Wilmington, North Carolina. Her steel hull was painted a light gray, and her giant side-wheels could drive her through the water at over fifteen and one-half knots. Her fifty-three man crew, with their English officers and Southern pilots, made the speedy *Banshee II* almost impossible to catch. She was the pride of the Anglo-Confederate Trading Company, and Taylor was eager to put her to work.[3]

The *Banshee II* had made three round trips into Wilmington before Taylor had an opportunity to sail in her. She left Wilmington in December of 1864, just before the attack and eventual fall of Fort Fisher, with Taylor's favorite captain at the helm, the fearless Jonathon Steele.

The fate of many. The remains of a blockade runner lie buried in the sand on a rocky Carolina shore.

The Library of Congress

The *Banshee II*. The speedy blockade runner could do more than fifteen knots, and was Tom Taylor's last steamer.

The adventures of Taylor and his *Banshee II* during these last desperate months of the war, as the Confederacy struggled for its very exisitence, are best told in his own words:

When Wilmington was on the point of falling there was nothing for it but to transfer our operations to Galveston, and to accomplish this I took the Banshee No. 2 over to Havana with a valuable cargo, accompanied by Frank Hurst, in order to make an attempt to run into Galveston: this proved to be my last trip, but it was far from being the least exciting.[4]

Frank Hurst was the agent for the Anglo-Confederate Trading Company at Nassau, in the Bahamas, but with the fall of Wilmington, Taylor transferred him to Havana. Surviving records indicate that the *Banshee II* slipped over the bar at the mouth of the Cape Fear River on December 28, laden with a valuable cargo of cotton. She was one of the last blockade runners to clear the North Carolina port before it was finally sealed when Union forces captured Fort Fisher. Taylor's damaged *Night Hawk* left three days later.[5]

When all was ready we experienced the greatest difficulty in finding a Galveston pilot, Taylor continued. *Though, owing to the high rate of pay, numbers of men were to be found ready to offer their services, it was extremely hard to obtain competent men. After considerable delay we had to content ourselves at last with a man who said he knew all about the port, but who turned out to be absolutely worthless. We then made a start, and with the exception of meeting with the most violent thunderstorm, in which the lightning was something awful, nothing extraordinary occurred on our passage across the Gulf of Mexico, and we scarcely saw a sail—very different from our experiences between Nassau and Wilmington, when it was generally a case of "sail on the port bow " or "steamer right ahead" at all hours of the day.*[6]

It was 725 nautical miles from Havana to Galveston. The problem was not so much the distance between the two ports, as the lack of transportation from Texas to the rest of the Confederacy. With the fall of Vicksburg and Port Hudson on the Mississippi River in 1863, very little in the way of supplies could reach the eastern half of the country. Most of the munitions, provisions, and consumer goods arriving at Galveston, therefore, were shipped by rail to Houston and distributed throughout the Trans-Mississippi Department. Records are incomplete, but it was in the month of March, 1865, that the *Banshee II* cautiously approached the Texas coast.[7]

The third evening after leaving Havana we had run our distance, and, on heaving the lead and finding that we were within a few miles of the shore, we steamed cautiously on in order to try and make out the blockading squadron or the land. It was a comparatively calm and very dark night, just the one for the purpose, but within an hour all had changed and it commenced to blow a regular "Norther," a wind which is very prevalent on that coast. Until then I had no idea what a "Norther" meant; first rain came down in torrents, then out of the inky blackness of clouds and rain came furious gusts, until a hurricane was blowing against which, notwithstanding that we were steaming at full speed, we made little or no way, and although the sea was smooth our decks were swept by white foam and spray. Suddenly we made out some dark objects all around us, and found ourselves drifting helplessly among the ships of the blockading squadron, which were steaming hard to their anchors, and at one moment we were almost jostling two of them; whether they knew what we were, or mistook us for one of themselves matters not; they were too much occupied about their own safety to attempt to interfere.

As to attempt to get into Galveston that night would have been madness, we let the Banshee drift and, when we thought we were clear of the fleet, we steamed slowly seaward, after a while shaping a course so as to make the land about thirty miles to the south-west at daylight. We succeeded in doing this and quietly dropped our anchor in perfectly calm water, the "Norther" having subsided almost as quickly as it had risen. Having seen enough of our pilot to realize that he was no good whatever, we decided after a conference to lie all day where we were, keeping a sharp look-out and steam handy, and determined as evening came on to creep slowly up the coast until we made out the blockading fleet, then to anchor again and make a bold dash at daylight for our port.

All went well; we were unmolested during the day and we got under weigh towards evening, passing close to a wreck which we recognized as our old friend the Will-o'-the-Wisp, which had been driven ashore and lost on the very first trip she made after I had sold her. Immediately afterwards we very nearly lost our own ship too. Seeing a post of Confederate soldiers close by on the beach, we determined to steam close in and communicate with them in order to learn all about the tactics of the blockaders and our exact distance from Galveston. We backed her close in to the breakers in order to speak, but when the order was given to go ahead she declined to move, and the chief engineer reported that something had gone wrong with the cylinder valve, and that she must heave to for repairs. It was an anxious moment; the Banshee had barely three fathoms beneath her, and her stern was almost in the white water. We let go the anchor, but in the heavy swell it failed to hold: the pilot was in a helpless state of flurry when he found that we were drifting slowly but steadily towards the shore, but Steele's presence of mind never for one moment deserted him. The comparatively few minutes which occupied the engineers in temporarily remedying the defect seemed like hours in the presence of the danger momentarily threatening us. When, at length, the engineers managed to turn her head we on the bridge were greatly relieved to see her point seawards and clear the breakers. I have often thought since, if a disaster had happened and we had lost the ship, how stupid we should have been thought by people at home.

As soon as we reached deep water the damage was permanently repaired, and we steamed cautiously up the coast, until about sundown we made out the topmasts of the blockading squadron right ahead. We promptly stopped, calculating that, as they were about ten to eleven miles from us, Galveston must lie a little farther on our port bow. We let go our anchor and prepared for an anxious night; all hands were on deck and the cable was ready to be unshackled at a moment's notice, with steam as nearly ready as possible without blowing off, as at any moment a prowler from the squadron patrolling the coast might have made us out. We had not been lying thus very long when suddenly on the starboard bow we made out a cruiser steaming towards us evidently on the prowl. It was a critical time; all hands were on deck, a man standing by to knock the shackle out of the chain cable, and the engineers at their stations. Thanks to the backing of the coast, our friend did not discover us and to our relief disappeared to the southward.

After this all was quiet during the remainder of the night, which, fortunately for us, was very dark, and about two hours before daylight we quietly raised our anchor and steamed slowly on, feeling our way cautiously by the lead, and hoping, when daylight fairly broke, to find ourselves inside the fleet opposite Galveston and able to make a short dash for the bar. We had been under way some time, when suddenly we discovered a launch close to us on the port bow filled with Northern blue-jackets and marines. "Full speed ahead," shouted Steele, and we were within an ace of running her down as we almost grazed her with our port paddlewheel. Hurst and I looked straight down into the boat, waving them a parting salute. The crew seemed only too thankful at their narrow escape to open fire, but they soon regained their senses and threw up rocket after rocket in our wake as a warning to the blockading fleet to be on the alert.

Daylight was then slowly breaking, and the first thing we discovered was that we had not taken sufficient account of the effects of the "Norther" on the current; instead of being opposite the town with the fleet broad on to our starboard beam, we found ourselves down three or four miles from it and the most leeward blockader close to us on our bow. It was a moment for immediate decision: the alternatives were to turn tail and stand a chase to seaward by their fastest cruisers with chance of capture, and in any case a return to Havana as we had not sufficient coal for another attempt, or to make a dash for it and take the fire of the squadron. In an instant we decided to go for it, and orders to turn ahead full speed were given; but the difficulty now to be overcome was that we could not make for the main channel without going through the fleet. This would have been certain destruction, so we had to make for a sort of swash channel along the beach, which, however, was nothing but a cul-de-sac, and to get from it into the main channel. Shoal water and heavy breakers had to be passed, but there was now no other choice open to us.

By this time the fleet had opened fire upon us, and shells were bursting merrily around as we took the fire of each ship which we passed. Fortunately there was a narrow shoal between us, which prevented them from approaching within about half a mile of us; luckily also for us they were in rough water on the windward side of the shoal and could not lay their guns with precision. And to this we owed our escape, as, although our funnels were riddled with shell splinters, we received no damage and had only one man wounded. But the worst was to come; we saw the white water dead ahead, and we knew our only chance was to bump through it, being well aware that if stuck fast we should lose the ship and all our lives, for no boat, even if it could have been launched, would have lived in such a surf.

With two leadsmen in the chains we approached our fate, taking no notice of the bursting shells and round shot to which the blockaders treated us in their desperation; it was not a question of the fathoms but of the feet we were drawing: twelve feet, ten, nine, and when we put her at it, as you do a horse at a jump, and as her nose was entering the white water, "eight feet" was sung out. A moment afterwards we touched and hung; and I thought all was over, when a big wave came rolling along and lifted our stern and the ship bodily with a crack which could be heard a quarter of a mile off, and which we thought meant that her back was broken.

She once more went ahead: the worst was over, and, after two or three minor bumps, we were in the deep channel, helm hard a-starboard and heading for Galveston Bay, leaving the disappointed blockaders astern. It was a reckless undertaking and a narrow escape, but we were safe in, and after an examination by the health officer we steamed gaily up to the town, the wharves of which were crowded by people, who, gazing to seaward, had watched our exploit with much interest, and who cheered us heartily upon its success.

I found Galveston a most forsaken place; its streets covered with sand, its wharves rotting, its defenses in a most deplorable condition, very different from those at Wilmington, and if the Northerners had taken the trouble I think that they could easily have possessed themselves of it. But our welcome *was warm, and during the Banshee's long stay we had a real good time; General Magruder was in command, and many a cheery entertainment we had on board with him and his staff as guests, who were all musical. We had a capital French cook, and as plenty of game, fish, and oysters were procurable, and our good liquor was plentiful, we had all the necessary ingredients for many most sociable evenings—this was the bright side of the picture.*[8]

The "dark side" for Taylor was that he had to travel all the way to Houston in order to secure an outbound cargo of cotton for his vessel. This he finally acheived and after shipment over the worn-out rail line to Galveston, the *Banshee II* cleared Galveston for Havana without incident. By the time the Cuban port was reached, however, the war was over and Taylor sent the speedy runner home to England where she was eventually sold for less than one-tenth of her original cost. Thus, the career of one of the last blockade runners was over.[9]

***

The *Owl*, too, belonged to that new class of blockade runners that came along toward the close of the war. These vessels, which were constructed in Liverpool under the watchful eye of James Bulloch and owned by the Southern government, also included the *Bat*, the *Stag*, and the *Deer*. The *Owl* was a 771-ton side-wheeler with a low rakish molded steel hull. She was 230 feet long, 26 feet abeam, drew 10.5 feet of water, and her twin Watt engines could drive her at speeds up to 16 knots. She could carry eight hundred bales of cotton and her oversized coal bunkers gave her extra range. Being careful to comply with

The *Banshee II* under fire as she runs into Galveston, Texas, in March of 1865.

English neutrality laws, the *Owl* under the command of British master Matthew J. Butcher, left Liverpool bound for Halifax, Nova Scotia, on July 29, 1864.[10] (Butcher was the same British captain who had contracted with Bulloch to deliver the *Enrica* to the Azores. The *Enrica* later became the famous CSS *Alabama*.)

The *Owl's* cargo had been personally selected by Bulloch, and he elaborated on its contents in a letter to Secretary Mallory, stating that it contained goods for the Navy Department as well as the Ordnance Bureau. Bulloch also explained that he was sending a consignment of wire and a magnetic exploder with 100 fuses for electric torpedoes. The supplies for the torpedoes were most likely the result of experiments which were being carried on by Commander Matthew Fontaine Maury.

Arriving at Halifax, the *Owl* attracted the attention of the U.S Consulate who telegraphed on August 29, that she was in port and expected to leave shortly. Two days later, Consular M. M. Jackson rushed another telegram off to the U.S. Government: *British Blockade-running iron steamer Owl, 330 tons, has just cleared for Nassau with large valuable cargo, real destination, doubtless, Wilmington. Steamer, schooner rigged; has two pipes, one abaft the other. Is long and low and painted light-red color. Takes nearly 100 seamen, probably to supply another vessel at Wilmington.*[11]

Butcher did indeed head for Wilmington, but stopped first at Bermuda to pick up a pilot, arriving in the North Carolina port about September 19. Ten days prior to the *Owl's* arrival, Commander John Newland Maffitt was opening a telegram from Confederate Navy Secretary Mallory: *Sir: You are hereby detached from the command of the C.S. (ram) Albemarle, and will proceed to Wilmington, N.C., and report to Flag-Officer William F. Lynch, commanding, for the command of a blockade runner.*[12] The vessel Maffitt was being transferred to was the eagerly anticipated *Owl*. It would be Maffit's final command of the war, but it would be several exasperating months before he would take her to sea.

While she was docked at Wilmington, Confederate naval officers attempted to transfer the *Owl* to government registry, but for some reason Butcher did not consider the process properly executed and he refused to relinquish command. On the night of October 3, he crossed the bar at the mouth of the Cape Fear and headed for Bermuda with a full load of government-owned cotton. In spite of the moonless night, the Owl was spotted by the Federal blockaders who proceeded to send nine shots screaming over and around the speeding Confederate vessel. Several shells exploded in close proximity, slightly wounding Butcher and several crewmen, but the *Owl* reached St. George safely a few days later. Butcher was now informed that a Confederate naval officer would take his place for the return trip to Wilmington, and the disgruntled English captain sailed for Liverpool. First Lieutenant John W. Dunnington took command of the *Owl*, and guided by the experienced pilot Tom Burroughs, arrived uneventfully back at Wilmington on December 2.[13]

While Maffitt waited impatiently in Wilmington for the transfer of the *Owl* to naval registry, he received a series of instructions from Secretary Mallory. The naval secretary was convinced that the most efficient use of the fast steamers that were now entering service was to operate them strictly as Confederate navy vessels, officered and crewed by regular naval personnel. In a letter dated September 14, Mallory emphasized that: *The Owl is the first of several steamers built for and on account of the Confederate Government, and which are to be run under the direction of the Secretary of the Navy. Naval officers are to be placed in command, and you are selected to take charge of the Owl.... As the Owl will soon be followed by several other vessels under this Department, it is important that uniformity, as far as practicable, be observed in their management.*[14]

Five days later, no doubt further contemplating the extreme importance of the navy operated runners, Mallory sent an urgent telegram to Maffitt at Wilmington:

It is of the first importance, he wrote, *that our steamers should not fall into the enemy's hands. Apart from the specific loss sustained by the country*

in the capture of blockaded runners, these vessels, lightly armed, now constitute the fleetest and most efficient part of his blockading force off Wilmington.

As commanding officer of the Owl you will please devise and adopt thorough and efficient means for saving all hands and destroying the vessel and cargo whenever these measures may become necessary to prevent capture. Upon your firmness and ability the Department relies for the execution of this important trust.[15]

Again on November 25, Mallory wrote: *Before leaving port you will station your crew for the different boats of the steamer, having placed in them water and provisions, and also nautical instruments.*

First Lieutenant John W. Dunnington, captain of the *Owl* on her run into Wilmington on December 2, 1864.
Author's Collection

When capture, in your judgment, becomes inevitable, fire the vessel in several places and embark in the boats, making for the nearest land.... The Department leaves to your discretion the time when and the circumstances that must govern you in the destruction of the Owl in order to prevent her falling into the hands of the enemy.[16] Although Mallory's obsession with the possible capture of the *Owl* is indicative of the desperate straits that the Confederacy now found itself, the recommendations to a bold and imaginative commander such as John Newland Maffitt were most certainly unnecessary.

Upon the arrival of the *Owl* at the beginning of December, Maffitt was at last able to take command of the speedy runner. On the dark night of December 21, Maffitt drove the *Owl* across the bar at the mouth

Commander John Newland Maffitt, captain of the blockade runner *Owl*.

Author's Collection

Lieutenant E. Maffitt Anderson who served
with Commander Maffitt on the *Owl*.
Sinclair, *Two Years on the Alabama*

of the Cape Fear River and set a course for Bermuda. Stacked in the hold and on deck were 780 bales of valuable Southern cotton. The *Owl*, as Maffitt later wrote, "ran clear of the Federal sentinels without the loss of a rope yarn."[17] Arriving at St. George, Maffitt found several blockade runners awaiting the results of the expected Union assault against Fort Fisher. By the first part of January, word reached the islands that Butler's assault against the Confederate bastion had failed, and Maffitt prepared to return to Wilmington.

On or about January 12, 1865, with her cargo hold stuffed with assorted hardware for the Army of Northern Virginia, the *Owl* stole out of St. George and sped toward the North Carolina coast. On the dark night of the 15th, Maffitt approached Old Inlet at the mouth of the Cape Fear River. Luck was with the *Owl*, for the lookouts spotted only one blockader which was easily avoided. Crossing the bar on a high tide at 8:00 p.m., Maffitt eased the big steamer up to the wharf at Fort Caswell. Wisps of escaping smoke spiraled from her twin stacks as crewmen, elated over their easy and successful run through the blockade, rapidly drew the anchor lines taut. Presently a small boat pulled alongside. The occupants, Confederate soldiers from the fort, had some disturbing news. Fort Fisher had fallen earlier that same day to a combined Federal land and navy force, and at this very moment, Southern forces were evacuating Fort Caswell and preparing to retreat toward Wilmington. Several Union warships had already crossed the bar at New Inlet and were in the river. The *Owl* must leave at once![18]

Knowing that he had only minutes to make his escape, Maffitt acted immediately. Just as he was about to give the order to slip the chain, his pilot begged for a short delay. He pleaded for Maffitt to wait, if only for ten minutes, in order that he might slip ashore to check on his ailing wife. The pilot presented his case in such imploring terms that Maffitt was moved to grant his request, but only upon the strict condition that he return quickly. Giving his word, the pilot bounded onto the wharf and disappeared into the darkness. Maffitt nervously paced the steamer's deck. Calling the engine room, he ordered the engineer to maintain the highest steam pressure possible, and to be ready to start the engines at a moment's notice. Lines were ordered cast off and the chain unshackled. Upriver, shadowy forms of several blockaders could be seen, and they appeared to be moving in the *Owl's* direction. The minutes seemed like hours as the officers and men anxiously waited. As steam hissed softly from the engine room, Maffitt once more checked his watch. Ten minutes; fifteen minutes; they must leave now! Suddenly, the faithful pilot came bounding out of the night. The moment his feet hit the deck, the *Owl's* big paddle wheels began to revolve. The chain was slipped, her head turned southeastward, and the powerful steamer ran for the open sea. The nearest Federal immediately opened fire, her shells exploding around the fleeing runner, showering her with shrapnel, but doing no damage. Soon the speeding *Owl* was lost in the velvet folds of darkness.[19]

Maffitt must have had mixed feelings as the throbbing engines drove the *Owl* on into the night. He and his vessel had escaped capture, but with Wilmington gone, he was now completely isolated from his family and his homeland. As the *Owl* drove seaward, the muffled explosions caused by the destruction of Fort Caswell were clearly audible. Maffitt wrote that they "rumbled portentously from wave to wave in melancholy echoes." Watching the distant flashes of light, the Confederate commander "in poignant distress...turned from the heartrending scene." It was more than he could bear.[20]

With his coal supply dangerously low, Maffitt returned to Bermuda under easy steam, arriving there on January 21. His arrival was in time to stop five blockaders which were preparing to depart for Wilmington. Being the ranking Confederate officer in the islands, Maffitt called John Wilkinson and John Low to the home of the Confederate quartermaster, Major Norman S. Walker. There, amid the gloom of the most recent news, the three navy officers discussed possible strategies for reaching the struggling Southern armies with their supplies. When word reached the group that Charleston had not yet fallen, Maffitt and several others determined to sail for that port.

My cargo being important, he wrote, *and the capture of Fort Fisher and the Cape Fear cutting me off from Wilmington, I deemed it my duty to make an effort to enter the harbor of Charleston in order to deliver the much needed supplies.*[21] Accordingly, on January 26, the *Owl* cleared St. George bound for Charleston. Although several Federal warships were sighted on the departure from Bermuda, the speedy runner soon left them far behind.[22]

Arriving off Charleston in the dead of night, Maffitt placed the government mail and his journal, including his log of the cruise of the CSS

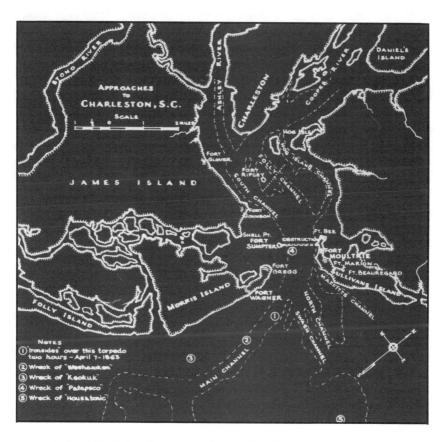

A chart depicting the approaches to Charleston, South Carolina.

Florida, in two weighted bags and slug them over the side secured by a heavy line. A trusted sailor was ordered to stand by the line with a hatchet, and if capture appeared imminent, he was to send the pouches to the bottom of the sea. Many Federal blockaders, freed from their service at Wilmington, now crowded the entrances to the channels leading into Charleston, and the Maffitt steamed the *Owl* slowly back and forth trying to locate an opening. *When on the western tail end of Rattlesnake Shoal,* he wrote, *we encountered streaks of mist and fog that enveloped stars and everything for a few moments, when it would become quite clear again. Running cautiously in one of these obscurations, a sudden lift in the haze disclosed that we were about to run into an anchored blockader. We had bare room with a hard-a-port helm to avoid him some fifteen or twenty feet, when their officer on deck called out, "Heave to, or I'll sink you!" The order was unnoticed, and we received his entire broadside, that cut away our turtleback, perforated the forecastle, and tore up the bulwarks in front of our engine room, wounding twelve men, some severely, some slightly. The quartermaster stationed by the mail bags was so convinced that we were captured that he instantly used his hatchet, and sent them, well moored, to the bottom; hence my meager account of the cruise of the Florida.*[23]

Instantly the area was illuminated by burning drummond lights and numerous rockets which sputtered up into the blackened sky. The *Owl,* her paddle wheels now driven at full throttle, was silhouetted in the flickering light, and the guns of the blockaders roared, sending their shells screaming indiscriminately in all directions. There seemed to be swarms of enemy vessels everywhere, but owing to the confusion, Maffitt was enabled to thread his way through the mêlée. The *Owl,* although badly damaged, finally reached the perimeter of the surrounding blockaders, and with engines still at full power, drove steadily onward into the darkened Atlantic. There appeared to be no way that they could make it into Charleston, and a disheartened Maffitt reluctantly ordered the course set for Nassau.[24]

The *Owl* limped into the Bahamian port, Maffitt recorded, "with a shot through her funnel, several more through her hull, her standing rigging in rags and other indications of a hot time." The Confederate commander wished to try running into Charleston again, but while the *Owl* was undergoing repairs, word reached Nassau that the South Carolina city had been evacuated. Only one Southern port still remained accessible now, and that was the distant Texas town of Galveston. Maffitt still had a full cargo of essential supplies on board the *Owl,* and he was determined to land it somewhere in the Confederacy.

The decision was made to sail to Havana, and from there, try to reach Galveston. On the way, however, Maffitt agreed to drop off three passengers on the North Carolina coast. Thomas Conolly, a wealthy member of the British Parliament, had approached him in Nassau, asking for his assistance in reaching the Confederacy. He was the bearer, Conolly explained, of important dispatches from James Mason in England to the government officials in Richmond. It was imperative that he reach the Confederate States as soon as possible. Maffitt, eager to be on his way, agreed, and although the repairs to the *Owl* were incomplete, he steamed out of Nassau on February 23, and set his course once more for the Carolina coast.[25]

Just before dawn on the morning of February 26, the *Owl* approached the coast of North Carolina near Shallotte Inlet. With much difficulty, in a cold driving rain, a boat was lowered, and Conolly and two others set out for the sandy shore which was barely visible in the fog and spray. The heavy surf swamped the boat, but the three men, cold, wet, and miserable, made it to the beach. Conolly successfully made his way to Fayetteville where he visited Maffitt's family before journeying on to Richmond. There he met President Davis, dined with General Robert E. Lee, and was witness to the sad evacuation of the Confederate capital.

After dropping off Conolly and the two other passengers, Maffitt steamed for Havana where he arrived around the first part of March. There he found other blockade runners, including Tom Taylor's *Banshee II*, preparing for the long run to Galveston. It took four to five days to steam the 725 miles from Havana to Galveston, and with the prospect of finding no coal at the Texas port, the steamers had to carry enough fuel for the round trip. Only the largest steamers had the bunker capacity to carry that much fuel, but even then, their draft might be too great to allow passage over the bar at Galveston. The *Owl* still had her full load of supplies, and while her fuel supply might be marginal, and she might have trouble crossing the bar, Maffitt resolved to give it a try anyway.

Before heading for Galveston, however, Maffitt was asked to execute one more courier mission. On March 24, Assistant Surgeon D. S. Watson and First Assistant Engineer E. R. Archer were landed on the Florida coast some nine miles from St. Marks.[26] The reason or necessity for their mission is unknown, but after the war, J. Thomas Scharf in his *History of the Confederate States Navy* described how Maffitt, *left Havana about the middle of March, within "a quarter of an hour" after the USS Cherokee steamed out of the harbor. Passing Morro Castle, the Owl hugged the coast toward the west, followed by the Cherokee—the chase continued for an hour or more; the Owl had the speed, and Maffitt the seamanship, to throw "dust into the eyes" of his pursuer by changing her coal from hard to soft, and clouding the air with dense black smoke, under cover of which the Owl turned on the Cherokee, and steaming away to the stern of the cruiser, disappeared in the darkness of night and storm.*[27]

Sometime during the first few days of April (records are incomplete), Maffitt left Havana again, this time for Galveston. Arriving off the Texas port, the *Owl's* commander found sixteen blockaders guarding the entrance to Galveston Bay. Pressing on in the face of heavy fire, the *Owl* managed to cross the bar, but ran aground on Bird Island Shoals. The Federal commanders were determined to destroy the helpless steamer, and they increased their fire, their shells dropping all around the *Owl*. Maffitt stood on the bridge, as exploding shrapnel whizzed about him, and directed the efforts to free the runner. Her powerful paddle wheels labored in reverse, but she would not budge. The Union fire was becoming more accurate, and it looked as though the vessel was lost, when, suddenly, someone pointed to a steamer that was coming out of Galveston Bay. It was the little CSS *Diana*, captained by James H. McGarvey. Seeing the plight of the *Owl*, McGarvey, heedless of the screaming shot and shell falling around the runner, steamed out into the storm and threw her a towline. With the help of the *Diana*, the *Owl* was finally freed and steamed safely into the Bay. It had been a narrow escape.[28]

Near the first of May, long after the hardened veterans of Lee and Johnston had stacked their arms for the last time, Maffitt ran the blockade out of Galveston and was back in Havana on May 9. When word arrived there that all Confederate forces west of the Mississippi had also surrendered, Maffitt and his fellow officers had to face the reality that their country and their cause was lost. Deciding that the best course of action was to return to Liverpool and deliver the *Owl* to Fraser, Trenholm and Company, Maffitt sailed from Havana for the long ocean crossing. During the voyage, he maintained a wary eye for Federal cruisers which were under urgent orders to apprehend him. Stopping at Nassau for coal, the *Owl* reached Liverpool without incident and steamed up the Mersey River on July 14.

The following day, July 15, 1865, Maffitt gathered the entire crew on the quarterdeck of the *Owl* and addressed them for the final time as their commander: *This is the last time we meet as sailors of the Confederate States Navy.... The Confederacy is dead. Our country is in the hands of the enemy, and we must accept the verdict.... I am grateful to you for your loyalty to me, and to the South.* Maffitt then paid off the men, spliced the main brace one last time for the Confederacy, and to the accompaniment of three resounding cheers from the crew, slowly lowered the Confederate flag.[29]

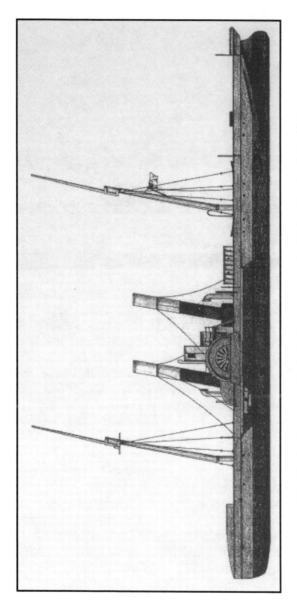

The blockade runner *Owl*, the last command of John Newland Maffitt.

Chapter Nine

The Rendezvous

October is always a beautiful time of year in London, England, and the fall of 1864 was no exception. The numerous shade trees along the ancient cobblestone boulevards were just beginning to display their brilliant hues of red, brown, and orange. It was Friday, the seventh, and the streets were a scene of feverish activity as merchants and financiers hurried to complete their weekly transactions. At Wood's Hotel, just north of the Thames in the Holborn district, a young impatient man from Virginia, dressed in immaculate business attire, sat alone at a corner table in the hotel's coffee room. Peering over the *London Times*, which he was ostensibly reading, he nervously eyed the other patrons in the restaurant, debating in his own mind whether any could possibly be a United States agent.

Tucked securely in his inner coat pocket was a letter dated October 6, from Commander James D. Bulloch, senior Confederate naval agent in Europe, which read in part: *You will proceed to London by the 5 p.m. train today, and go to Wood's Hotel, Furnival's Inn, High Holborn. Take a room there, and give your name as Mr. W. C. Brown, if asked. It has been arranged for you to be in the coffee room of the hotel at 11 a.m. precisely tomorrow, and that you will sit in a prominent position, with a white pocket-handkerchief rove through a buttonhole of your coat, and a newspaper in your hand. In that attitude you will be recognized by Mr. ———, who will call at*

166

the appointed time, and ask if your name is Brown. You will say "Yes," and ask his name. He will give it, and you will then retire with him to your own room, hand him the enclosed letter of introduction, and throwing off all disguise, discuss with him freely the business at hand.

Presently an English businessman with a bundle of papers under his arm entered the coffee room and studied each of the guests. Spying the white handkerchief, he casually approached the table in the corner.

"Is this Mr. Brown?" he inquired.

"I am Mr. Brown," the gentleman at the table responded, as he rose to shake hands. "Please come with me."

The two men climbed the stairs to Brown's room, entered, and locked the door behind them. There, where they were secure from the prying eyes and ears of Union agents, they could speak freely. "Mr. Brown" was in actuality an officer in the Confederate States Navy and destined to become the executive officer on the South's last sea-roving cruiser. The man now sitting on the edge of the bed and unfolding his bundle of documents was Richard Wright, an Englishman and friend of Bulloch's, who had just purchased the steamer *Sea King* for the Confederacy. Amid this "cloak and dagger" atmosphere the remarkable cruise of the CSS *Shenandoah* was born.

The tragic news that the CSS *Alabama* had been sunk by the USS *Kearsarge* off Cherbourg, France on June 19, 1864, struck like a thunderbolt among the Confederate officers stationed in Europe. The *Alabama* had cruised the oceans for two years, destroying or bonding 65 enemy merchant ships, but now she and 21 members of her crew were resting on the bottom of the English Channel. Only the *Florida* remained to press the war against the Northern commerce. Little did the saddened Southern officers realize that she, too, would soon be lost. In spite of the anguish and distress over the loss of the *Alabama*, Commander Bulloch immediately began formulating plans to replace her.

At the same time, on July 18, 1864 Secretary Mallory penned a letter to Bulloch emphasizing the urgent need to find a replacement: *The loss of the Alabama was announced in the Federal papers with all the manifestations of joy which usually ushers the news of great national victories, showing that the calculating enemy fully understood amd appreciated the importance of her destruction. You must supply her place if possible, a measure...of paramount importance.* A short time later Mallory wrote: *The blows of our cruisers have destroyed the foreign trade of the enemy, and given great discouragement to his whale fisheries, the tonnage of which has declined to its limit of 1840, while our naval operations here, including the construction of a few ironclads, have constrained him to add at least a hundred millions to his expenditure to meet them.*[1]

Commander James D. Bulloch, Confederate naval agent in
Europe. Bulloch was responsible for the acquisition of the
CSS *Shenandoah*.

Scharf, *History of the Confederate States Navy*

Bulloch was quite aware, however, that public and official opinion
in Europe was beginning to turn away from the Confederacy. The destruction caused by the *Alabama* and the *Florida*, in addition to other
Confederate raiders, while acknowledged as legal, was nevertheless
becoming distasteful to Southern supporters in England and France.
With every Southern reverse in the field in America, British and French
officials began to worry about facing a victorious and angry United
States once the conflict was ended. While both countries had strived to
maintain a position of neutrality, there was no denying the fact that
great amounts of arms and ammunition had been supplied, and the
ships to carry them had been built or acquired within the borders of
England and France. The *Alabama* and the *Florida* had been constructed
in English shipyards, and a vindictive United States was unlikely to

forget that fact. There was now, Bulloch believed, no possibility of building another cruiser disguised as a merchant vessel, and if completed, even less of a possibility of ever getting her to sea. Pressure from the United States would cause the British or French governments to seize any vessel that bore the slightest suspicion of being built for the Confederacy. The only alternative, at this late stage of the war, was to purchase an existing vessel.

During the summer of 1863, while searching the Clyde River dockyards for suitable blockade runners with Lieutenant Robert R. Carter, Bulloch had come across the *Sea King, a fine, composite, full-rigged ship, with something more than auxiliary steam power,* he wrote, *and all the necessary arrangements for disconnecting and lifting her screw. We were charmed with the ship, but could only make a very hasty and imperfect inspection of her, as she was in all the bustle of loading for her first voyage. I took, however, a careful note of her, and learned that she was bound for Bombay, and would return to England in due course, probably in eight to ten months.*[2]

Lieutenant Carter later returned to the Confederate States, and when word arrived concerning the loss of the *Alabama*, Secretary Mallory called Carter and Commander John M. Brooke to his office to discuss what could be done to maintain the pressure on Northern commerce. Brooke recommended that the American Pacific whaling fleet, an industry of enormous importance to the North, and one that had so far escaped molestation, be attacked. Carter concurred, and recalling the fine ship that he and Bulloch had seen the previous year, suggested that a similar vessel be purchased and dispatched against the Pacific whaling fleet. Mallory wrote out the necessary instructions, and ordered Carter to return to England and deliver their recommendations to Bulloch.

Meanwhile, Bulloch had not waited for instructions, but knowing that he could not search for vessels himself, for he would most surely be recognized by Federal agents, had employed Richard Wright to look for a suitable replacement for the *Alabama*. By coincidence the *Sea King* had returned to Glasgow by early September, 1864, and she was now for sale. Wright telegraphed Bulloch with the exciting news, asking for instructions, and Bulloch instantly wired back for him to purchase the ship immediately in his own name. Wright completed the transaction on September 30, without arousing any suspicion among the numerous Union spies lurking about, and placed Captain Peter Corbett, a British master of merchant ships and an old friend of Bulloch's, in command. Corbett was instructed to sail for London where the *Sea King* would take on a load of coal, ostensibly to be delivered to Bombay. Tucked away in his coat pocket was a power-of-attorney granting

Corbett "permission" to sell the *Sea King* anytime within the next six months for not less than £45,000.[3]

By the time that Wright entered "Mr. Brown's" room at Wood's Hotel on October 7, he had all of the ship's papers in his possession, and she stood loaded at the London docks and ready to sail. Little did they realize, as they began their conversation, that at that very moment, half a world away in the neutral harbor of Bahia, Brazil, the only Confederate cruiser still prowling the oceans of the globe, the CSS *Florida*, was being illegally seized by a United States warship. Blissfully ignorant of this tragedy to Southern arms, the two men carefully unfolded Wright's bundle of documents, and quickly began to realize what a magnificent vessel the *Sea King* really was. Bulloch, in a letter to Mallory dated September 16, had already described her details:

I have the satisfaction to inform you of the purchase of a fine composite ship, built for the Bombay trade, and just returned to London from her first voyage. She is 1,160 tons builder's measurement, classed A1 for 14 years at Lloyd's, frames, beams, etc., of iron, but planked from keel to gunwale with East India teak. She is full rigged as a ship, with rolling topsails, has plenty of accommodation for officers of all grades, and her between decks are 7 feet 6 inches high, with large air-ports, having been fitted under government inspection for the transport of troops. Her engines are direct acting, with two cylinders 47 inches in diameter and 2 feet 9 inches stroke, with ample grate and heating surface, nominal horsepower 220, but indicating 850 horsepower, and she has a lifting screw....Yesterday she went into a graving dock to have her bottom examined and the screw shaft carefully inspected, and the report on both these points was favorable. The log of the ship shows her to be a fast sailer under canvas, for with screw up she has made 330 miles in twenty-four hours by observation (13.75 mph). You will be gratified to learn of this good fortune in finding a ship so admirably suited to our purpose, and I will only now assure you that no effort will be spared, and no precaution neglected, which may help to get her under our flag.[4]

Bulloch's efforts now included organizing a staff of officers, shipping a crew, purchasing the heavy guns, small arms, and munitions, and finding a suitable tender to carry all these necessary items to a rendezvous point that would result in the *Sea King* becoming a Confederate cruiser. Requesting from Flag Officer Barron, senior Confederate naval officer in Europe, that a commanding officer be assigned, Barron dispatched First Lieutenant James Iredell Waddell to be the new cruiser's commander.

James I. Waddell was born on July 13, 1824, in Pittsboro, North Carolina. Appointed a midshipman in the United States Navy on September 10, 1841, at the young age of seventeen, he was assigned to duty on the USS *Pennsylvania*, at Portsmouth, Virginia. (This was prior

First Lieutenant James I. Waddell, commanding officer of the Confederate cruiser, CSS *Shenandoah.*

Author's Collection

to the establishment of the naval academy at Annapolis.) Early in his naval career, a duel, fought with another midshipman, left a bullet lodged in his hip, causing him to limp slightly. After serving several years at sea, Waddell, now married to a Baltimore girl and promoted to lieutenant, was appointed to the naval academy at Annapolis as assistant professor of navigation. After teaching for ten years at the academy, he was serving with the East India Squadron when North Carolina seceded. Upon the confirmation of his state's withdrawal from the Union, Waddell tendered his resignation, stating his "unwillingness to bear arms against his father's home and relatives in the seceded states."[5]

Arriving in Richmond, he was appointed a lieutenant in the Confederate Navy on March 27, 1862, and ordered to New Orleans, where he joined other Southern officers on the still unfinished ironclad CSS *Mississippi.* When Union Admiral Farragut's fleet passed the forts below New Orleans on April 24, Waddell was left on board the immovable *Mississippi* with instructions to set her on fire and destroy her as soon as the Federals hove into view. This unwelcome duty was performed, and he retreated upriver in an open boat as the fiercely burning ironclad drifted downstream toward the approaching Federals. Escaping ahead of the Union fleet, and reaching Vicksburg by steamboat, Waddell was recalled to Richmond where he was ordered to Drewry's Bluff just south of the city as an ordnance officer. After some brief service at Charleston, the North Carolina lieutenant slipped through the blockade and headed for his new assignment in England. Although an intelligent and capable officer, Waddell was thought by his men to be too schooled in the old traditions of the navy to be an aggressive cruiser commander. Because of this, he would never garner the fame, nor the devotion from his crew, as such famous officers as Raphael Semmes or John Newland Maffitt.[6]

"Mr. Brown, " the stranger in the Wood's Hotel coffeehouse, was First Lieutenant William C. Whittle from Norfolk, Virginia, and he would soon prove to be the real strength of the *Shenandoah*. Waddell would quickly learn to entrust all of the day-to-day operations of the Confederate cruiser to his reliable executive officer. Born in 1840, Whittle entered the United States Naval Academy in 1854 and was graduated from that prestigious institution in 1858. After serving with the Gulf Squadron in the Caribbean, he was ordered back to the academy for examinations where he earned his promotion to passed midshipman. Upon the secession of his native state, Whittle resigned his commission and was appointed a lieutenant in the Virginia State Navy. When that service was absorbed by the national government in Montgomery, Lieutenant Whittle was transferred to the Confederate Navy.[7]

The young lieutenant was assigned to the CSS *Nashville*, which was about to sail to Europe under Robert B. Pegram, and he accompanied that cruiser on its voyage to England in 1861. After a lengthy stay where the European powers recognized the belligerent rights of the new Confederacy, Whittle and the *Nashville* returned, entering Beaufort, North Carolina, in February of 1862. Left in command of the cruiser, Whittle, who was determined not to allow the speedy sidewheeler to fall into the hands of the Federals advancing on New Bern, ran her out under heavy fire and arrived safely in Georgetown, South Carolina. (See chapter 2 for the story of the *Nashville*.) In March of 1862, he was ordered to New Orleans as third lieutenant aboard the unfinished ironclad, CSS *Louisiana*. Commanding that ship's forward guns during her brief encounter with Farragut's warships at the Battle of New Orleans, Whittle was taken captive upon that vessel's destruction and spent four months at Fort Warren in Boston harbor before being exchanged. After a brief period as commander of the CSS *Chattahoochee*, on the river of that same name, he was ordered to Europe as part of a cadre of officers who expected to serve on the ironclads and cruisers which

First Lieutenant William C. Whittle, Jr., executive officer of the Confederate cruiser, CSS *Shenandoah*.

Author's Collection

were being built there. It was here that Commander Bulloch chose Whittle to be the *Shenandoah's* executive officer.[8]

Other men came from the large pool of officers then stationed in Europe, and included Lieutenants John Grimball, who had served on the CSS *Arkansas*; Sidney Smith Lee, Jr., nephew of General Robert E. Lee; Francis T. Chew, who along with Waddell had been assigned to the *Louisiana*; and Dabney M. Scales who had also served on the ironclad *Arkansas*. A number of officers of lesser grades rounded out the *Shenandoah's* complement, and they were all young and eager to strike a blow at the enemy. (See appendix I for a complete list of the *Shenandoah's* officers.)

In the meantime, Bulloch continued to quietly assemble a crew for the new cruiser and forwarded them to Waddell in Liverpool where he and his wife maintained an apartment on Clegg Street. As quickly as they arrived, the men were scattered about the city in various rooming houses and told to await further instructions. To transport these men, guns, and equipment to a rendezvous, Bulloch purchased the fast screw steamer *Laurel*, which was berthed in Liverpool. He then placed newly appointed Lieutenant John F. Ramsay of the Confederate Navy in command. Ramsay also held a British Board of Trade master's certificate and could easily pass as a legitimate English officer. Some of the men being sent to Waddell, such as Boatswain George Harwood, Boatswain's Mate Andrew Bachman, Carpenter John O'Shea, Sailmaker Henry Alcot, and Gunner's Mates John Guy and William Crawford were former *Alabama* men. Bulloch hoped that these dedicated men would use their influence among the crews of the *Laurel* and *Sea King* to encourage many of them to enlist as crewmen on the *Shenandoah*. By the time "Mr. Brown" had seated himself in the coffee room at Wood's Hotel in London, both vessels were ready to sail.[9]

While Waddell and the secretly gathered officers would sail as passengers on board the *Laurel*, Bulloch instructed Whittle to take passage on the soon to be *Shenandoah*. *The object in your going out on the Sea King, he wrote, is to acquaint yourself with her sailing and other qualities, and to observe the crew. You can also inspect the internal arrangements, and discuss with Captain Corbett the necessary alterations, and you can learn the stowage of the provisions and other stores, and pick out the position for magazine and shell room. Perhaps the construction of these might be actually begun under...Captain Corbett. You will bear in mind that until she is regularly transferred, Captain Corbett is the legal commander of the Sea King... (and) you will express all your wishes in the form of requests. When you reach Maderia (an island off northwest Africa) and the Laurel joins company, you will report to Lieutenant Commanding Waddell, and thereafter act under his instructions.*[10]

Lieutenant John F. Ramsay (*right*), captain of the *Laurel*, when she rendezvoused with the *Shenandoah*. The other officers are Lieutenants Hilary Cenas (*left*), and Thomas L. Domin.

Author's Collection

At 3:00 a.m. on Saturday, October 8, 1864, the *Sea King* stood with only a couple of lines securing her to the dock on the Thames. Other vessels moored nearby were hushed and dark. On the *Sea King*, however, shadowy forms could be discerned hustling about her deck. Her sleek black hull, moistened by the cold damp night air, glistened in the light of the few gaslamps that still burned along the wharves and alleys of the waterfront. Occasionally, light from inside the ship itself could be seen coming from an unshaded porthole or an open hatch. Steam hissed faintly from somewhere within her bowels, and wisps of grayish smoke spiraled lazily up from her funnel and into the darkness. Suddenly, the figure of a man staggered onto the dock—a drunken sailor, no doubt, returning to his ship. Quickly he approached the ship's rail, and with one giant heave, "Mr. Brown" swung himself aboard. Instantly the lines securing the vessel were cast off and she began to move. Steaming slowly through the maze of anchored shipping, the *Sea King* reached the middle of the Thames, turned downstream, and headed for the Channel. The cruise of the CSS *Shenandoah* was about to begin.

Bulloch received a coded telegram early that morning in Liverpool that the *Sea King* had sailed from London successfully, and he immediately dispatched a note to Lieutenant Ramsay: *You will proceed to sea tonight in command of the steamship Laurel, and carry Lieutenant Commanding James I. Waddell, his staff of officers, and the other passengers of whom you have been advised, to Funchal, in the island of Madeira, with quick dispatch.*[11]

As had been prearranged, Ramsay, upon receiving Bulloch's signal, sent a messenger scurrying to each of the boardinghouses in Liverpool where the passengers were staying. The men were instructed to report that evening to Prince's Landing Stage where a tug would be waiting to transport them to the *Laurel*. Their personal belongings, uniforms, and side arms had already been packed aboard the steamer. By nightfall, a chilly October mist had enveloped the city as individually, or in groups of two or three, the men shuffled down the wet, slippery streets leading to the landing. They avoided acknowledging one another as they plodded along, and with their collars turned up against the cold rain, tried their best to be as inconspicuous as possible.

As they converged on the landing, they continued to avoid conversation as they waited patiently in line while an English clerk dutifully stamped each man's receipt indicating that he had paid £32.00 for the passage to Havana, Cuba. Shortly after midnight, all were aboard the rickety harbor tug. Wheezing and hissing, the old boat cast off and headed slowly for the dark, misty shape that was anchored out in the Mersey River. By 4:00 a.m., all of the men had been checked in on the steamer and shown to their quarters. Ramsay ordered the anchor raised, and signaling the engine room, the engines were started. Swiftly, silently, the *Laurel* slid down the Mersey, disappeared into the mist, and headed for the open sea.[12]

Bulloch, as usual, had accomplished the impossible. At this late stage of the war, with Federal armies all but strangling the life out of the Confederacy, with European nations turning away from supporting the South, Bulloch had gotten another cruiser to sea. Not only had he purchased and dispatched the *Sea King* from right under the noses of numerous Federal agents without arousing their suspicion, but he had also bought her tender, the *Laurel*, assigned the *Sea King's* officers, shipped men for her crew, purchased and loaded aboard the *Laurel* the cruiser's guns, munitions, and supplies, assigned her commander and dispatched her to a rendezvous off the coast of Africa. The naval agent had made it appear easy, but it had encompassed enormous hours of hard work, numerous trusted confidants, and the patience and determination to see the task through. The Confederate nation owed much to this inconspicuous naval commander who labored far from her strife-torn shore.

The *Laurel* proved faster than expected, and the lush flower-strewn mountains of Maderia that rise over six thousand feet out of the stark gray Atlantic appeared through the bluish haze to Ramsay on October 15. Bulloch had instructed Captain Corbett to time his voyage so as not to arrive with the *Sea King* before the 17th. This would allow Ramsay sufficient time to take on a full load of coal and to be prepared to meet the cruiser when she arrived. Now, anchored in the harbor of the Portuguese island's capital, Funchal, Ramsay watched and waited, while the *Laurel* was being loaded with all the coal her voluminous bunkers could hold.[13]

Tuesday night, October 18, was a warm, clear night in Funchal harbor. A full moon cast its light over the harbor and threw its rays against the ancient stone fortress guarding the entrance. Waddell kept a lookout high on the mast where he could see the ocean across the breakwater at all times. Late in the evening the lookout came scurrying down from aloft and ran to Ramsay's cabin. Breathlessly he reported that a full-rigged ship with a dark hull had just rounded the edge of the island. Upon overhearing the lookout's report, every man on deck scrambled into the rigging. "That's her!" someone shouted, "It must be her!" Majestically the sleek hulled vessel steamed past the harbor entrance, her red and green signal lights burning brightly. She passed out of sight around the island, but soon she returned, steaming slowly by the breakwater. Ramsay could do nothing that night, for the *Laurel's* papers, as per regulation, were at the customhouse ashore and could not be retrieved until morning. The rendezvous would have to wait until daylight.[14]

As the sun rose from behind the island's august mountains, the black vessel was back. Waddell and his officers could see that she was now flying the British ensign at her stern, and high atop her mainmast streamed the *Laurel's* own pennant, the prearranged signal of recognition. Ramsay ordered steam raised, while a boat was dispatched to retrieve the ship's papers. Soon the *Laurel* was steaming out of Funchal and headed in the direction of the *Sea King*. In his memoirs, Waddell recorded that...*the 19th day of October 1864 was fine and the wind blew from the southwest. As soon as the Laurel drew near the steamship I saw on her port quarter three words in large white letters, "Sea King, London." Each of us asked instinctively, what great adventures shall we meet in her? What will be her ultimate fate? The Sea King was directed to follow her consort, and together we sought refuge on the north side of Desertas,* (Las Desertas, an uninhabited island) *where we found smooth sea and good anchorage.*[15]

Lashing the two vessels together, Lieutenant Whittle clambered across to the *Sea King* and reported to Waddell. The crew of both vessels soon had tackles rigged and began swinging the heavy wooden crates, stenciled "Machinery," from the *Laurel's* hold to the deck of the *Sea King*. It was difficult and back-breaking work, but both crews fell to the task with enthusiasm. All day and into the night the men toiled to transfer the ten tons of guns, powder kegs, barrels of shot, tackle, clothing, bread, and salt provisions. Cabin boys scurried between the two ships carrying grog for the men. By evening the heavy guns were aboard—four eight-inch smoothbores, and two rifled Whitworth 32-pounders. As a merchantman, the *Sea King* was already equipped with two small 12-pounders. Unlike other Confederate cruisers, these would eventually be mounted in broadside, meaning that the *Shenandoah* had no pivot guns.

The urgency of the moment was felt by the men of both vessels, for British subjects or not they would be totally defenseless if a United States cruiser happened upon them. Everyone pitched in, officers alongside the men. Even Portuguese fishermen who sailed inquisitively close by were impressed into service. By 9:00 p.m. the men were exhausted. Whittle ordered a one-hour rest, and dinner was provided from the galley below. No lights were allowed because of the powder being transferred, so the work continued by moonlight. A heavy wooden crate slipped from its tackle, fell to the deck and burst open, scattering solid round-shot about the deck as though they were marbles. By 2:00 a.m., some men were beginning to collapse and Whittle called a halt. Officers and men dropped where they were and went soundly to sleep. Within three hours they were kicked and shaken awake, and work resumed.[16]

By 10:00 a.m. the next morning everything was at last aboard the *Sea King*. The deck, however, was strewn with barrels, crates, ropes, lines, and every other conceivable piece of equipment. The last item to be swung aboard from the *Laurel* was a heavy iron safe. As four men rolled it to the captain's cabin, the jingling of gold coins could be distinctly heard. When everything was aboard, the crews of both vessels were ordered aft on the *Sea King*. Presently Corbett and Waddell emerged from the cabin and stood before the men. Waddell had changed his clothes and was now attired in the steel-gray uniform of a Confederate States naval officer.

Captain Corbett addressed the men first, explaining that he had sold the *Sea King* to the Confederacy, and stating that he was offering a bonus of two months' pay for any man who would enlist in her service. Waddell then announced that they were now aboard the Confederate cruiser *Shenandoah*, and read his commission as the vessel's commanding officer. He ended by offering high pay, promised prize money, and asked all who wanted to enlist to step forward. Two individuals stepped forward, a cabin boy and a fireman. Waddell was flabbergasted, for he had expected to be able to recruit at least fifty men from the crews of the *Sea King* and the *Laurel*. Several of the men shouted at Captain Corbett, accusing him of breaking faith with them because they were told that this was to be a peaceful voyage to Bombay. Corbett assured them that anyone who did not wish to ship on the Confederate cruiser could return to England with him on the *Laurel*. In the meantime Waddell had ordered a bucket of sovereigns brought from his cabin and now stood running his hands through the gold coins. Men edged more closely for a better look. Waddell offered a bounty of £12, then £15, and finally £17 for a six-months' enlistment. Another cabin boy and an engineer stepped forward. Disgusted, Waddell returned to his cabin and Corbett swung across the rail to the *Laurel*. Out of the 55 men who comprised the *Sea King's* original crew, 51 followed him.[17]

The minimum complement needed to sail and man the guns of the *Shenandoah* was 150 men. Five sailors from the Laurel had volunteered, and counting the four from the Sea King, plus ten that had shipped as "passengers," the Confederate cruiser could boast of only nineteen crewmen and twenty-three officers—a total of only forty-two.

Twenty-three years in the regular navy had not prepared Waddell for such a problem as this. Accustomed to stepping upon a warship where all was neat and shipshape, and with a sailor manning every station, an angry Waddell called Corbett and Ramsay, both experienced seamen, to his cabin for a conference. Both men advised against beginning the cruise, stating that to sail in such a condition with so few crew members was totally impractical.

Waddell summoned his second in command: *As his executive officer, he naturally consulted me,* Lieutenant Whittle recalled, *saying that it was his judgment that he should take the ship to Tenerife* (in the Canary Islands), *communicate with Captain Bulloch and have a crew sent to him. I knew every one of the regular officers personally. They were all "to the manner born."*[18]

Whittle was convinced that to take such a course would result in...*ignominious failure, (and) I strenuously advised against it. I said, "Don't confer, sir, with parties who are not going with us."* (Brazen advice coming from a 24-year-old lieutenant.) *"Call your young officers together,"* he continued, *"and learn from their assurances what they can and will do." They were called together; there was but one unanimous sentiment from each and every one, "Take the ocean!"*[19]

Waddell yielded to the unanimous opinion of his officers and gave the orders to prepare to get under way. Summoning his small crew to the quarterdeck, he read the articles officially commissioning the CSS *Shenandoah* as a Confederate warship and signaled for the national ensign to be raised. As the breeze caught the white folds, the *Shenandoah's* men broke into three lusty cheers. "It was a sort of a white flag," one of them later wrote, "with a blue cross up in the corner and a lot of stars—a right pretty flag."[20]

Abruptly the alarming cry of "Sail ho!" came from the masthead of the *Laurel*. A ship was approaching, which judging from the rake of her sails, had the distinct cut of a man-of-war. The *Laurel* had just been cast loose from the *Shenandoah*, and Ramsay quickly pointed her toward the oncoming vessel and steamed at full throttle to investigate. Waddell, acting quickly, gave the order to hoist the *Shenandoah's* anchor, while Whittle rushed to the engine room with instructions to start the engines. The Confederate cruiser was totally defenseless with her guns still packed in their crates. Her only option was to run. Ramsay, meanwhile, had reached the stranger, and making a complete sweep around her, determined that she was nothing more than a harmless merchantman. Returning to the *Shenandoah*, he lowered a boat, and three of the *Laurel's* crewmen, who had changed their minds about shipping on the cruiser, were rowed to her side.

It was now near 6:00 p.m., on October 20, and the clear western sky had turned a bright red-orange as the crimson disk of the sun slipped below the horizon. Steam began to hiss from the *Shenandoah's* escape pipes as pressure rose in her boilers, while on deck the men of both vessels lined the rails and climbed into the rigging to bid each other a final farewell. Ramsay was to take the *Laurel* to Tenerife for coal, and then to England to deliver Captain Corbett and the men. The *Shenandoah* would head southwest into the vast expanse of the South Atlantic. At last all was ready. Final salutes and farewells were conveyed, and as the two vessels parted, emotional cheers erupted from the throats of the men. The *Shenandoah's* helmsman spun the wheel, bringing her helm around to the south, while on deck, her crew stood and watched as the *Laurel* steamed away toward Tenerife. In a surprisingly short period of time, the steamer was but a smudge of smoke on the distant horizon. The *Shenandoah* and her skeleton crew were on their own.[21]

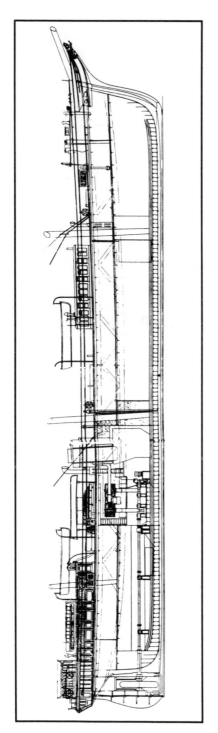

Cut-away view of the CSS *Shenandoah*.

Chapter Ten

An Arduous Beginning

The CSS *Shenandoah* drove south during the night of October 20, 1864. Her small crew was exhausted, and except for the helmsman and the deck watch, all hands fell fast asleep. After parting company with the *Laurel*, Waddell had ordered the cruiser put under short sail, and with her engines shut down and the screw lifted, she pushed on through the night. The following morning brought a full realization of the vessel's true condition: *We were now fairly afloat in a vessel of 1,100 tons, English measurement, constructed for peaceful pursuits but metamorphosed into an armed cruiser,* Waddell recorded. *The deck had to be cleared of the stores pitched on it pell-mell before the battery could be mounted on the carriages and gun ports must be cut, fighting bolts driven, gun tackle fitted, before that battery could be used in our defense. All of this service which was ordinarily done at a navy yard before a vessel is commissioned devolved upon us, out in mid-ocean, without even a hope of successful defense or a friendly port to take shelter in, if attacked in the interim.*[1]

Although the condition of his vessel the next morning must have seemed appalling to a traditionalist officer such as James I. Waddell, Lieutenant Whittle was not the least bit discouraged by the sight of the cruiser's cluttered deck: *Every officer and man pulled off his jacket and rolled up his sleeves,* Whittle wrote, *and with the motto "do or die," went to work at anything and everything. The captain took the wheel frequently in steering to give one more pair of hands for the work to be done. We worked systematically and intelligently, doing what was most imperative first.*

In twenty-four hours we had mounted and secured for sea two eight-inch guns and two Whitworths, and the next day the other half of the battery was similarly mounted and secured. We cleared the holds and stored and secured everything below, and in eight days, after leaving Desertas, had all portholes cut and guns secured therein. Under our instructions we had to allow sufficient time for Captain Corbett to communicate with England and have the customhouse papers canceled and all necessary legal steps connected with the bona fide sale taken before any overt act.[2]

Still, problems abounded. While John C. Lynch, the lone carpenter, may have managed to cut the gun ports and have the guns secured at their stations, another perplexing dilemma presented itself. Waddell pointed out that: *the bulwarks were discovered to be too weak for resistance to a shotted gun, and therefore some plan must be devised for strengthening them.*[3] Lynch was able to brace the attachments, but once the bulwarks were reinforced to withstand the recoil of the guns, Whittle made the startling discovery that there were no gun tackles to be found anywhere on the cruiser. They had either been left on the *Laurel*, or else had never been shipped in the first place. There was a sufficient quantity of rope on board, but if the guns were fired without the tackles they were likely to recoil through the railing on the far side of the ship. Even the fighting bolts that secured the blocks and tackles to the bulwarks could not be found. They were finally discovered a few days later, deep in the ship's hold, where they were packed in a wooden barrel labeled "Beef."[4]

With the guns lashed into position and their muzzles protruding from the sides, the *Shenandoah* might have appeared formidable to a passing merchant vessel, but the only weapons that could be fired, other than small arms, were the little 12-pounder signal guns. Unfortunately, there was only one shell available for the 12-pounders, the remaining charges were blanks. In addition, as Waddell explained, there was no suitable place to store the powder: *The hold as well as half of the berth deck was filled with coal and not being able to move the coal from the forehold which was selected as the place for the magazine, the powder was placed under tarpaulins in my starboard cabin, while I occupied the port one. Was it not a warm companion?*[5]

While the men labored to create order out of chaos, Waddell maintained the *Shenandoah's* course toward the south. During the day the cruiser was kept under steam, but with the freshening breezes at night, the fires were banked, the propeller hoisted, and the vessel put under canvas. On numerous occasions, Waddell took the wheel himself, freeing the helmsman to rest or join in some needed labor. Lengthy periods at the helm gave the *Shenandoah's* captain ample time to reflect on his grave mission and the innumerable obstacles that challenged his officers and tiny crew. Writing in his journal, he recorded his thoughts on those dark lonely nights at the wheel:

Responsibility weighed upon my mind, and reflections often created an absence of everything in active movement around me. I was often aroused by some cheerful remark from an officer, whose responsibility was to the extent of four hours' duty each day, about his experience in the steamer, and it was kind of him to divert my attention even for a few moments; but no sooner would the conversation cease than my mind was again occupied with ship thoughts...and I have no doubt I very often appeared to those with me (as) an unsocial and peculiar man.... It was my first command, and upon the accuracy of all the calculations of my judgment in directing a cruise upon so vast a scale depended success or failure.... Those who knew me in a subordinate position elsewhere found me then changed in position, occupying responsibilities to a nation which was struggling for its very existence.[6]

After a week of constant labor, Waddell ordered that there be no work performed on the coming Sunday. After muster and divine services, the men lounged about the deck, grateful for the few hours of relaxation. Unfortunately, the wind died and five angry stokers had to be sent to the engine room to light the fires. Gradually, except for the missing gun tackles, which Whittle hoped could be obtained from a captured merchant vessel, the *Shenandoah* began to take on the order and polish of a man-of-war.

On October 25, Waddell recorded that the powder had been moved to a small compartment under his cabin. Although it was now below the ocean's surface, the cruiser's commander still considered it to be in a very insecure location. Still on her southward course, the *Shenandoah* was now entering an area of heavy seas, accompanied by high winds and driving rain. Waddell wrote that *to our horror, the decks leaked like sieves, and the seams of the hull were sufficiently open to admit a fine spray from the sea which had spent itself on her sides.*[7] After re-caulking, this problem, too, was resolved. The *Shenandoah* required only two additional items to make her a bona fide warship—additional crew members and the missing gun tackles. Waddell hoped that the first few prizes would supply both.

At 1:00 p.m., on October 28, the lookout, who was perched high on the mainmast, spotted a sail on the distant horizon. The cruiser was already under steam and had no sails deployed in an effort to ease the workload on the crew. Waddell immediately signaled the engine room for maximum revolutions, and promptly the chase was on. It was a delicate decision to attempt this capture, for Waddell had received explicit instructions from Commander Bulloch not to take a prize for at least thirty days after leaving Madeira in order to allow time for Captain Corbett to reach England and cancel the registry. But the *Shenandoah* needed men, and above all, the precious tackles for the guns. Without them the Confederate vessel was defenseless, and Waddell could not afford to spend three more weeks avoiding a chance encounter with a Federal cruiser.

The *Shenandoah* gained rapidly on the prize which all agreed had the definite cut of an American vessel. Through his marine glass Waddell could see that she had broken out the British ensign, and so as not to allay suspicion, ordered the English flag hoisted on the *Shenandoah*. By 4:00 p.m. the cruiser was sufficiently near for a warning shot, and Waddell gave the nod to Whittle. The young lieutenant rushed aft, and soon, with a crack and a puff of bluish smoke, the solitary 12-pounder shell streaked across the bow of the fleeing vessel. The stranger obediently hove to, and Whittle sent a boarding party commanded by Acting Master Bulloch to inspect her papers. Within an hour the boat was back. As it neared the cruiser's side, the disappointment apparent on Bulloch's boyish face conveyed the story. She was the *Mongul* out of London, and although American built, she had been sold legitimately the previous year and her papers were in order.[8]

Two days later, however, the first bona fide prize was captured. She had been spotted the evening before, but was so far off, and with darkness rapidly approaching, Waddell elected to maintain his course during the night. The next morning, at latitude 16°47' N., longitude 26°43' W., although a long way off, she was still there. When the propeller was lowered and the engines started, however, the gap narrowed rapidly. Whittle ran up the English colors, and all hands watched for the stranger's expected response. Soon a large Stars and Stripes unfurled from her stern, and throaty cheers erupted on the *Shenandoah*. The British ensign was quickly lowered and the Southern banner raised. A blank cartridge fired from one of the 12-pounders signaled the fleeing vessel to round to and she obediently complied. Once again Master Bulloch was dispatched with a boarding party. This time the news was good. The vessel was the brand new 574-ton bark *Alina* of Searsport, Maine, out of Newport, Wales, bound for Buenos Aires with a cargo of railroad iron.

Bulloch brought Captain Edward Staples, along with the bark's papers, back to the *Shenandoah*. Waddell had assembled a prize board consisting of Paymaster Breedlove Smith, Surgeon Charles E. Lining, and himself, and together they examined the *Alina's* documents. The vessel was admittedly American, but Captain Staples contended that her cargo was neutral. Waddell agreed, but pointed out that

Acting Master Irvine S. Bulloch, of the *Shenandoah*. Bulloch was the son of Commander James D. Bulloch, Confederate naval agent in Europe.

Author's Collection

according to maritime law, the ownership documents must be notarized and that no such seal was evident. Smith and Lining agreed, and the verdict was swift. The *Alina* was condemned.[9]

She was a valuable capture, Waddell wrote, *furnishing the blocks for the gun tackles, a wide variety of blocks which the steamer was in want of, and cotton canvas so very suitable for sail making. The officers partly fitted themselves out with basins, pitchers, mess crockery, knives, forks, etc. A spring mattress fell to my share, and a small supply of provisions was removed from the ship.*[10] By late afternoon the twelve-man crew and most items of value had been removed to the *Shenandoah*, and Waddell dispatched

Carpenter O'Shea to the *Alina* with instructions to bore holes in her bottom and scuttle her. That evening in the twilight, men from both vessels lined the cruiser's rail and watched as the stricken bark, her sails set, forged slowly ahead as she sank lower and lower in the water. Suddenly, her stern slipped below the surface, her bow rose high in the air, and with the sound of breaking and groaning timbers, the *Alina* slid backward beneath the waves. A deathly silence prevailed on the deck of the *Shenandoah*. No one spoke, no one cheered. Each man was engrossed in his own thoughts. The *Alina* belonged to the enemy and this was war, but it was always difficult to see a good ship die.

Seven men from the *Alina* joined the *Shenandoah's* crew bringing her complement to fifty-three. For a week the Southern cruiser continued her southbound course without spotting any additional American vessels. While several ships were boarded, they all proved foreign. Then, on the evening of November 4, as the *Shenandoah* neared the equator in latitude 7°35' N and longitude 27°49' W, a distant sail was spotted that appeared American. Waddell ordered the raider's course altered in order to keep pace with the stranger until daylight. The next morning a flat calm prevailed, but the sailing craft was still in sight, and soon steam was hissing in the *Shenandoah's* boilers and the engines were started. In no time the raider drew abreast of the diminutive 150-ton schooner *Charter Oak*, out of Boston and bound for San Francisco. A warning shot from one of the broadside guns brought the American flag fluttering out from her mast, and Whittle dispatched the customary boarding party. The captain of the small schooner had his wife, sister-in-law, and her child on board, and these, along with two mates and four Portuguese seamen, were transferred to the *Shenandoah*. After removing a large quantity of preserved fruit from the prize, she was set on fire. Waddell considered enlisting the *Charter Oak's* four sailors, but upon investigation, learned that they were deserters from the Union army and reasoned that they would just as quickly desert the *Shenandoah*.[11]

Two days later, on November 7, the old 399-ton bark *De Godfrey* was taken. She was laden with barrels of pork and bound from Boston to Valparaiso, Chile. The *Shenandoah's* galley needed the pork, but the boarding party reported that 40,000 feet of lumber was stowed on top of the barrels of meat, and it would take at least a day to remove it all. Waddell reluctantly ordered the bark, pork and all, put to the torch. *Darkness had settled when the rigging and sails took fire*, Master's Mate Hunt recorded, *but every rope could be seen as distinctly as upon a painted canvas, as the flames made their way from the deck and writhed upward like fiery serpents. Soon the yards came thundering down by the run as the lifts and halyards yielded to the devouring element, the standing rigging parted*

like blazing flax, and the spars si-
multaneously went by the board
and left the hulk wrapped from stem
to stern in one fierce blaze, like a
floating, fiery furnace.[12]

The *Shenandoah* now had almost as many prisoners on
board as crewmen and Waddell
was concerned. On November
9, the Danish brig *Anna Jane* was
encountered, and her captain
was persuaded to take the prisoners in exchange for a chronometer and several barrels of
provisions. Whittle and several
other officers argued against
freeing the prisoners at this time,
contending that they would
soon communicate the cruiser's
position, condition, and her mission. Characteristic of Waddell,
and a foreshadowing of his
future relationship with his
younger officers, he overruled
their judgment and ordered the
prisoners over the side. Writing
in his journal, Assistant Surgeon

Acting Master Cornelius E. Hunt.
Author's Collection

Charles E. Lining summarized the feelings of the junior officers: *We*
are glad to get them out of the ship, though I doubt the policy of letting them
go at this time, as it is very important for us to keep our movements unknown
for some time, and these men may surmise our destination and will certainly
describe our ship, her armament, etc.[13]

On the following day the *Shenandoah* captured one of the most curious vessels taken on the entire cruise. When first spotted she appeared
to be a side-wheel steamer, but there was no smoke and no smokestack. She was a decrepit 134-ton hermaphrodite brig by the name of
Susan, out of Cardiff, bound for southern Brazil with a load of coal. It
was all her exhausted crew could do to keep her afloat. *The prize was*
very old and rickety, Waddell wrote. *She leaked badly and got along at a*
snail's pace. Barnacles grew to her bottom and the crew was constantly em-
ployed at the pumps in keeping the water down during calm weather or very
light winds.... An ingenious plan had been devised before she left port to keep
her afloat. To the pump was attached a shaft one-half the beam of the vessel,

and to the other end a wheel and buckets which resembled one side of a steamboat. The immersion of the buckets depended on her draft of water and the quantity of water discharged by the pump depended upon the velocity of the vessel through the water.[14] Three of her men—two deck hands and a boy—along with a dog which the cruiser's sailors quickly adopted, joined the *Shenandoah's* crew. The *Susan* was quickly scuttled.

At 5:00 p.m. on Friday, November 11, a large vessel was reported bearing southeast from the *Shenandoah's* course. The stranger's nationality, however, could not be ascertained in the fading light. The cruiser was still under sail, as was the practice during daylight hours, and it was soon evident that she could never catch the elusive craft on sail power alone. With a nod from Waddell, Lieutenant Whittle barked out the orders. Engineers and firemen scurried down the ladder to the engine room, and soon steam pressure was building in the boilers.

On deck, additional crewmen cranked the winch to lower and couple the propeller, and soon the engines were started. By now darkness had settled over the waters, but the speedy ship with her snow white canvas could still be seen in the distance. The signal gong rang in the engine room as Waddell ordered "All ahead, full," and the *Shenandoah* picked up speed as she raced after the fleeing vessel.

It was the first night-time chase, and every Confederate sailor crowded the rails to watch and speculate on the distant vessel's identity. Crewmen, swaying to and fro with every rise and fall of the bow, conversed in subdued tones and listened to the hiss of the copper-sheathed bow as it knifed its way through the cold Atlantic. The rumble from below and the vibration of the deck conveyed the unmistakable message that the engines were running at full throttle. The *Shenandoah's* wire

Lieutenant Sidney Smith Lee, Jr., of the *Shenandoah*. Lee was the nephew of Robert E. Lee, and had served on the *Louisiana* at New Orleans and on the cruiser *Georgia*.

Author's Collection

rigging hummed in the stiff night breeze as her sailors urged her onward; her towering masts creaked and groaned as her sails bit into the wind. The gap was closing ever so slowly. She was a fast one.

A little after midnight, the stranger was off the port side; a large, graceful clipper ship with spindly tall masts and an overhanging bow. Whittle shouted an order, and one of the *Shenandoah's* broadside guns fired, its muzzle flash blinding those nearby who had failed to look away. Instantly the 1,100-ton *Kate Prince* took in her sails and was skillfully brought into the wind. The Confederate cruiser lowered a boat, and a boarding party, commanded by First Lieutenant Sidney S. Lee, Jr. was soon on its way to the side of the clipper. Within one-half hour, Lee was back accompanied by the prize's captain, Henry Libby and his first mate, William Corfield.

The *Kate Prince* was an American vessel out of Portsmouth, New Hampshire, but her notarized papers proved that her cargo of British coal was owned by a neutral party. Waddell quickly announced his decision. The *Kate Prince* would be bonded for $40,000, but Lieutenant Lee interrupted the proceedings. While on board the clipper he had spoken with Captain Libby's wife. Mrs. Libby, he said, had insisted that she was a devoted Southern women, and claimed that the clipper's entire twenty-one man crew earnestly desired to join the *Shenandoah*. Captain Libby supported his wife's claim; however, Waddell was adamant in his decision. Because of the neutral cargo, the bond must stand. Several officers, including Whittle, remonstrated with the cruiser's commander, pointing out that, the neutral cargo be damned, here was an opportunity to increase the *Shenandoah's* crew by twenty-one ardent Southern supporters. Waddell still refused, and Libby and his first mate were sent back to their vessel. As the *Kate Prince* sailed off into the night, the *Shenandoah's* assistant surgeon was again recording in his journal the bitter disappointment felt among the officers: *This, I think, was a great mistake. A ship worth so much money and ransomed for the sake of a cargo not worth over seventeen thousand dollars at the most. Better to have burned her and let our governments settle about the cargo afterwards.*[15]

The following afternoon, the *Adelaide* was stopped, an obvious New England bark in spite of the Argentine flag that she flew. The ship's master, Captain Williams, could produce no bill of sale and admitted that he was out of New York bound for Rio with a cargo of flour belonging to Phipps & Company of New York. Williams insisted, however, that a Mr. Pendergrast of Baltimore, "a good Southerner," owned the vessel and had transferred her registry to Argentina only in order to save her from the hated "Yankees." Waddell was not convinced and ordered the *Adelaide* destroyed. The prize crew began knocking down bulkheads, smashing furniture, and spreading tar and kerosene all over the deck in preparation for setting her on fire.

In the midst of all this commotion, Master Bulloch discovered a bundle of letters on the *Adelaide* which he hurriedly sent over to the *Shenandoah*. Upon opening several of these, Waddell discovered that not only did Pendergrast own the vessel, he owned the cargo as well. In addition, it appeared that the Marylander was a loyal Southern shipping merchant who had somehow managed to maintain his business without attracting the attention of Federal agents. Waddell wrote an apology to be delivered to Pendergrast, and to allay suspicion as to why the *Adelaide* was not destroyed, bonded the vessel for $24,000. Although the bark was now in shambles, a joyful Captain Williams was only too happy to return to his ship and continue his voyage.[16]

On Sunday afternoon of November 13, while only one degree above the equator, another sail was spotted. After a spirited chase, in which the power of the engines had to be added again to that of the sails, the crisp little *Lizzie M. Stacey* was finally captured. The 140-ton vessel was out of Boston bound for the Sandwich Islands (Hawaii), and carried an assorted cargo of pine, salt, and iron bars. The schooner and her cargo were quickly condemned, and after the small crew was removed, Waddell dispatched Lieutenant Grimball to set her afire. Within a short period of time, the speedy vessel, with all of her sails set, was a mass of flames. Suddenly the wind shifted, and to their horror, the men of the *Shenandoah* saw the *Lizzie M. Stacey* standing directly for the Confederate cruiser. Whittle rushed to the deck shouting orders, the yards were braced back, and the *Shenandoah* turned slowly to starboard just as the blazing schooner rushed by only a few feet away. A near disaster had been averted by the quick thinking of the *Shenandoah's* executive officer.[17]

Two days later, the officers and men of the Confederate cruiser experienced a time-honored tradition of the sea which is still practiced today. Lieutenant Whittle described their first encounter with "King Neptune:" *On November 15, 1864, at 11:30 a.m., we crossed the equator, or "crossed the line," and an amusing break in routine and monotony occurred. There were many officers and men on board who had never before gone into the Southern Hemisphere, I among the number. I was approached, as executive officer to know if I had any objection to King Neptune's coming on board to look after and initiate those on board who had never crossed his domain before. I did not object. It was nearly calm. At 7:30 p.m. a loud hail was heard from under the bows and a brilliant light shone, asking permission from King Neptune to visit the ship. It was granted. A giant-like figure came over the bow, with an immense harpoon in his hand, and a chafing mat for a hat, and came aft, followed by a well disguised retinue or suite, to look after King Neptune's new subjects.*

Lieutenant Chew was first seized. The first question was, "Where are you from?" Woe to the man who opened his mouth to answer. It would be filled with a mixture of soap, grease and molasses. If no answer was given your face was lathered with a mixture and you were shaved with a long wooden razor, and then the pump was started, which nearly drowned you, to wash it off. Dr. McNulty, on being asked where he was from, replied "Ireland," and his mouth was filled with the mixture. This was too much for his Irish blood and he knocked the barber full length on the deck. I, as executive officer, for that reason thought I would be let off, particularly as I had given permission for the fun, but I was shaved also. The sport all went off very well and was a break in the shipboard life.[18]

First Lieutenant John Grimball, of the *Shenandoah.*

Battles and Leaders

Lieutenant Grimball, too, assumed he would be immune, as he was on duty as deck officer, but just as the unfortunate Whittle was being hosed off, Waddell stepped forward and relieved him as officer of the deck. The protesting lieutenant was dragged to his fate much to the merriment of the cheering crew.

By now the secret was out that the *Sea King* had been transformed into the *Shenandoah*. Captain Corbett had arrived in England, and upon canceling the registry, explained that the ship had been sold to the Confederates. In addition, Captain Libby of the *Kate Prince* had arrived at Bahia, Brazil, and upon questioning by United States authorities, acknowledged that he had been captured by the *Shenandoah* and elaborated on her description and the shorthandedness of her crew. The USS *Onward* was on station at Bahia, but she was a light sailing vessel and no match for the Confederate cruiser. Her Federal commander had no need to fear such an encounter though, for instead of cruising off the coast of Brazil, as other Confederate raiders had done, the lone Southern warship was pushing deeper and deeper into the remote expanse of the South Atlantic Ocean. Soon, after rounding the southern tip of Africa, her prow would turn eastward toward the vast Indian Ocean and the distant shores of Australia.[19]

Before rounding the Cape of Good Hope, however, Waddell was persuaded by Surgeon Lining to investigate Tristan da Cunha, a remote cluster of islands lying deep in the South Atlantic. The islands had been a favorite hunting ground for whalers in days gone by, but excessive hunting had decreased the number of mammals, and most of the New England whalers had moved to more distant waters in the Pacific. Still, it was worth a look, and as the cruiser neared the islands on December 4, 1864, the lookout reported a vessel hove to near the shore. Greasy black smoke spiraled upward from her trypots, a sure sign of a whaler busy with the grizzly task of cutting up and boiling blubber to extract the oil. More importantly, the American colors hung limply at her blackened stern. She was the *Edward*, an old 274-ton whaling bark just four months out of New Bedford. Her crew was so involved in their work that they never noticed the approach of the menacing-looking vessel with the long black hull. Lieutenant Grimball led the boarding party and was greeted by the *Edward's* captain, Charles P. Worth, who accepted his fate with some humor by complimenting the young lieutenant on the appearance of the fine looking cruiser that lay alongside.[20]

The *Edward* was well provisioned and Waddell wanted the stores, but not the twenty-five angry seamen who crowded her deck. *The outfit of the Edward was of excellent quality,* he wrote, *and we lay by her (for) two days, replenishing the Shenandoah with what we were in want of. We removed from her 100 barrels of beef and as many pork, besides several thousand pounds of ship biscuits, the best we had ever eaten, put up in large whiskey-seasoned hogsheads capable of holding 300 gallons of oil.... Two of her boats were new and they were removed to the Shenandoah in place of her old and worthless ones. She was burned, and I visited a settlement on the northeast side of Tristan da Cunha and arranged with the chief man, (a Yankee) of the island who was called governor, to receive the crew of the Edward, most of whom were Sandwich Islanders.*[21]

Spreading the rumor among the landed seamen that the Confederate cruiser was headed for Cape Town, Waddell waited until the islands dropped below the horizon and then ordered the raider's course set south by southeast. That night, December 7, a faint grating sound which seemed to come from the propeller shaft kept Waddell awake. He sent for Matthew O'Brien; however, the chief engineer could hear nothing amiss. The next morning, when the propeller was hoisted and the vessel put under sail, O'Brien discovered a crack entirely across the brass band on the coupling of the propeller shaft. Screws were inserted as a temporary repair, but the *Shenandoah* would require the facilities of a first class shipyard to replace the band. Although Cape Town was near, Waddell decided to keep the cruiser under sail, using the engines sparingly, and push on to Melbourne, 6,000 miles away.[22]

By now life on board the *Shenandoah* had taken on a more organized aspect. The clutter and disorder of the deck were gone, wood-
work and brass fittings were polished, and all ropes and lines coiled
and stowed in the prescribed manner. The two Whitworth rifles were
mounted and ready at the forward ports, while the four 32-pounders,
two per side, stood ready in broadside. The two small 12-pounders
remained secured aft. The area below deck amidships had been cleared
and provisions made for the accommodation of the crew. Hammocks
had been slung, while tables, chairs, and sea chests taken from the
prizes constituted their furniture.

Farther aft, eight staterooms, originally intended for wealthy passengers, were allocated to the commissioned officers. These cabins
opened upon a central saloon that served as the wardroom where the
off-duty officers read, played backgammon, chess, and other board
games, in addition to taking their meals. Books brought on board by
the officers, when added to those captured on the prizes, endowed the
wardroom with a prolific library of over 600 volumes. The two aft-
most cabins in the stern of the vessel had been petitioned off and were
reserved for Waddell. No longer was this "the most cheerless and offensive spot I ever occupied," as he once described it, but now contained a new plush carpet, a fine bed with a deep mattress, a sofa, a
mahogany table lined with books, and an easy chair. As was the custom on any nineteenth-century man-of-war, Waddell ate his meals
alone in his cabin.[23]

The officers ate the same fare as the men, although the cooks probably saw that they received the best of the portions. Typical meals consisted of hardtack, which was an unleavened biscuit, salted beef, and
duff—a mixture of lard, flour, and yeast, boiled until hard and served
with molasses. Delicacies and vegetables were taken from the prizes,
while fresh meat was provided by livestock which was kept in a pen
on the topgallant forecastle. A daily ration of grog was served to the
men.

The crew was issued Confederate Navy uniforms, but these were
seldom worn except on Sunday muster, when all had to answer the
call dressed in regulation gray jackets and white ducks. For the officers, Waddell issued orders stipulating the wearing of their uniform
coats any time they left the wardroom. Dark trousers were permitted,
but no slouch hats were allowed. The regulations were enforced even
when the *Shenandoah* was sailing through the humid seas of the
tropics. The order was grudgingly obeyed, but it was extremely
unpopular and served to fuel the dissension between Waddell and
his junior officers. No one challenged Waddell's authority directly, but
several of his juniors, when talking among themselves, openly questioned

his judgment. A case in point was the commander's insistence that the *Shenandoah* be kept under short sail at night which diminished her speed. This was done as a safety measure, but many of the officers felt the restriction was overly conservative.[24]

The *Shenandoah*, passing south of Cape Town, now entered an area of constant storms and monstrous seas as she plowed her way eastward through the vast Indian Ocean. Frequent storms with driving rain, sleet, and snow buffeted the cruiser, causing her to roll dangerously. At one point the raider was caught in a revolving gale, the winds increasing hour by hour. A colossal wave, the largest Waddell had ever seen, crashed down upon the deck. The ship groaned under the impact and her forward motion stopped. Many of the men thought they felt her settling. Another huge wave and she might founder. Water was up to the edge of the bulwarks, and above the howling wind came the shrill voice of Whittle: "Clear the ports! Clear the ports!" Men half-swam, half-waded to the rails, and with axes and crowbars smashed open the gun ports, allowing the water to drain out before the next wave hit.[25]

Waddell ordered a course change to the north in an attempt to find better weather. *It became evident,* he wrote, *that to continue the course would be hazardous, and by changing the course to the north of east the ship would make better weather in a short time. She rolled so heavily that sea after sea tumbled in over her railing and her preparations for freeing herself were so indifferent that water was several inches deep, flooding all the apartments on that deck.*

On Christmas day the cook managed to kill and prepare the last goose from the forecastle pen. At the appointed time the officers seated themselves in the wardroom. There was little holiday spirit among the sullen men gathered around the bare wooden table. Each was cold and soaked to the skin. Rivulets of sea water trickling from their beards left little puddles on the table. They sat in silence, their thoughts a thousand miles away, as smoky kerosene lamps, used to light the narrow room, swung violently from side to side. Waddell, who had joined his officers for this occasion, sat at one end of the table. Presently the cook entered, proudly balancing the goose and miraculously navigated his way to the assembled group. Waddell began to carve. The cruiser shuddered from another jarring wave, and the goose slid from the table. Without hesitation, the bird was retrieved; the carving resumed. Finally, all were served and they began to eat, but another monster wave broke over the *Shenandoah*. Water cascaded down the hatch and into the wardroom, sweeping dishes, cups, and the water-soaked goose again from the table. Dispirited and disgusted, the officers returned to their cabins, pulled on their sou'westers, and climbed out onto the heaving deck to stand their watch. So much for Christmas.[26]

The weather improved slightly with the more northerly course. An angry sea, however, still caused the *Shenandoah* to roll drunkenly among the swells. Squalls of fine rain, driven horitizontaly by a stiff wind, engulfed her, cutting visibility to a scant few miles. At 9:00 a.m. on the morning of December 29, the lookout spotted a sail far astern. She was visible only sporadically among the squalls, but it appeared that she was on the same course as the *Shenandoah* and gaining on her. The raider was running slowly under short sail, and Waddell ordered her course and speed maintained so as to allow the unsuspecting vessel to overtake them. As the morning progressed, she drew near enough that those with powerful telescopes could see that she had a white-painted hull trimmed in green slender masts and white canvas, all good indicators of an American.

As she drew near astern, the *Shenandoah* hoisted the British ensign. The approaching vessel raised a badly faded Stars and Stripes and a cheer erupted on the deck of the cruiser. As she drew abeam under a cloud of canvas and sailing very fast before the wind, a seaman held up a blackboard inquiring as to the correct longitude and latitude. Waddell did not respond, but ordered the English flag hauled down and the Confederate colors hoisted. Whittle shouted an order to the aft gun crew, and one of the 12-pounders barked out its command for the speeding vessel to stop. The *Shenandoah's* officers could now discern the word *Delphine* painted on her stern, and rather than stopping, she was pulling rapidly away. Another blank cartridge was fired, and Confederate sailors rushed to clear the forward Whitworth. The few remaining seamen scrambled aloft to deploy more sails. A solid shot was rammed down the Whitworth. There would be an opportunity for only one shot, for by the time the gun's crew could reload, the stranger would be out of range. Then unexpectedly, the *Delphine* furled her sails and hoved to.[27]

The trim vessel was a 705-ton bark out of Bangor, Maine, in ballast for Akyab for a cargo of rice. When her captain, William G. Nichols, was informed that his vessel was a prize of the Confederate raider, he pleaded with Waddell to spare his vessel because his wife who was on board was gravely ill, and it might cause her death if she were moved. Waddell sent Surgeon Lining to the *Delphine* to examine Mrs. Nichols, who found that "she is a women of some culture, in perfect health and very decided."

Lillias Nichols was a tall, shapely, temperamental woman of twenty-six years, and accustomed to having her own way. In addition, her father was the owner of the *Delphine*. Two boats were required to bring her, her son, her maid, baggage, a library, and her caged canary to the *Shenandoah*. Because the sea was rough, a boatswain's chair had to be rigged to the main yard in order to hoist the women aboard. Lieutenant Whittle greeted Nichols as her feet touched the deck and offered to escort her aft to the captain's cabin which would be her quarters. Contemptuously she huffed, "If I had been in command, you would never have taken the *Delphine!*"

As she approached the aft cabin, Waddell stepped on deck, and seeing the gold stripes on his sleeve, Mrs. Nichols stopped and demanded, "Are you the pirate chief?"

"I have the honor to be captain of the Confederate States steamer *Shenandoah*, Madam," said Waddell.

"What do you intend doing with us? I demand that we be put ashore immediately."

"The nearest land is St. Paul's Island," Waddell remarked dryly. "Would you care to be landed there?"

Lillias Nichols knew of St. Paul. It was uninhabited, 4,000 miles from nowhere, and one of the most isolated spots on earth. "Oh no, never!" she exclaimed, and turning on her heels, entered the cabin and slammed the door in Waddell's face. "As you desire, Madam, and now I must excuse myself." Removing the bark's eleven-man crew, six of whom joined the Confederate service, the *Delphine* was set ablaze.[28]

On the last day of 1864, Waddell paused to reflect upon the past year, and on the status of conditions at home. Undoubtedly his thoughts turned to loved ones in North Carolina, especially his wife Ann. From newspapers taken from the prizes he knew that Sherman's infamous bummers were advancing on his beloved Old North state, burning and pillaging as they went. Writing in his memoirs some years after the close of the conflict, his anxiety and sorrow were still very much in evidence: *Thus closed the thirty-first day of December, the last day of the year, amid fire, smoke and ruin, and the fourth year since the Civil War began. How many of our dear friends and companions had in that time gone to that undiscovered country from whose bourne no traveler returns. Full of hope in the commencement as we then were, how many had seen the light of hope go out with their lives, their dying eyes fixed upon a struggling country, upon desolated homes, broken family ties, and all lost that makes life enjoyable. Such thoughts gave me food for reflection.*[29]

On January 2, 1865, the *Shenandoah* stopped off the island of St. Paul deep in the south Indian Ocean halfway between Cape Town and Australia. Waddell sent a boat ashore to search for some signs of habitation. The cruiser's commander wanted to check his chronometer against a known point, and in addition, hoped that an American whaler might have stopped at the island to replenish her provisions. After the boat had departed Lillias Nichols came on deck, and seeing the towering mountains of the desolate island, remembered Waddell's offer to deposit her there. Master's Mate Hunt attempted to reassure her that no Confederate officer would ever commit such a barbarous act as leaving a defenseless women stranded in such a desolate place. Unconvinced, the fearful Mrs. Nichols retreated to her cabin.

The officers that Waddell had sent ashore discovered a small French fishing village on the island and brought back a supply of fresh fish, live chickens, and a penguin. Some wag on the *Shenandoah* tied a scarf around the penguin's neck, and it waddled about the deck emitting a call which sounded like the bray of a donkey, much to the hilarity of the rest of the crew. Even the apprehensive Mrs. Nichols joined in the laughter.[30]

The *Shenandoah* continued on her easterly course, and on January 17, when only 100 miles off the southwestern coast of Australia, the clipper ship *Nimrod* was overtaken and stopped. She was indeed American built, but like so many of her sister merchant vessels, had been sold to British interests the year before. The *Nimrod* was released, and the Confederate cruiser continued on her course for Melbourne. Westerly winds and a strong current from the east retarded the *Shenandoah's* progress, and Waddell ordered steam raised and the propeller lowered, a risky prospect considering the condition of the propeller shaft. The cruiser's commander was intent, however, on reaching Melbourne in time to post a report to Flag Officer Barron in Paris. The British mail steamer was scheduled to depart on January 26.

While the *Shenandoah* plodded along under steam, between intermittent rain showers another sail was spotted at a great distance. The cruiser's officers studied the far away vessel through their telescopes, but Waddell pronounced it to be the recently detained *Nimrod*. Lieutenant Whittle and others disagreed and urged their commander to give chase, but Waddell did not want to spend the time on a long chase, for he was still convinced that she was the English clipper. It was probably just as well that the *Shenandoah's* officers were not aware of the information that Lillias Nichols had acquired. She, too, had been on deck and had inspected the vessel through a telescope loaned to her by one of the raider's officers. She kept her thoughts to herself, however, for she had instantly recognized the *David Brown*, another one of her father's ships.

At noon on January 25, the *Shenandoah* stood off Port Phillip, Melbourne. A pilot came on board and soon the cruiser was gliding through the heads and across Hobson's Bay toward Australia's most southern city. The word had been telegraphed ahead and fleets of yachts and pleasure craft came out to escort the Confederate warship to her berth. Some dipped their flags as they passed, while passengers waved and cheered; others watched glumly, however, as the black hulled raider glided past. The Confederate cruiser and her crew would find many friends in the land down under, however, it was apparent that not everyone was in agreement with the cause that her red and white ensign represented.[31]

Chapter Eleven

Australian Interlude

On the evening of January 25, 1865, Waddell sent Lieutenant Grimball ashore to communicate with Governor Sir Charles H. Darling and to request the use of repair facilities. At the same time, Paymaster Breedlove Smith was instructed to obtain the paroles of all the prisoners on board, and then release them. When finding that Mrs. Nichols had not performed the formality of signing, Smith approached her with the document. Lillias Nichols protested that because she was a non-combatant, she was not a prisoner of war, and therefore not required to sign a parole. After Smith assured her that it was only a matter of protocol, she reluctantly affixed her signature to the paper. She then asked, contemptuously, if her son, little Phinny, was required to sign. "No Madam," Smith replied. "We are much more afraid of you than we are of him."[1]

It was 6:00 p.m. when the *Shenandoah* dropped her anchor at the Australian metropolis, and immediately she was surrounded by a flotilla of small craft, many of which were filled with correspondents from Melbourne's local newspapers. The reporters clamored to come aboard, but Waddell refused permission until a reply was received from the governor.

The cruiser's commander retired to his cabin to work on the final paragraphs of his report to Secretary Mallory, but was soon interrupted

The CSS *Shenandoah* anchored in Hobson's Bay near Melbourne, Australia.

by the officer of the deck. The lieutenant reported that Lillias Nichols had hailed a passing launch and persuaded them to take her ashore. She and her son had departed, taking all of their possessions with the exception of a copy of *Uncle Tom's Cabin*, which Lieutenant Whittle had thrown overboard. "Let them go," Waddell responded wearily, "as long as it is not the ship's boat they use."

The final defiant words of the feisty Mrs. Nichols, as the launch shoved off from the cruiser's side, were heard by all of the Confederate officers gathered by the rail. Pointing an accusing finger at the black hull she exclaimed: "I wish that that steamer may be burned!"[2]

The lights flickered late in Waddell's cabin that night as he worked to finish his report. Once completed, it would go out with the British mail packet the following morning. After briefly relating the events of the vessel's cruise, including the ships captured and destroyed, he ended with a poignant paragraph: *God has been very merciful and kind unto us, and in all our danger and necessities stretched forth His right hand to help and defend us. I shall be detained here a few days, making some repairs and coaling, and will then proceed on my cruise. We are all well and cheerful, but anxious for an honorable settlement of our national difficulties.*[3]

Word reached the cruiser at 3:00 p.m. on the 26th, that the executive council, after consultation with the governor, had granted permission for the ship to remain in port for repairs and coaling. Immediately assuming the role of a diplomat, Waddell opened the vessel for visitors. Word had spread rapidly among the 50,000 Melbourne residents that the Confederate cruiser was in port, and all day the short railroad running from the metropolis to the seaport towns of Sandridge and Williamstown was crowded with passengers. Small craft of every description constantly shuttled the curious between the raider and the shore. At times her decks became so crowded that many boats had to lay off and wait their turn before their passengers could come aboard.

The multitude of absurd questions with which we were plied by the gaping crowd would have made a stole laugh, Master's Mate Hunt wrote afterwards. *A large percentage of our visitors seemed to entertain the notion that human beings were removed from the vessels we captured, or not, as convenience dictated, prior to their destruction, and solemnly queried of us to the manner in which the Yankees bore themselves while awaiting the approach of the devouring element on a burning ship, or waiting to be engulfed with a scuttled one. But notwithstanding this hard character they were ready to ascribe to us, they vied with each other in showing us every courtesy in their power, and the ladies in particular were well pleased when they could secure the attendance of a gray uniform to escort them on their tour of inspection.*[4]

Waddell and the rest of the *Shenandoah's* officers were showered with invitations to numerous balls and concerts where they were hosted

Visitors crowd the deck of the *Shenandoah* in Melbourne, Australia.

as the guests of honor. One of the most notable was a large reception at the Craig's Hotel in Ballarat, a bustling mining town forty miles north of Melbourne. Wearing their best dress uniforms, the officers of the Confederate warship traveled the two-hour train ride to where: *the wealth, beauty, and fashion of Ballarat were out in full force,* Master's Mate Hunt remembered. *Every attention that kindness and courtesy could suggest was shown us, and more than one heart beat quicker at such convincing evidence of the existence of sympathy in this country of Antipodes. Many a gray uniform coat lost its gilt buttons that night, but we saw them again ere we bade a final adieu to Australia, suspended from watchguards dangling from the necks of bright-eyed women, and we appreciated the compliment thus paid, not to us but to our country. God bless the gentle women of Melbourne and Ballarat.*[5]

Not everyone, however, was enthralled by the Confederate warship's presence. The U.S. consul, William Blanchard, had never been popular in the mostly pro-Southern city of Melbourne, but he now perceived an opportunity to destroy the "Rebel pirate," and he worked diligently to achieve his goal. Collecting the paroled prisoners from the *Shenandoah*, he compiled precise reports which gave accurate details concerning the vessel, her officers, and crew. These he forwarded to Minister Adams in London and to the United States consul in Hong Kong. Blanchard protested the raider's acceptance into the port to Governor Darling, claiming that she was the *Sea King*, and that she had been carrying out "piratical activities."

The authorities of the Crown colony of Victoria rejected Blanchard's claim, however, stating that "whatever may be the previous history of the *Shenandoah*, the government of this colony is bound to treat her as a ship of war belonging to a belligerent power." But the persistent American consul was not to be dissuaded. Spreading the word that he would protect any crew member from the captured prizes who wished to desert, fourteen men immediately slipped ashore. Waddell prohibited any additional shore leave and appealed to the local law officers for assistance in apprehending his errant seaman, but the police refused to become involved.[6]

By the first of February, the *Shenandoah* had been hauled up on the slip owned by Langlands Brothers & Company. Engineers informed Waddell that it would take at least ten days to make all the necessary repairs. (It was while on this slip that the famous photograph of the cruiser was taken.) With the Confederate warship out of the water and now immobilized, the persistent U.S. consul determined to advance another notion. Convinced that Waddell was enlisting British subjects as replacements for his deserters in violation of the Foreign Enlistment Act, the ill-tempered Blanchard demanded that the Australian

The CSS *Shenandoah* hauled out of the water for repairs at the Williamstown slip of Langlands Brothers & Company, Melbourne, Australia, February 1865. Note the Confederate ensign.

The acting chief engineer of the *Shenandoah*, Matthew O'Brien.

Sinclair, *Two Years on the Alabama*

government do something. On Friday, February 10, after securing an affidavit from one of the deserters that a "Charlie the cook" was one of the new enlistees, Blanchard demanded that the "pirate" be seized and searched. Governor Darling postponed the confrontation for the weekend, hoping that the repairs might be completed and the vessel could sail, but on Monday the *Shenandoah* was still sitting solidly on the slip.

On Monday, with Waddell on shore, Lieutenant Grimball was officer of the deck when later in the day a number of police and a company of fifty militia surrounded the vessel. Superintendent Lyttleton and Inspector Beam from the Victoria police came on board carrying a magistrate's warrant to search the ship. Grimball escorted the two police officers to Whittle, who, as executive officer and in Waddell's absence, was in command of the warship. Lyttleton presented the search warrant, but Whittle, claiming that no such person as "Charlie the cook" existed among the crew, refused to allow the search. Instead, he suggested that the law officers should return the following day when Waddell would be present. Lyttleton reluctantly agreed, and the militia and police were withdrawn.[7]

On Tuesday morning the tenacious policeman and his militia returned, and Waddell met him at the rail. The Confederate commander emphatically denied that he had enlisted anyone since the arrival of the vessel in Hobson's Bay, and sternly denied permission for the British law officers to search the ship. The deck of the *Shenandoah* was Confederate territory, he stated emphatically, his anger growing, and any attempt to violate that territory would be met with resolute force. *It is only by courtesy that you were allowed to come on board at all, sir.* Waddell's anger and frustration were mounting to a boil. *I think that a great injustice has been put upon me and upon my country by your government in sending you aboard the ship with a warrant, a police warrant. I believe, sir, that the word of the master of a ship, of an officer and gentleman should be taken in preference to that of men who had probably deserted from the ship and have been hired by the American consul to annoy us. If I allowed you to take one man from my ship, you might come afterward and take fifteen or twenty. If such warrants are to be honored, the American consul would perhaps lay information against me as being a buccaneer or pirate. I think, sir, that I have been very badly treated in this port. I get no cooperation from you in regard to my deserters, and yet you come and offer such an insult as this.*

Then, Captain, you refuse to allow me to look for the man for whom I hold a warrant in my hand, Lyttleton stammered.

Yes, sir! I refuse! I will fight my ship rather than allow it![8]

Lyttleton departed and reported Waddell's refusal to allow the search to Governor Darling, who immediately called the executive council into an emergency session. The council's decision, after a heated debate, was to draft a letter to Waddell asking him to reconsider his refusal, and at the same time ordering the police to surround the slip and prohibit any repairs to be carried out on the vessel by Australian subjects. Waddell was forewarned of the council's decision by a Southern sympathizer, and persuaded the slip manager to retain the repairmen on board in order to thwart the council's orders. At 4:00 p.m., the police and militia surrounded the slip and prohibited any Australian citizen from entering or leaving the work area. From the deck of the cruiser a detachment of artillery was spotted which wheeled into position on the Williamstown Road where they could fire upon the *Shenandoah*. The situation was fraught with difficulties, and tension grew on the deck of the immobile warship. At 6:00 p.m., the message from the council arrived.[9]

Waddell took his time in responding. At 10:00 p.m. he addressed two letters to Commissioner of Trade and Customs James G. Francis, informing him that he should be ready to sail by February 19. In the second message, Waddell informed the governor that "execution of the warrant was not refused, as no such person as the one therein specified was on board; but permission to search the ship was refused."[10] A thorough search of the vessel had been made by two of the ship's officers, Waddell stated, and no one was found on board who was not part of the crew when the cruiser arrived.

While Waddell was penning these notes, however, Constable Alexander Minto of the Williamstown water police noticed four men descending the gangway of the cruiser and departing in a small boat. The constable pursued the suspects and apprehended them, two at a nearby railway station and two more hiding in a water closet. Although they denied the accusations, all four men, Australian citizens, were jailed on suspicion of attempting to evade the Foreign Enlistment Act. One of the four, a James Davidson, bore a striking resemblance to the person known as "Charlie the cook." It is likely that the *Shenandoah's* crew brought hopeful enlistees on board the Confederate warship, and that Davidson, unknown to Waddell, may have indeed been the much sought after "Charlie."[11]

The following morning another emergency session of the executive council was held. Reviewing the messages sent by Waddell, the governor worked to avoid an explosive situation. News of the impoundment had spread throughout Melbourne, and angry crowds called for a demonstration meeting at the Criterion Hotel for 3:00 p.m. to protest the seizure. Darling wanted to avoid a confrontation, and shortly before the demonstration was scheduled to convene, the Crown Court issued a directive stating "that the government has not the power which they claim. A ship of war commissioned by a foreign government is exempt from the jurisdiction of the courts of other countries."[12]

With this ruling the police and militia were withdrawn, and work forged ahead on the cruiser. On the afternoon of February 15, to the cheers of onlookers along the wharf, the *Shenandoah* slid down the way and left the slip. Two days later, after loading 250 tons of coal, stores of lime juice, fresh vegetables, wine, rum, and bread, she was ready to sail. That evening, smoke curling from the *Shenandoah's* stack was the signal for which many had been waiting. Clouds blocked out the light from the moon and stars as men in groups of twos and threes began gathering in a patch of scrub along the Sandridge Pier. Quietly they waited until the police boat had passed and then hurried to board three watermen's boats which then pulled noiselessly toward the *Shenandoah*. From a pier not far away Constable Minto spied the boats heading for the Confederate cruiser, and although visibility was poor, he thought he saw a man wearing an officer's uniform directing operations.[13]

The ill-tempered American consul, Blanchard, also received word late in the night that suspected recruits were being sent to the *Shenandoah*, but because of the lateness of the hour he could find no Australian official who would venture any action. After repeatedly arousing various government members and demanding that they stop the "Rebel pirate," Blanchard stormed back to his office in disgust. It was now 4:00 a.m.

Daylight was breaking as the *Shenandoah's* anchor was slowly raised. Standing on the bridge next to Waddell was Edward Johnson, the same pilot who had brought the cruiser safely into Hobson's Bay. With the anchor up, Johnson ordered the engines started, and the Confederate warship steamed for the heads of Port Phillip and the entrance to the bay thirty miles away. Beyond was the open sea. Whittle had called all hands to quarters and the guns were loaded. It was always possible that a Federal cruiser might be lurking just outside the harbor.[14]

The rising sun of Sunday morning, February 19, 1865, found the *Shenandoah* steaming majestically across Hobson's Bay with Johnson still at the helm. Soon the rising of the bow indicated the swells from the ocean, and by 1:00 p.m. the cruiser was safely on the high seas. As Johnson descended the ladder to the waiting pilot boat, Waddell bade him good-bye, *but it was not like the farewell we exchange with friends who from the ship's side, return to our own dear native shore with letters and last words of affectionate greeting to those we leave behind,* the *Shenandoah's* commander wrote.

Impatiently we hurried our stranger pilot over the side, he continued, *and no one said God speed. The vessels in sight were steering for Port Phillip, where on their arrival (they) would report the direction taken by the Shenandoah. Soon after night, the steamer's head was turned eastward toward Round Island in Bass Strait.... The moon, with its soft sheen light, the clear atmosphere, the frosty air, and the sky seemed more distant than I had ever seen it before, and*

> "The stars that over sprinkle
> All the heavens, seemed to twinkle
> With a crystalline delight." E. A. P.[15]

Once at sea, some strange faces began appearing on deck as Master's Mate Hunt explained: *A surprise awaited us upon getting fairly outside. Our ship's company had received a mysterious addition of forty-five men, who now made their appearance from every conceivable place where a human being could conceal himself from vigilant eyes. Fourteen of the number crept out of the bowsprit, which was of iron and hollow, where they came very near ending their existence by suffocation; twenty more turned out of some water tanks which were dry; another detachment was unearthed from the lower hold, and at last the whole number of stowaways were mustered forward, and word was passed to the captain to learn his pleasure concerning them.*

Captain Waddell soon made his appearance, not in the best humor, and without any circumlocution demanded of our new recruits as to what country they belonged and for what purpose they were there. The old sea-dogs chuckled, rolled over their tobacco, hitched up their trousers, and with one accord protested that they were natives of the Southern Confederacy, and had come on board thus surreptitiously for the purpose of joining us.[16]

Waddell now had seventy-five men on deck of various ratings to work the ship. Uniforms were ordered from the ship's tailor, and Lieutenant Whittle formed the nucleus of a marine guard with the appointment of a sergeant, a corporal, and three privates. Although the new men had stayed hidden until the *Shenandoah* was beyond the three-mile limit, it is doubtful that the officers, including Waddell, were totally oblivious to their presence. The Confederate cruiser needed men, and in her commander's opinion, it was not up to him to see that the laws of the English colony were obeyed. *The Shenandoah's people were not the custodians of British law,* he wrote, *and least of all a British law which ran counter to our own immediate interests as the British Foreign Enlistment Act did. The British authorities are the proper custodians of British law; with them alone it rests to take care that no breach of neutrality does take place in the event of an armed vessel of a belligerent power entering their ports and harbors.*[17]

The *Shenandoah* turned east through Bass Strait, a deep indigo body of water that separates Australia from the island of Tasmania. After rounding the southeastern corner of Australia, Waddell ordered the cruiser's course set to the north. Ahead were the islands of Middletown, Lord Howe, and Norfolk which lie at the northern tip of New Zealand. Originally these islands had been the base for the South Pacific whaling fleet, but as Waddell supposed, the repairs in Melbourne had given the American consul ample time to spread the alarm. *If the ship had been favored with a good wind,* he wrote, *I would have visited the whaling ground of each of these islands, but to nurture the supply of coal was of the utmost importance.... The whaling fleet of that ocean, known as the "South Pacific whaling fleet," had received warning and had suspended its fishing in that region, and had taken shelter in the neighboring ports, or gone to the Arctic Ocean, which was most probable.*[18]

With unfavorable winds the cruiser plodded northward under sail alone, while her officers grumbled that Waddell was again too conservative and should be using the engines. North of New Zealand the warship was caught in a "revolving gale," as Waddell styled it. Hatches were battened down, her topsails close-reefed, and a tarpaulin laced in the mizzen rigging. Because many uncharted islands were in the region, lookouts, lashed to the deck by lifelines, kept a constant vigil as they peered ahead through the swirling spray. In spite of Waddell's aversion to using coal, steam was kept up and the propeller lowered in case the cruiser needed emergency power to avoid a possible rocky shore. For four days the *Shenandoah* tossed and rolled on the violent sea. *Never in my twenty-three years' service had I seen such succession of violent squalls,* Waddell wrote. *She was enveloped in a salt mist and tossed about by an angry sea like a plaything.*[19]

At the end of the four days the storm left as abruptly as it had arrived and a flat calm prevailed. Blistering sun, broken by occasional torrential downpours, baked the cruiser. No land was in sight; no birds; no fish. Surgeon Lining remarked that, "This region seems to be the abomination of desolation." For a full month the *Shenandoah* slowly worked her way northward. The islands of Fiji, Rotumah, and Ellice were passed, and not a single sail was spotted. Although a sharp lookout for American men-of-war was kept at all times, Waddell had no need for such vigilance. The only U.S. warship in the entire Pacific was the sailing sloop USS *Jamestown*, which was laid up for repairs at Shanghai. The USS *Iroquois* was en route to the Pacific in the Indian Ocean, and the USS *Wachusett*—the same warship that had captured the *Florida* in the neutral harbor of Bahia, Brazil the year before—had just received orders to speed to the Pacific in pursuit of the *Shenandoah*. The Federal Navy, however, made the mistake of believing that the raider was headed for the coast of Chile, while Waddell had his sights set thousands of miles farther north.[20]

On March 21, at latitude 8°35' S and longitude 172°51' E, Waddell, exasperated by the slow progress, finally ordered steam raised and the engines started. Three days later Drummond Island was raised. Pausing off the lush tropical shore, a canoe manned by three natives put out for the *Shenandoah*. Officers and crew alike crowded to the rail as the little dugout approached. The natives were short, copper-toned, and except for numerous tattoos, totally naked. Their canoe was loaded with fish and fruit for which they desired to trade for tobacco. To the surprise of all, one of the cruiser's Malay seamen began conversing with the natives in their own dialect. Whittle saw an opportunity to gather information and asked if any whalers had been seen around the island. Through a series of translations from English into

Portuguese into Malay, it was reported that no whalers had been seen for months. Bitterly disappointed, Waddell ordered the engines started, and with a blast from the ship's steam whistle, the *Shenandoah* moved off while the frightened natives, having never seen a steamer before, paddled furiously for shore. Now Waddell was even more convinced that his game lay much farther to the north.[21]

A low hanging layer of fog covered the ocean on the morning of April 1, but towering above the mist could be seen the lush jungle-covered peak of Totolom, the volcanic mountain that forms the island of Ponape. (At the time of the *Shenandoah's* visit the island was known as Ascension Island.) Ponape, the largest of the eastern Caroline group which now constitutes the Federated States of Micronesia, lies 750 miles southeast of Guam. The rising tropical sun quickly dissipated the obscuring fog, and an excited lookout pointed out four sails visible in the sheltered lagoon. An individual in a small canoe was seen coming out to meet them, and the cruiser's officers were pleasantly surprised when they were hailed by a generously tattooed man who spoke fluent English. His name was Tom Hardrocke, an escaped convict from Australia, who had married a native girl and settled on the island. Hardrocke agreed to lead the *Shenandoah* through the coral reefs to a safe anchorage, but to make sure of his fidelity, Waddell strapped on his revolver and climbed down into the canoe behind him. Slowly and cautiously the cruiser edged her way through the narrow channel. When the lagoon was reached, Whittle had the warship turned broadside to the opening and the anchor was dropped. Hawsers were run out from the stern and secured to coconut trees on the shore. The exit from the lagoon was now effectively blocked, and across the small body of water, not more than a few hundred yards away, were four American whalers.[22]

The four vessels welcomed the strange black-hulled steamer by running up their national colors—three American and one Hawaiian. Waddell responded by firing one of the twelve pounders, which frightened the natives who had gathered on the shore to see the strange steamer, and then raised the Confederate flag. Four of the cruiser's boats were lowered and boarding parties were dispatched to each of the whalers. Lieutenant Grimball returned with the papers from the *Edward Carey* of San Francisco; Lieutenant Chew from the *Pearl* of New London; Lieutenant Lee from the *Hector* of New Bedford; and Dabney Scales with documents from the *Harvest* of Oahu. Only the *Harvest* presented a question of ownership. Although she carried a bill of sale indicating her transfer to Hawaiian owners, she still carried American registry, had American flags on board, and was crewed by officers and men from New England. Waddell wasted little time and condemned all four vessels.

It was fortunate that these four whalers were taken this far south, for on board one of them was a complete set of up-to-date whaling charts. *The charts were all important,* Waddell pointed out, *because the ship (Shenandoah) was not furnished with such as whalers use, which show every track and where they have been most successful in taking whales. With such charts in my possession I not only held a key to the navigation of all the Pacific Islands, the Okhotsk and Bering Seas, and the Arctic Ocean, but the probable localities for finding the great Arctic whaling fleet of New England without a tiresome search.*[23]

On the following day, April 2, Waddell dispatched Master's Mate Hunt and Hardrocke inland in search of the native king in order to negotiate the disposition of the prizes. (Mercifully, unknown to the officers and men of the *Shenandoah* was that on that same day, Richmond was being evacuated.) The native ruler provided several tribal chieftains who set out to guide the two men up into the mountains to where the king held court. It was a rough and difficult trail, but Hunt and Hardrocke finally reached the king's thatched abode and were ushered in. *His majesty was seated on a platform raised a few inches above the floor, and on my entrance arose to meet me,* Hunt wrote. *He was a miserable little savage, scarcely more than five feet high, naked with the exception of a tappa made of grass worn about his waist, and smeared from head to foot with coconut oil. Like most of his followers he wore thrust through a hole made in the lobe of his ear for the purpose a huge misshapen tobacco pipe, an arrangement which however convenient did not add in the least to his personal appearance.*[24]

With the aid of Hardrocke's interpretative skills, Hunt was able to persuade the king to accompany him back to the lagoon and pay a royal visit to the deck of the *Shenandoah*. Within an hour the cruiser's gig, with the king aboard, and accompanied by seventy war canoes, was making its way to the side of the Confederate warship. Waddell had ordered his officers into dress uniform, and as the party approached the gangway, the sweaty officers were ceremoniously called to attention.

His majesty came up the side very cautiously, Waddell recorded later, *and arranging his apron, seated himself between the headboards of the gangway, smelling furiously of coconut oil, a protection against mosquitoes and almost anything else, and blocking the passage to the hereditary prince who was hanging on outside the vessel to a manrope. The pilot* (Hardrocke) *was still in the gig. It was impossible for me to speak to his majesty. He was therefore very unceremoniously introduced to the deck by motions of the head and hand. He stood perfectly erect, as if expecting a submissive bow from all present;*

and after his retinue reached the deck and arranged themselves in their respective orders with respect to their sovereign, I was presented to his majesty by the pilot, who simply said, with a backward motion of his head, "That's the king, sir."[25]

The king and his entourage were invited to Waddell's cabin where, after several rounds of schnapps, the native monarch became quite talkative and the conversation turned to the captured whalers. Waddell explained that the vessels belonged to his enemy, and he wished to destroy them without violating the neutrality of the king's domain. The monarch appeared a little puzzled at the word "neutrality," but Waddell continued, stating that he would allow the tribe to remove anything they wanted from the prizes, after which the vessels would be burned. The king agreed to accept the prisoners from the whalers as long as Waddell promised not to fire the big guns which had frightened his people. The Confederate commander agreed, and to sweeten the deal, consigned seventy old muskets and ammunition to the chieftain. Pleased with the arrangement, the king presented a basket of coconuts and two dead hens wrapped in coconut leaves. Waddell offered a silk scarf. Not to be outdone, the king offered Waddell the royal princess. Through delicate negotiations, handled by Hardrocke, the offer was declined without offending his royal majesty.[26]

Over the next several days all valuable items were taken from the whalers, and they were then run upon shore where the natives swarmed over them, dismantling them piece by piece. What remained of the vessels was then put to the torch, and with all of the 130 prisoners landed, except for seven men who joined the *Shenandoah*, Waddell ordered the anchor raised and the engines started. On April 13, 1865, with Hardrocke leading the way, the Confederate cruiser eased her way through the coral reefs and was soon on the open sea. The cruiser steamed eastward until she had rounded the island, and then with a nod from Waddell, Whittle ordered the helmsman to bring the cruiser's head around to the north. The *Shenandoah's* commander knew from his captured charts where he would most likely find his next prizes. The Arctic whaling fleet, however, was still a long way over the northern horizon. Meanwhile, as the black-hulled warship surged her way through the blue Pacific swells, half a world away the surrendered veterans of the Army of Northern Virginia were just beginning their long painful trek home.

Chapter Twelve

The Long Voyage Home

For six long weeks the *Shenandoah* worked her way northward. Crossing the equator again, this time with no celebration, she continued her monotonous course under a blistering sun and stifling heat. By the time she had passed the 43rd parallel, however, the weather was beginning to change. Waddell wrote that: *the weather became cold, foggy, and the winds were variable and westerly in direction, but unsteady in force, and that ever-reliable friend of the sailor, the barometer, indicated atmospheric convulsion—change in weather. She was prepared for a change of weather, which was rapidly approaching; the ocean was boiling from agitation, and if the barometer had been silent I would have called the appearance of the surface of the deep a famous tide rip. A black cloud was hurrying toward us from the northeast, and so close did it rest upon the surface of the water that it seemed determined to smother and blot out of existence forever the little vessel; and there came in it a violence of wind that threw the vessel on her side, and she started like the affrighted stag from his lair, bounding off before the awful pressure. Squall after squall struck her, flash after flash surrounded her, and thunder rolled in her wake, while every timber retorted to the shakings of the heavens. It was a typhoon; the ocean was as white as the snowdrift. Such was the violence of the wind that a new maintopsail, close-reefed, was blown into shreds.*[1]

For ten storm-tossed hours the *Shenandoah* was battered by the tempest. Finally the howling winds and driving rain moved off to the west and the sea began to calm. The cruiser continued her northward journey between intermittent rain showers and clearing weather, and gradually the temperature began to change. Whittle kept a sharp eye on the thermometer which was now falling as they pressed farther and farther north. Thick banks of fog enveloped the cruiser, and blinding wind-driven snow pelted the deck. Winter clothing was issued, and Surgeon Lining suggested that the men remain below deck unless absolutely needed topside. By May 21, the snow-capped peaks of the Kuriles, a chain of volcanic islands stretching between the northern tip of Japan and the Kamchatka Peninsula, became visible over the bow. Steam was raised and the *Shenandoah* moved carefully through the Amphrite Strait and into the Okhotsk Sea.[2]

The weather grew steadily colder, and the crew watched apprehensively as patches of floating ice drifted past the cruiser. Lookouts were doubled, and men lay awake in their hammocks at night listening to the unsettling thump of the floes as they brushed against the raider's side. Referring to the charts taken at Ponape, Waddell kept the cruiser headed toward Shantaski Island, northwest of Sakhalim, where the whalers occasionally rendezvoused. At noon on May 27, a sail was spotted to the north across a floe of ice. The vessel was moving roughly parallel to the *Shenandoah* and appeared to be about five miles distant. Through the early afternoon the two ships kept pace with one another until a shout from the lookout high on the cruiser's main mast announced that a channel had been found through the floe. The *Shenandoah* swung into the break, raised the Russian flag, and was soon within a quarter mile of the stranger. At 500 yards the forward gun crew fired a blank round and the Confederate ensign was raised, but the whaler paid no heed until Whittle, being close enough to be heard, shouted "Heave to on the starboard tack, damn quick!" The *Abigail* of Massachusetts heaved to.[3]

Captain Ebenezer Nye of the whaler was indeed an unfortunate captain, for he had lost a ship to the *Alabama* almost three years earlier. Dabney Scales and the boarding party found nothing of value on the *Abigail*, except for an extensive cargo of whiskey, brandy, rum, pure alcohol, and cases of wines which Nye had intended to trade for furs. It did not take long for Scales' men to discover this vast supply, and they decided to pause for a small celebration. When they did not return to the cruiser, Waddell dispatched another boarding crew.

When the second crew arrived at the whaler, they found her still in the hands of her own men with the raider's first boat crew below deck knocking open the various liquor kegs and having a grand time. The second boarding party told the *Abigail's* crew to take their own boats and row to the *Shenandoah*, which they obediently did, and then the Confederate sailors descended below to join in the festivities.

Waddell was surprised when the captured crew arrived at the cruiser's side with no guards. The prisoners were placed in irons in the forecastle, and Lieutenant Whittle was ordered to take another crew to find out what had happened to the first two boats. He found the whiskey-soaked men floundering about the whaler's lower deck and sent his men below to haul them topside. A few too drunk to stand were dragged on deck, but when Whittle's men returned for more, they, too, paused to celebrate. Whittle signaled the *Shenandoah* for help, and Waddell dispatched the marines. Predictably, sailors and marines were soon frolicking below in various states of intoxication. Waddell next dispatched a boat of officers who quickly appropriated Captain Nye's private stock and proceeded to become intoxicated in a more gentlemanly manner. Finally, several of the more sober of the officers and men were able to persuade their comrades to return to the boats. They rowed an unsteady course to the cruiser, and when they arrived the men were dropped on the deck and told to sleep it off, while the drunken officers were locked in the wardroom. Two officers, Assistant Surgeon McNulty and the ship's carpenter, John Lynch, were so unruly that they had to be gagged and tied in their beds.

Master's Mate Hunt wrote: *It was the most general and stupendous spree ever witnessed. There was not a dozen sober men on board the ship except the prisoners, and had not these been ironed, it might have proved a dearly bought frolic.* Midshipman Mason, however, was stunned: *Had it been merely the men who became intoxicated it would not have been so bad, but I regret to say that some few of the officers committed themselves.*[4]

Waddell was furious. On May 29, while the *Abigail* burned, he penned a strict order and handed it to Whittle: *Private appropriation of prize property is prohibited. All articles sent from prizes to the ship must be sent to you, to be transferred to the paymaster's department. You will be pleased to call the attention of the officers to this order, and require rigid adherence to it. Any violation of it, coming under your observation, must be brought to my knowledge.*[5] Still critical and distrusting of their commander's judgment, many of the officers and much of the crew simply ignored the order.

Fourteen men from the *Abigail* joined the Southern navy, and with the crew sober, for the time being, the *Shenandoah* continued to push farther north. The ice began to thicken, and several days later the crew was drunk again from the liquor they had smuggled aboard. Although he usually dined alone, on the evening of June 3, Waddell entered the wardroom in full dress uniform with several bottles of champagne slung under his arm. The irony of the visit, after the drunken sprees and the strict order from the commander, was not lost upon the group gathered at the mess table. It was Jefferson Davis' fifty-seventh birthday, however, and Waddell felt it was time for a small relaxed celebration. After a dinner of roast pork, which had been confiscated from the *Abigail*, the officers toasted the Confederacy and their esteemed president. Little did they realize that at that moment, half a world away, their government no longer existed, and their president was a prisoner at Fortress Monroe. It would be a bitter moment when the news finally arrived.

Later that night the birthday celebration was interrupted by the watch officer who reported the wind rising and the barometer falling rapidly. Waddell went on deck for a closer look. The midnight sun had just slipped below the northern horizon, but visibility was still fairly good in the Arctic twilight. Black clouds were boiling toward the cruiser, but more disturbing was the massive ice floe that ran parallel to the vessel. She was sailing upwind from the ice, and if driven upon its huge jagged twenty-foot walls by the approaching storm, the cruiser would be dashed to pieces just as surely as though she had run upon a rocky shore. Waddell ordered the engines started, and the raider was quickly put under steam. Lookouts scurried aloft to see if an opening could be found in the floe. If the Confederate warship could be moved to the lee side of the ice she would not be driven against it. The biting wind began to howl through the wire rigging as the cruiser approached the floe. By the time a channel was found a fierce gale was blowing.

The helmsman swung her head toward the opening. The ice was shifting, and the possibility existed that the cruiser could become trapped in the channel before reaching the open water on the other side. With infuriating but necessary slowness, the man at the wheel guided the raider through the narrow chasm. High rough walls of ice loomed on every side; chunks of ice banged against the hull, and the freezing wind intensified. *She entered that passage,* Waddell later wrote with an air of nonchalance, *and in a short time was lying under close sail, and the floe to windward, which a little time before was our dreaded enemy, was then our best friend, for the fury of the seas was expended on it and not against the sides of the Shenandoah, and acting as a breakwater for her. She lay perfectly easy; the water was as smooth as a mill pond, while expended seas on the farther edge of the floe broke furiously, throwing sheets of water 20 feet high. It was a majestic sight, resembling an infuriated ocean wasting itself against an iron-bound coast.*[6]

For nine hours the *Shenandoah* endured the shrieking winds and driving rain. Her engines labored at times at full power as the helmsman endeavored to hold her stationary with her head into the wind. But in spite of all efforts the cruiser was gradually pushed into the middle of another floe. By morning the winds had abated, and when the men came on deck they found that they were completely surrounded by ice. *On every side of us, as far as the eye could reach extended the ice field*, Hunt wrote. *As the ponderous floes came together, the crushed and mangled debris rose up into huge mounds of crystal blocks, seemingly as immovable and imperishable as the bluffs on shore. Indeed it was impossible, while gazing off over the scene of wildness and desolation, to conceive (of) the possibility of an avenue of escape.*[7]

The cruiser was also encrusted with ice. Waddell wrote that the braces, blocks, yards, sails, and all the rigging were coated with ice up to two inches thick. *The rosy tints of morn prepared us for a scene of enchantment, and when the sunlight burst upon the fairy ship she sparkled from deck to truck as if a diadem had been thrown about her, awakening exclamations of enthusiastic delight. The crew was ordered aloft with billets of wood to dislodge the ice and free the running gear. The large icicles falling from aloft rendered the deck dangerous to move upon, and it soon became covered with clear beautiful ice. The water tanks, casks, and every vessel capable of receiving it were filled.*[8]

After the ice was cleared from the deck, warps and grapnels were run out onto the floe and secured to large blocks of ice. With Lieutenant Lee in charge of the deck, the *Shenandoah* was gradually worked out of the dangerous floe. By June 6, it was obvious that further progress was impossible, and Waddell ordered a reversal of course. The cruiser headed south toward Jonas Island which was situated near the center of the Okhotsk Sea and was a favorite hunting ground for the New England whalers. Even in this direction huge chunks of ice were everywhere, and for the first time the crew showed signs of being truly frightened. Unlike the sturdy whalers, the *Shenandoah's* fragile hull was not designed for crashing through the floes of ice. At any moment her hull could be torn open by one of the jagged blocks, and in the cold waters death would come quickly.

Later that night, Hunt could not sleep. *As I lay in my berth*, he wrote, *I could hear the huge blocks thundering and chafing against the side of the ship as though they would dash her to pieces. It was an anxious night to all on board. None of us were familiar with Arctic cruising, and consequently were in a great extent incompetent to judge of the imminence of the danger, but the hours of darkness wore away at last, without leaving us to mourn any serious accident.*[9]

The *Shenandoah* continued her careful way through the ice fields toward Jonas Island. Many of the officers were upset that Waddell had decided to look for whalers in the Okhotsk Sea at this season of the year. Hunt spoke for all of them when he wrote: *We had had enough of the route to Jonas Island, which may be a most desirable locality for whalemen*

The *Shenandoah* eases her way through patches of ice in the Okhotsk Sea.

and other amphibious animals who enjoy a temperature below zero and have an affinity for ice fields and fogs.... The plain truth was, we were running too much risk in taking our cruiser through this sort of navigation for which she was never intended.[10] Waddell evidently finally reached the same conclusion, for he now ordered a course set for the Amphrite Strait, the exit from the frozen and forbidden Okhotsk Sea.

After passing through the strait, Waddell turned the cruiser northward again, toward the Bering Sea and the Arctic Sea beyond. A strong wind pushed the raider onward, and as the warm Japanese currents mixed with the cold waters, dense fogs developed. Waddell's intent was to pass into the Bering Sea between the island of Attu, which is the westernmost island of the Aleutian chain, and the Komandorskies, a group of islands off the coast of Siberia. The fog became so dense that light barely penetrated, but on June 21, it lifted enough for a glimpse of the Siberian coast not more than five miles off the port beam. "Sail ho!" was shouted by the lookout, and the *Shenandoah* began the chase. In the swirling mist the "sail" turned out to be a rock, but floating pieces of blubber indicated that the long sought-after whaling fleet was not far ahead.

On June 22, at latitude 62°23′ N and longitude 179°46′ E, two ships were spotted. Steam was raised and the propeller lowered, and flying the Russian flag, the *Shenandoah* bounded after the strangers. The whalers were preoccupied with their fishing and paid little attention to the approaching black-hulled steamer. The 495-ton *William Thompson* from New Bedford had a whale lashed to her side, and her crew was busy cutting up the large chunks of blubber and boiling them in the vessel's trypots. Waddell dropped off a prize crew under the command of Midshipman Orris Browne as he passed and continued on after the second ship. A blank shot from one of the 12-pounders announced the cruiser's intentions, and the 364-ton *Euphrates* was boarded by the second prize crew led by Lieutenant Lee. Removing the sextant, three chronometers, and the small crew, Lee's men had the *Euphrates* ablaze within thirty minutes.[11]

The *Shenandoah* hurried back to the *William Thompson*, but as provisions were being transferred from the whaler to the cruiser, the shout "Sail ho!" was shouted from the masthead. The distant vessel was five points off the port bow and with all her canvas deployed was standing north. Crewmen raced aloft to deploy the cruiser's sails as gongs rang in the engine room signaling for maximum power. Smoke poured from the warship's stack as she raced after the third prize of the day. It was close to 7:00 p.m. before she drew near enough to fire a shot across her bow. The speedy whaler turned into the wind, stopped, and ran up the English flag. She proved to be the *Robert L. Townes* of Sydney,

Australia's only ocean-going whaler. Once again the *Shenandoah* re-traced her route back to her first prize. What few provisions that could be garnered from the *William Thompson* were loaded aboard the cruiser, and with her prisoners added to those from the *Euphrates* secured be-low, the largest of New England's whalers was put to the torch. As the *Shenandoah* steamed slowly away, the gray Arctic night was illumi-nated by the glow of the two oil-soaked whalers as they burned to the waterline.

Midshipman Browne, however, carried a disturbing message with him when he finally clambered back aboard the cruiser. He reported to Waddell that while on board the *William Thompson*, he had gone with her captain, Francis Smith, to the ship's cabin. While retrieving his papers from the safe, Smith had vehemently protested the seizure stating that the war was over and that the Army of Northern Virginia had surrendered. He could provide no definite proof, however, and Waddell, hoping that it was just another false rumor, determined to continue.[12]

The following day, which happened also to be June 22, 1865 be-cause the cruiser had crossed the international date line, brought a dismal day with fog and snow squalls. The *Shenandoah*, her engines turning slowly, pushed carefully through a field of mushy ice. Around noon the sun broke through with enough force to lift the mist, and the lookouts distinguished five sails ahead. By 4:00 p.m., the unusually bright sunshine revealed eight whalers in sight. A solid mass of ice, however, separated the cruiser from her prey. Hunt remembered the scene well:
The sun was shining with more than its accustomed radiance as we advanced toward them. As its rays reflected from the glittering fields of ice, the effect was indescribably beautiful.

Away on the starboard bow we could distinguish a boat and its crew glid-ing swiftly through the water, towed by a large white whale they had just fastened, and the vessel to which it belonged was standing slowly after, to keep it in view. Other ships we could see far off in the ice field....

On the starboard beam stretching away as far as the eye could reach was a seemingly unbroken sea of ice, while on the port beam rose up the cold, dreary shores of North Asia, (Siberia) as sterile and inhospitable a region as my eyes ever looked upon. The two vessels nearest us had foreign ensigns flying at their peaks, but the next three in order sported Uncle Sam's gridiron....[13]

Flying the Russian flag, the *Shenandoah* approached the first whaler. Painted on the stern of her white hull was the name *Milo* of New Bedford. Waddell dropped off a prize crew, and when the *Milo's* captain came aboard he expressed surprise that the raider, which he had heard was still in Australia, was now in the Bering Sea. He, too, had heard the war was over, but could produce no documentary

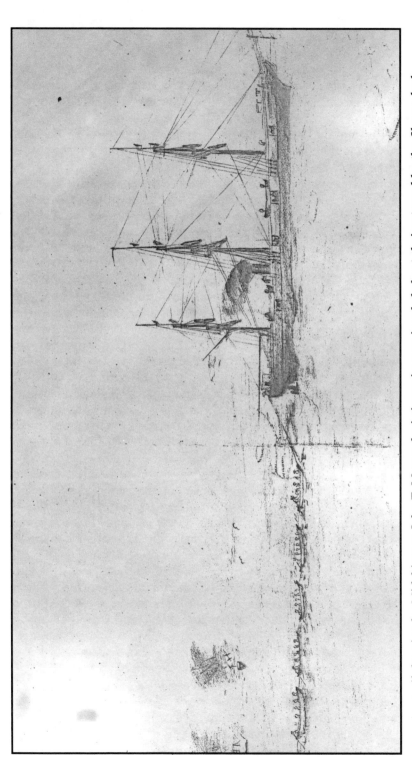

A pencil drawing by Midshipman John T. Mason depicting prisoners in whale boats being towed by the *Shenandoah*.
Courtesy Eleanor S. Brockenbrough Library, Museum of the Confederacy

evidence. Whittle ordered the *Milo's* crew on board the cruiser to prevent the whaler's escape, and with steam hissing in the *Shenandoah's* boilers, she set out after the remaining American vessels. One of the whalers was endeavoring to make her escape among the floes, and Waddell ordered a shot fired from the forward Whitworth. The gun crew rushed to their positions, and within a few minutes the big piece thundered its message across the frozen sea. The shot howled by the whaler's bow, barely missing the figurehead, but she still did not stop. Another thunderous report and another shell tore through the main topsail and exploded in a shower of iron and ice splinters a short distance beyond. Moses Tucker, master of the 426-ton *Sophia Thornton* determined that that was close enough, and hauled his vessel around and awaited his fate.[14]

Dabney Scales with his prize crew went aboard and ordered Captain Tucker and his mates to proceed quickly to the *Shenandoah*. The Confederate cruiser then steamed after the next whaler which, with all of her sails spread, was making for the Siberian coast. After a three-hour chase the cruiser drew near enough for the Whitworth rifle to do its work. With a thunderous roar, the English-built gun sent a round shrieking across the whaler's stern. The shot was thoroughly convincing, and though only a mile from the sanctuary of the marine league, the *Jireh Swift* of New Bedford hauled around and lowered her sails. The pristine bark, at 428 tons, was one of the largest and fastest of the New England whalers. Within thirty minutes of her capture the *Jireh Swift* was a mass of flames.[15]

Four more sails were visible, but two of them were securely locked behind fields of ice; the others were of foreign registry. Consequently, the *Shenandoah* steamed back to the *Milo*. On the way, Waddell questioned the *Jireh Swift's* master, Thomas Williams, on his opinion of the status of the war. Williams stated that he "did not believe the war was over, but that the South would yield eventually." The whaler's comments were made in the presence of all of the cruiser's officers and served to buoy their hopes that their government still existed.[16]

It was 9:00 p.m. when the *Shenandoah* rejoined the two captured prizes. Waddell sent all the prisoners to the *Milo*, but when her master protested that he did not have sufficient provisions to feed 300 men, Waddell instructed him to take all that he needed from the *Sophia Thornton*, providing he destroyed the vessel before departing. To eliminate any temptation of salvaging the vessel, the cruiser's carpenters were sent aboard to saw down her masts. Three more sails were in sight and the Confederate commander was anxious to be off. As soon as the carpenters clambered back aboard, signal gongs rang in the engine room, and black smoke poured from the raider's stack as she steamed away. Hunt remembered the scene well: *As we glided seaward, still standing toward the frozen region of the Arctic Circle, we could see the disabled vessel, with her masts dragging alongside, and the paroled prisoners with their whaleboats, transferring from her to the Milo whatever suited their fancy. I have no doubt the craft was thoroughly ransacked, but ere the sun made its brief disappearance below the horizon, a bright tongue of flame shot heavenward, telling us that the prisoners had performed their distasteful task. A more unpleasant duty, I trust, will never be assigned to them.*[17]

At 8:10 a.m. on June 23, the crew of the *Susan Abigail* watched with intense curiosity as the black-hulled steamer flying the Stars and Stripes slowly approached. The 159-ton whaler was still in San Francisco when the guns of the Presidio thundered the news of Lee's surrender. Her flag had been lowered to half staff at the news of Lincoln's assassination. When she sailed, only the region west of the Mississippi was still holding out. The skipper of the *Susan Abigail* was eager to continue his celebration with the captain of the "Federal" cruiser that was now only a short distance away, and so lowering a boat, quickly rowed to her side. Clambering over her rail, he was flabbergasted to be confronted by officers in faded gray uniforms. Glancing above, he was even more horrified to see that Old Glory had been replaced by the Confederate banner. Despite the captain's incessant pleading, the *Susan Abigail* was quickly condemned.

Five sailors from the whaler joined the *Shenandoah*, but newspapers brought from the *Susan Abigail* told of the crushing defeats in the South. Waddell hoped that the news stories were exaggerated. In spite of the distressing articles, there were several reports that offered a ray of hope. *The California papers contained a number of dispatches,* Waddell recorded in his journal, *and among them was one that stated that the Southern government (had) removed to Danville and the greater part of the army of Virginia had joined General Johnston's army in North Carolina, where an indecisive battle had been fought against General Sherman's army; also that at Danville a proclamation was issued by President Davis, announcing that the war would be carried on with renewed vigor, and exhorting the people of the South to bear up heroically against their adversities.*[18]

Waddell called a meeting of his officers. After reading the accounts, they all agreed that the *Shenandoah* should continue her war against the New England whalers. Hunt explained their decision: *So far as we knew, our armies, though repulsed at many points and sadly depleted in numbers, were still making a gallant stand against the Northern hordes, which eventually overran our unhappy country, bearing down all resistance before them; consequently our hearts were buoyed up with the thought that we were still aiding the great cause to which we had devoted our lives and fortunes.*[19]

The *Shenandoah* tows whaleboats filled with prisoners from three prizes, June 25, 1865.

The terrible news could not be ignored, however, and in spite of Hunt's "buoyed heart," a sense of foreboding prevailed. Surgeon Lining poured out his feelings in his journal later that night: *If it proves true it will be terrible. First that Charleston was captured; this I was expecting, as I did not think we could hold it against Sherman's army. Next that Richmond and Petersburg were taken. I was looking for their evacuation, so it did not surprise me much. But when I heard that General Lee had surrendered with the whole of the Army of Northern Virginia, I was knocked flat aback— can I believe it? And after the official letters which are published as being written by Grant and Lee can I help believing it? It is either true, or the Yankees are again publishing official lies. God grant that it may not be true.*[20]

Continuing toward the northeast, St. Lawrence Island was passed, and the Bering Strait—the gateway to the Arctic Ocean—was not far ahead. The Confederate cruiser was now so far north that night and day had become as one. Thick fields of ice were visible over the bow, but slowly and carefully, the *Shenandoah* continued to push on. The following day on June 25, the 419-ton *General Williams* out of New London was captured and burned. To the north, three more sails were in sight, but an almost solid field of drift ice barred the way. While it was bitterly cold, a perfect calm prevailed, and the three whalers eyed their drooping sails helplessly as the black-hulled steamer slowly made her way through the narrow channels in the ice. At 1:00 a.m., with the midnight sun resting on the horizon, the *Shenandoah* broke out into clear water. Within thirty minutes her boarding parties had secured the 389-ton bark *William C. Nye* of San Francisco, the 384-ton *Catherine* of New Bedford, and the 340-ton *Nimrod*, also out of New Bedford.

Captain James Clark of the *Nimrod* knew what was coming as he observed the Confederate cruiser approaching. Two years earlier he had lost the *Ocean Rover* to the *Alabama*, and now he watched with horror as Acting Master Bulloch climbed over his railing. "My God, no!" he gasped. "We meet again, Captain," Bulloch responded with a smile. Bulloch had led the boarding party from the *Alabama* when the *Ocean Rover* was captured.[21]

The crews of the three whalers were hurried over to the *Shenandoah*. Her decks became crowded with more than 200 prisoners, much too many for the cruiser's small marine guard to control. Waddell was in a hurry, however, for five more prizes were in sight. Lieutenant Grimball offered a solution, and Waddell agreed. The officers were confined in the coal bunkers, and the remaining prisoners were distributed among twelve whaleboats which were then taken in tow by the cruiser. *It was a singular scene which we now looked out upon,* Hunt recorded. *Behind us were three blazing ships, wildly drifting amid gigantic fragments of ice; close astern were the twelve whaleboats with their living freight; and ahead of us were five other vessels now evidently aware of their danger but seeing no avenue of escape. It was a tortuous way we now had to pursue, winding about among the ice floes like the trail of a serpent. Six knots an hour was the highest speed we dared attempt, so intricate was the navigation, but we at length succeeded in penetrating the little fleet for which we were steering.*[22]

Waddell passed up the nearest prize, for the prisoners warned him that smallpox was on board. The next vessel boarded was the *General Pike* of New Bedford. *The General Pike had lost her captain, Waddell recorded, and the mate was in charge of her, who asked as a special favor of me to ransom the Pike, as I should have to ransom one of the vessels. I asked his reason, and he said, "Captain, if you ransom the vessel her owners will think me well to do in getting her out of this scrape, and it will give me a claim on them for the command."* Waddell liked the mate's candid appeal. He ransomed the *General Pike* for $30,000, and placing the prisoners on board, directed her to sail for San Francisco.[23]

Before the *General Pike* was released, two more prizes were rounded up, the 315-ton *Isabella* and the 360-ton *Gypsey*. Their crews were hustled over to the *General Pike*, bringing the *Pike's* total complement to 250. The captains of the *Isabella* and *Gypsey* begged Waddell to spare their vessels, stating that they believed that the war was over, but the cruiser's commander, following his president's order to carry on the war with "renewed vigor," condemned them both. The *Isabella* was lashed alongside the *Shenandoah*, and provisions and water were transferred to the cruiser. When all was secure she was cast loose, and soon the two whalers were a mass of flames, their fires being fed by $37,000 worth of whale oil stored in their holds.[24]

The *Shenandoah* continued steaming slowly northward through thickening ice floes and into the Bering Strait. At 6:30 a.m. on June 27, the 327-ton *Waverly* out of New Bedford became an easy prize and was soon a blazing inferno. A large number of sails, eleven in number, were reported to the north, and Waddell came on deck to study the situation. *I felt no doubt of their nationality, he wrote, and to attempt the capture of any one of them while the wind blew would be the loss of the greater part of them. (We) lowered the smokestack and continued in the rear of the whalers, keeping a luff and retarding her progress as much as possible, so as to arouse no suspicions among the Yankee crowd ahead. On the 28th at 10:30 a.m. a calm ensued; the game were collected in East Cape Bay, and the Shenandoah came plowing the Arctic waters under the American flag with a fine pressure of steam on. Every vessel hoisted the American flag.*[25]

One of the whalers visible up ahead was the New Bedford bark, the *Brunswick*, which had recently stove in her side on a jagged piece of ice. Seeing his vessel a total wreck, Captain A. T. Potter had hauled her over on her side to keep from sinking and had set out to bargain with his fellow captains for the purchase of his whale oil. A thick fog had rolled in as Potter desperately made the rounds of the nearby whalers seeking their assistance. Anxious to fill their own casks with oil, the neighboring captains had all refused. As the fog began to lift, Potter saw a black steamer moving slowly among the whaling fleet. Help was at hand, he thought, and he quickly rowed to her side. *While the boats were being armed preparatory to taking possession of the prizes,* Waddell recalled, *a boat from the whale ship Brunswick came to the steamer, and the mate in charge of the boat, still ignorant of our nationality, represented that the Brunswick a few hours before had struck a piece of ice which left a hole in her starboard bow twenty inches below the waterline, and asked for assistance, to which application Lieutenant Whittle replied, "We are very busy now, but in a little time we will attend to you." The facetiousness of the reply coaxed a smile from me.*[26]

Before Potter left, Whittle asked him to point out the *James Maury*. While at Ponape, Waddell had learned of the death of the whaler's captain, S. L. Gray, and that his wife and two small children were still on board. Command of the *James Maury* had been transferred to First Mate Cunningham, and the distraught Mrs. Gray had had her husband's body preserved in a barrel of whiskey in order to carry him home for a proper Christian burial. Lieutenant Chew was sent to ransom the whaler, and to inform Mrs. Gray that she had nothing to fear, "that she and the children were under the protection of the *Shenandoah* and no harm would come to her or the vessel, that the men of the South did not make war upon women and children."[27]

The *Shenandoah* was now ready. She lay in the midst of the fleet where her guns could command every vessel. All five of her boats had been lowered, and their armed crews had each been assigned two whalers. At a given signal a blank cartridge was fired, the United States flag hauled down, the Confederate ensign raised, and the five boats pulled for their respective targets. Ten American flags were hauled down instantly, but one whaler, the *Favorite* of Fair Haven, refused to lower her flag. The *Favorite* had been assigned to Lieutenant Whittle and his boarding party, but as they approached, the *Shenandoah's* executive officer could see the whaler's master, Captain Young, a burly gray-haired man, standing on deck next to the harpoon gun. He held a cutlass in one hand and an old-fashioned navy revolver in the other. Along the bulwarks, sighting down the barrels of their leveled muskets, could be seen the heads of his men.

"Boat ahoy!" the old captain bellowed when the cruiser's cutter drew near enough to be hailed.

"Ahoy!" shouted Whittle.

"Who are you and what do you want?"

"We come to inform you that your vessel is a prize to the Confederate steamer *Shenandoah*."

"I'll be damned if she is, at least just yet. Now keep off, you, or I'll fire into you."

Young swung his harpoon gun around and trained it on the approaching boat. Whittle decided the old gentleman was just crazy enough to do battle and ordered his crew to return to the *Shenandoah*. Waddell steamed the cruiser alongside the *Favorite*, and the four broadside guns were run out. Young's cutlass had now been discarded, and a whiskey bottle had taken its place.

"Haul down your flag," Grimball shouted.

"Haul it down yourself, damn you!" Young roared. By now the old gentleman was beginning to sway a bit as he waved his whiskey bottle over his head.

"If you don't haul it down, we'll blow you out of the water in five minutes!"

"Blow away, my buck," Young shouted back, "but I may be eternally blasted if I haul down that flag for any cussed Confederate pirate that ever floated!"

Waddell had had enough. He ordered Whittle and his boat's crew to board the *Favorite*. Gunners rammed explosive shells into the Whitworths and stood poised with firing lanyards in hand. As Whittle approached, he could see the old captain standing his ground, but his crew, perhaps without the fortification of the bottle were not as confident. They had thrown down their muskets, removed the cap from the harpoon gun without Young's knowledge, and taken to the boats.

Whittle's boat bumped alongside.

"Haul down your colors!" Whittle shouted.

"I'll see you dead first!" Young roared while waving his bottle.

"If you don't I'll have to shoot you!" Whittle sighted his revolver.

"Shoot and be damned!"

Whittle lowered his pistol and ordered his men to carry the *Favorite* by boarding. Quickly they clambered onto her deck and rushed the still shouting Captain Young. Sagging by the harpoon gun, the defiant old sea dog gave up without further resistance. Not only had the harpoon gun been disarmed, but Whittle found that Young had neglected to cap his revolver. *It was evident,* Hunt wrote, *that he had been seeking spirituous consolation; indeed to be plain about it, he was at least three sheets to the wind, but by general consent he was voted to be the bravest and most resolute man we captured during our cruise.*[28]

By 5:00 p.m., the *Shenandoah* had captured and condemned ten New England whalers. In addition to the *James Maury*, the *Brunswick*, and the defiant *Favorite*, there were the *Hillman*, the *Martha*, the *Covington*, the *Nile*, the *Nassau*, the *Isaac Howland*, and the *Congress*.

The prisoners, 336 in all, were made to sign their paroles and by 7:00 p.m., all had been transferred to the *James Maury* and the *Nile*. Nine men joined the *Shenandoah*, bringing her total complement of men and officers to 132, a significant improvement over those early days when the cruiser was so shorthanded. Of these last nine men, Waddell recorded in his journal that: *They were all intelligent soldiers, men who had been educated to use the Enfield rifle and to respect military position. The enlistment of these men in Confederate service was evidence at least that if they had heard any report of the military failure of the South they considered it so unreliable that it failed to embarrass their judgment in seeking service in the Shenandoah. It is not to be supposed that these men would have embarked in a cause which they believed to be lost.*[29] Waddell prayed that the Southern nation's heart still beat, and grasped for any evidence that would support his hopes.

By 10:00 p.m., eight whalers were blazing infernos. *It was a scene never to be forgotten by any who beheld it,* Hunt wrote. *The red glare from the eight burning vessels shone far and wide over the drifting ice of those savage seas; the crackling of the fire as it made its devouring way through each doomed ship, fell on the still air like unbraiding voices. The sea was filled with boats driving hither and thither with no hand to guide them, and with yards, sails, and cordage, remnants of the stupendous ruin there progressing. In the distance, but where the light fell strong and red upon them, bringing out into bold relief each spar and line, were the two ransomed vessels, the Noah's arks that were to bear away the human life which in a few hours would be all that was left of the gallant whaling fleet.*[30]

Some of the prisoners had reported that a fleet of sixty whalers had passed through the strait several days earlier and were headed north. Waddell doubted the accuracy of these reports, but felt it justifiable to at least investigate them. At 1:00 a.m. on Thursday, June 29, with Siberia off the port beam and Alaska to starboard, the *Shenandoah* pushed on into the desolate Arctic Ocean. A few days before the waters had been clear, but great floes of ice had been pushed southward by the currents, and as far as the lookouts could see there was nothing but one great unbroken sea of ice. The cruiser steamed along the rim of the craggy floes for several hours, but no opening in the massive ice fields could be found.

She continued northward amid snow and iceberg until she reached latitude 66°40' N, Waddell wrote, *when in consequence of her great length, the immensity of the icebergs and floes, and the danger of being shut in the Arctic Ocean for several months, I was induced to turn her head southward, and she reached East Cape just in time to slip by the Diomedes when a vast field of ice*

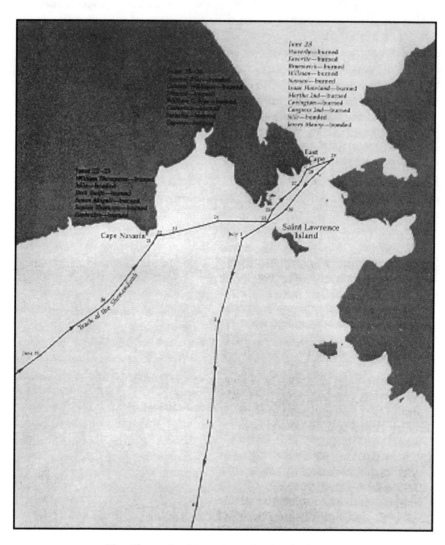

The *Shenandoah's* path to the Arctic Ocean.

was closing the strait. She was forced to enter the ice, but very slowly, and every caution was observed to save her from injury. For hours she winded her way through that extreme danger, and I hoped it would be the last to encounter, for although we had become familiarized with it, still it was an unpleasant companion and one we desired to avoid.[31]

Off St. Lawrence Island the *Shenandoah* broke into relatively clear water and the wind freshened out of the northwest. Waddell ordered the propeller hoisted and all sails deployed. With a collective sigh of relief from her officers and crew, the Confederate warship skimmed over the open waters of the Bering Sea at six knots with her head at last set to the south. On July 5, the cruiser passed through Amukta Pass of the Aleutian Island chain, and with the deep swells of the North Pacific once again under her keel, Waddell ordered her course set for the coast of California.

For the next few days the *Shenandoah* sailed on under clearing skies that soon revealed the majestic Aleutian mountains off her port beam. Giant snow-covered ranges broken by black basalt ridges, coupled with the deep blue of the northern sky, all presented a panorama of incredible beauty. *It was a relief to feel we were again bound for the general region of the tropics,* Hunt recalled. *Our intention was now to cruise on the Pacific Coast in the hope of capturing one or more of the rich steamers that ply between San Francisco and Panama. How others may have felt I know not, but for myself, I am free to confess that I had had enough of Arctic cruising, and if I never look again upon those icy seas and barren shores, fit residences only for Eskimos, seals, and Polar bears, it will not occasion me one moment's regret.*[32]

On July 18, word finally reached San Francisco of the raider's attacks on the northern whaling fleet. Two days later the rumors were confirmed when the *Milo* limped into port bringing the first load of hungry survivors. David McDougal, commandant of the Mare Island Navy Yard, dispatched an urgent telegram to the Secretary of the Navy in Washington: "Ship *Milo* arrived today from the Arctic with crews of ten whalers destroyed by the *Shenandoah*. Admiral Pearson notified by steamer *America*, which sailed today for Panama."

The message went astray, and it was not until August 18, that word finally reached the Federal capital. By that time, Waddell's mission had dramatically switched from one of destruction to that of survival.

Before operations commenced along the California coast, it was imperative that Waddell put his mind at ease on the course of the war. It was with a mixture of relief and apprehension, therefore, that the *Shenandoah* stopped the British bark *Barracouta* on August 2. The English vessel was only thirteen days out of San Francisco. Waddell sent Bulloch to inspect the bark's papers. After examining the vessel's registry,

"Captains of the Whaleships," photographed in San Francisco. *Left to right:* Captains Smith, Tucker, Hawes, Hathaway, and Williams.

Bulloch, apologizing for the intrusion, thanked the British captain, and then asked for the latest news about the war.

"What war?" was the puzzled response.

"The war between the United States and Confederate States," answered Bulloch.

"Why, the war has been over since April. What ship is that?"

"The Confederate steamer *Shenandoah*."

"Good God almighty. Every navy in the world is after you."

Bulloch's heart sank. The captain led the stunned Confederate officer to the bark's cabin, and there produced the latest newspapers from San Francisco. The Englishman assured him that the news was true. It was almost more than the young officer could bear. Returning to the boat, the crew rowed silently back to the *Shenandoah*.

The officers hurriedly gathered in the wardroom. It was too terrible to be true, but the papers told the story. Lee's and Johnston's armies had surrendered. The Trans-Mississippi Department, too, had been given up. Jefferson Davis, shackled in irons, languished in prison, and as the *Barracouta's* captain had exclaimed, every navy in the world seemed to be searching for the "pirate *Shenandoah*." The news seemed too crushing to be true, and yet, as Whittle recorded in his journal, *coming as it did from an Englishman, we could not doubt its accuracy. We were bereft of country, bereft of government, bereft of ground for hope or aspiration, bereft of a cause for which to struggle and suffer.*[33]

Hunt scribbled in his journal: *It was as though every man had just learned of the death of a near and dear relative.*[34]

Surgeon Lining was even more despondent: *This is doomed to be one of the blackest of all the days of my life, for from today I must look forward to begin life over again, starting where I cannot tell, how I cannot say—but I have learned for a certainty that I have no country.*[35]

Under the date of August 2, 1865, Dabney Scales made the following entry in the ship's log:

> Having received by the bark *Barracouta* the sad intelligence of the overthrow of the Confederate Government, all attempts to destroy the shipping or property of the United States will cease from this date, in accordance with which the first lieutenant, William C. Whittle, Jr., received the order from the commander to strike below the battery and disarm the ship and crew.
>
> D. M. Scales[36]

For the cruiser's commander, the news was especially devastating, for it was under his authority that the destruction of the whaling fleet occurred after the cessation of hostilities. He was determined, however, to steel his heart for whatever might lie ahead: *My life had been checkered,* he wrote of the moment, *and I was tutored to disappointments;*

the intelligence of the issue of the fearful struggle cast a deep stillness over the ship's company, and would have occupied all my reflection had not a responsibility of the highest order rested upon me in the course I should pursue, which involved not only my personal honor, but the honor of that flag entrusted to me, which had been thus far triumphant.[37]

With no real government to back his authority, Waddell sought the advice of his officers. Some suggested blowing up the ship after landing the men in some remote country. Others argued that because all former Confederate property now belonged to the United States, the raider should be sailed to the nearest American port and surrendered. A third group pressed for the *Shenandoah* to be taken to a British or French port and surrendered as public property, and because the men now belonged to no specific government, they should be free from arrest. Several officers expressed concern that the crew, consisting of many nationalities, might mutiny once they learned that Waddell's authority lacked government backing. They, too, had seen the newspapers calling them "pirates," and each knew what the consequences would be if caught and prosecuted as such.

After endless debates there was still little agreement among the officers, but Waddell had made his decision. The next day, August 3, he headed for Sidney, Australia, where be believed they would find a sympathetic reception in the British crown colony. The following day, however, he changed his mind. England was home to the majority of the crew, and it did not make sense, in his judgment, to deposit them half a world away. Even though it would mean running a greater risk of being intercepted by a Federal cruiser, Waddell determined to head for Liverpool.

The following morning the crew presented the *Shenandoah's* commander with a petition requesting that he make his intentions clear. At 1:00 p.m., all hands were piped aft to the quarterdeck where Waddell addressed the crew: *My men,* he began, *I have received your communication, which is a very proper one. The spirit in which it was written is a subordinate one. A commanding officer can ask for nothing more. What you say here is true. The South has been subdued. At the same time you must know that the position of myself and all of my officers is far worse than that of any of you. You ask where we shall go. I tell you this. I shall take the ship into the nearest English port. All I have to ask of you men is to stand by me to the last.* (There were cries of, "We will! We will!") *As for our cruise, it is a record which stands for itself. All you have to do is to be proud of it.* (More cries of, "We are! We are!")

No man among you has any reason to blush for the service in which he has been engaged. Waddell continued, his voice breaking, *Our cruise was projected and prosecuted in good faith. It has inflicted heavy blows upon the commerce of our late enemies which will not soon be forgotten. But now there is nothing more to be done but to secure our personal safety by the readiest and most efficacious means at hand. You must trust in me.* (Shouts of, "We do! We do!")[38]

Many of the men and officers were brought to tears. For the moment, at least, they were all united in a common bond to do their duty and see the *Shenandoah* safely to an English port. It was soon apparent to the officers and crew, however, that Waddell had not specified which port he meant when he referred to the "nearest English port." While the speculation grew, and would eventually split the crew and officers into two bitter camps, the "Cape Towners" and the "Liverpoolers," Waddell kept his own council. *I first thought that a port in the South Atlantic would answer all my purposes*, he explained,... *but upon reflection I saw the propriety of avoiding those ports and determined to run the ship for a European port, which involved a distance of 17,000 miles—a long gauntlet to run and escape.... I considered it due the honor of all concerned that to avoid everything like a show of dread under the severe trial imposed upon me was my duty as a man and an officer in whose hands was placed the honor of my country's flag and the welfare of 132 men.*[39]

Running before the fresh northwest winds that sweep down the Pacific side of the North and South American continents, the *Shenandoah* continued her southward course. Lookouts perched high on her swaying mast kept a sharp eye out for other vessels, not as prospective prizes, but as vessels to avoid. But the morale of the crew was somber. Hunt noted that: *the hilarity which had so long been observable through the ship was now gone, and there were only anxious faces to be seen in the cabin, wardroom and forecastle....*[40]

The long weeks of monotonous sailing, the constant vigil to avoid other vessels, the uncertain future, all began to dampen the spirit of the men. By the time the cruiser had rounded Cape Horn at the southern tip of South America, discontent and discord had broken out among the officers and crew. Arguments and fights erupted, pistols were pointed, and even Waddell lost patience. Scales was relieved from duty for oversleeping, Hunt and Browne for arguing with the commander, and Lee for smoking on deck while on watch. Waddell cooled off and restored the officers to duty, but the actions only served to fray the already taut nerves of all concerned.

Everyone on board had by now taken a keen interest in navigation. By September 26, the cruiser had reached a position in the deep South Atlantic Ocean where a few more days of sailing would indicate the vessel's destination—Cape Town or Liverpool. The men and officers were fiercely split, some favoring the South African port, others England. Two days later six officers presented a signed petition to Waddell requesting that the *Shenandoah* be taken to Cape Town. They pledged, however, that whatever their commander's decision might be, they would support him and abide by it. A second petition, signed by ten junior officers, was more critical and seemed to question Waddell's judgment. The document had been drawn up by James Blacker, the captain's clerk, and Waddell stormed at Blacker, "I will be captain, sir, or die on this deck!"[41]

With control of the *Shenandoah* teetering on the brink of chaos, Waddell called a council of several of his officers. Some would claim later that he invited only those whom he had reason to believe would support his position. Whittle, who favored Cape Town, declined to vote on the grounds that as executive officer he was duty bound to support his commander. Before the ballot was cast, however, a final petition was presented at the cabin door. It was signed by seventy-one petty officers and men, most of whom were British, all of whom pledged their complete reliance and trust in their commander's decision to take the vessel to England. Chew, Grimball, Scales, and Lee voted three to one to proceed to Liverpool.[42]

The vote of the officer's council settled the question of the *Shenandoah's* destination and most of the men and officers were satisfied. Still, hard feelings abounded. On the day following the vote, the raider crossed the path of her outbound tract, and Waddell sent a bottle of champagne to the wardroom with a note congratulating his officers for having served on the only Confederate warship to have circled the globe. Three of the Cape Town supporters arose and walked out.[43]

On Wednesday, October 11, the equator was crossed for the fourth time. There was no celebration.

Two weeks later the cruiser was "fanning along," as Waddell described it, with slight breezes when the often longed for cry of "Sail ho!" resounded from the masthead. The cry brought everyone to their feet, and anxious faces strained skyward to the lookout's perch, waiting for the next report.

Glasses swept the northern horizon in search of the stranger, Waddell wrote, *but she was visible from aloft only. I sent a quartermaster aloft with orders to communicate to me only what he could ascertain from the appearance of the sail. He reported her under short sail with her mainsail up or furled, and that from the spread of her masts (she seemed) to be a steamer. She was standing a little more to the east of north than the Shenandoah was heading. The sun was thirty minutes high and the sky was cloudless. I could make no change in the course of the ship or the quantity of sail she was carrying, because such evolution would have aroused the stranger's suspicion.... Communication was undesirable to me. After the sun had gone down, leaving a brilliant western sky and a beautifully defined horizon, I sent the quartermaster aloft again with orders similar to those he had previously received. He reported her to be a cruiser and he believed her awaiting in order to speak.*[44]

For once the men cursed the *Shenandoah's* speed. Rapidly she had come upon the sail in daylight, and now there seemed to be no way of retarding her progress enough for nightfall to overtake them. The propeller was lowered for its drag, and buckets were swung from the stern for the same effect. Engineers and firemen rushed to the engine room to begin raising steam. The engines had not been used since crossing the equator on the Pacific side. Onward she rushed as the men held their breath and prayed for darkness.

She could already be seen from on deck, Waddell continued, *and darkness came on more slowly than I had ever before observed it. The situation was one of anxious suspense; our security, if any remained, depended on a strict adherence to the course; deviation would be fatal; boldness must accomplish the deception. Still she forged toward the sail, and it would be madness to stop her. Darkness finally threw her friendly folds around the anxious heart and little ship, and closed the space between the vessels. What a relief! She could not have been more than four miles off.*[45]

The *Shenandoah* was turned toward the south and the engines started. She was burning Cardiff coal which left only a thin white trail of vapor. Signal gongs clattered in the engine room calling for, "All ahead full," and the engineers applied power to the faithful propeller. On deck sailors clambered aloft to furl the sails so they would not be visible in the tropical moon which would rise at 9:00 p.m. With the welcome feel of the engines throbbing beneath his feet, Waddell ordered a course change, and the black-hulled *Shenandoah,* now almost invisible in the total darkness, steamed off due east. Waddell kept her running east for fifteen miles and then turned north again. When the sun rose the following morning the suspected enemy cruiser was nowhere in sight.[46]

Pushed by the southwest trades, the *Shenandoah* pressed up to within 700 miles of Liverpool—and then the wind died. The ship was becalmed with not a breath of wind, and numerous sails were visible on the horizon. At nightfall, Waddell ordered steam raised on the precious little coal that was left, and the *Shenandoah* forged ahead. Three more days of steaming by night and sailing by day brought her almost within sight of Ireland. Gulls wheeled overhead, and old seaman claimed they could smell the bogs.

On the fourth of November, Hunt wrote, *our reckoning showed us to be near land, and all eyes were anxiously scanning the horizon for a glimpse of old England. We knew not what reception was in store for us, for momentous changes had taken place since we set forth on that adventurous pilgrimage around the world, but we were weary of suspense and all were desirous of making port and learning the worst as soon as possible. Night, however, closed around us with nothing but the heaving sea with which we had been so long familiar in sight.*

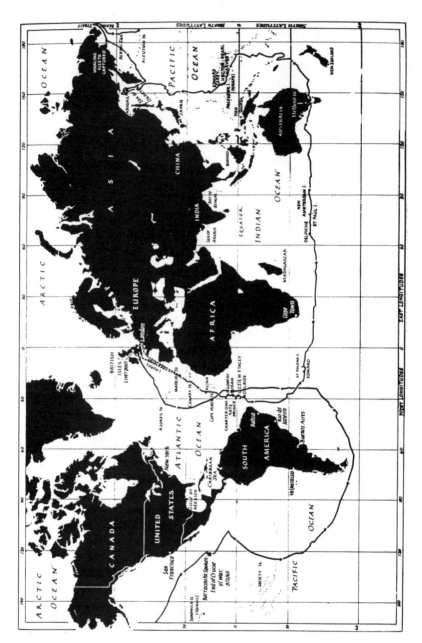

Map depicting the route taken by the *Shenandoah* on her around-the-world cruise.

The following morning a dense fog was hanging over the water, effectu-
ally concealing everything from view at a ship's length distance. Extreme
caution was now necessary as we had only our chronometers and the patent
log towed astern to rely upon for showing us our position, but we steamed
slowly ahead with all sails furled, laying our course for St. George's Channel.
Soon the fog lifted (and) revealed to our view the green shores of Ireland off
our port beam, the first land we had seen since we lost sight of the snow-clad
bluffs of Northern America.[47]

The *Shenandoah* had traveled a total of 58,000 miles over a span of
thirteen months. She had destroyed 32 vessels and bonded six others,
all at an estimated value of $1,290,823. It had been 122 days since her
men last saw those "snow-clad bluffs of Northern America." During
that time the *Shenandoah* had traveled 23,000 miles without sighting
land, and now their navigator, young Master Irvine Bulloch, the son of
James D. Bulloch, the Confederate Navy's unheralded agent in Europe, had placed the cruiser exactly where she was supposed to be.
Waddell was impressed, "The navigation was very beautiful."

During the day the cruiser continued steaming northeast toward
Holyhead, that peninsula of land that juts into the Irish Sea on England's
west coast. Paymaster Smith was kept busy paying off the men, and by
sundown the cruiser had rounded Holyhead and turned east for
Liverpool. Around midnight the lights of a pilot boat were seen.

Very early in the morning, November 6, 1865, the pilot boat pulled
alongside. The pilot scampered up the gangway and was met at the
rail by Whittle who wished him good morning.

"Good morning. What ship is this?"

"The late Confederate steamer *Shenandoah*," Whittle responded.

"The hell you say. Where have you fellows come from?"

"From the Arctic Ocean."

"And you haven't stopped at any port since you left there?"

"No, nor been in sight of land either. What news from the war in
America?"

The *Shenandoah's* officers had all gathered around the pilot, many
still hoping against hope that the San Francisco papers had been in
error.

"Why the war has been over so long people have got through talking about it. Jeff Davis is in Fortress Monroe, and the Yankees have a
lot of cruisers out looking for you."

At daylight in a thick fog, the *Shenandoah*, guided by the pilot, started
up the Mersey. After some consultation with his officers, Waddell ordered the Confederate flag raised. Slowly, carefully, she glided along.
With fog swirling over the river, few early morning passersby took
notice of the black-hulled steamer with the red and white ensign at her

The CSS *Shenandoah* anchored in the Mersey River, November 6, 1865.

The Illustrated London News

stern. *The fog shut out the town from our view,* Hunt wrote, *and we were not sorry for it, for we did not care about a gaping crowd on shore witnessing the humiliation that was soon to befall our ship.*[48]

A fleet of British warships were in the harbor, and Waddell instructed the pilot to position the *Shenandoah* alongside the H.B.M. ship of the line *Donegal*, commanded by Captain Paynter, R. N. At 8:00 a.m., the anchors were let go. Steam hissed from the escape valves, as seamen hurried to draw the lines taut. A few minutes later a British officer from the *Donegal* came on board and was escorted to Waddell's cabin. There he officially informed the *Shenandoah's* commander what he already knew—the American war was over. The Confederacy was no more.

Waddell dispatched a lengthy letter to Lord Russell, explaining the reasons for not learning of the war's end, and offering to surrender the vessel to the British government. At 10:00 a.m., the officers and crew were called aft where Waddell appeared in full dress uniform. He spoke for only a few minutes, thanking the men for their faithful service, assuring them that they had nothing to be ashamed of, and pledging that he would exert every effort on their behalf.

Both officers and men stood at silent attention as Waddell spoke. Many were struggling to control their emotions. Relief at reaching port was mixed with the uncertainties of what lay ahead. For the officers, most of whom were Southerners, it was terribly agonizing. Lieutenant Whittle stood to one side of the assembled men, his arms folded across his chest, and tears streaming down his weathered cheeks. It was a painful moment.

When Waddell had finished, he signaled the quartermaster. The old seaman stepped forward, and in dead silence, slowly lowered the last flag of the Confederacy. Reverently he folded the ensign, and at the pace of a funeral march, carried it and presented it to Waddell. The cruise of the CSS *Shenandoah* was over.[49]

Left to right: Sidney Smith Lee, John T. Mason, Orris A. Browne, and William C. Whittle. The four *Shenandoah* officers posed for the photographer after their return from the Arctic Ocean.

A photograph taken late in 1865 at Lemington Spa, England, after the return of the *Shenandoah*. Standing to the far left is Irvine S. Bulloch, and seated on the table is the cruiser's former surgeon, Charles E. Lining. The others are former Assistant Surgeon Edwin G. Boothe (seated), Passed Assistant Surgeon Bennett W. Green (left), and Lieutenant William H. Murdaugh.

Epilogue

The lowering of the *Shenandoah's* flag on that cold foggy November morning constituted the final act in the life of the Confederate Navy, and indeed, of the Confederacy itself. The more than four years of struggle was over. For the Southern officers who stood on the cruiser's deck listening to Waddell's final words, most had been there from the beginning. Whittle had served on the *Nashville* when she became the first warship to carry the flag of a new nation to the shores of Europe. Grimball and Dabney Scales had served the smoking guns of the *Arkansas* when she fought her way through two Federal fleets to the sanctuary of Vicksburg. Irvine Bulloch sailed aboard the *Alabama* and had gone down with that vessel when she was sunk by the guns of the USS *Kearsarge* off Cherbourg. Chew and Smith Lee had served together on the *Louisiana* at New Orleans, the same station where Waddell was charged with the duty of destroying the mighty but unfinished *Mississippi*.

Indeed, as the crimson and white banner was carefully furled, an uncertain future awaited the officers of the *Shenandoah*. But of immediate concern was the impending fate of the 109 enlisted men. For two days the British authorities debated the thorny issue of what to do with the crew. Finally, the officers of the court ruled that as a cruiser of a belligerent power, the *Shenandoah* had every legal right to conduct the

246

raid on the Arctic whaling fleet. The Confederate vessel was to be turned over to American authorities, and all crew members who were not British subjects would be free to go. Any English citizen discovered among the crew would be prosecuted for violating the Foreign Enlistment Act. If the American minister still insisted that acts of piracy had been committed, he would have to prosecute those responsible for such acts in the British courts.

Captain Paynter of the Royal Navy had taken charge of the *Shenandoah* and ordered that no one was to leave the ship. When the law offices reached their decision, Paynter informed Waddell that any British subjects found on board would be detained. On November 10, the entire ship's company was assembled, and the men fell into formation with knowing smiles. Paynter asked Waddell to point out the British subjects. Waddell responded that he had paid no attention to nationality, and assumed that, except for the Hawaiians and the Swedes, that they were all American. Whittle stepped forward and began calling the roll. As each man answered to his name, a British officer asked his nationality. With thick Irish and Cockney dialects, every man responded that he was from Virginia, or Georgia, or Alabama, or some other Southern state. When the roll call was finished, Paynter shrugged his shoulders and released them all.

Writing thirty years after that sad arrival in Liverpool, Whittle seemed to speak for all who had worn the Confederate uniform: *These men were not politicians, but when the war clouds gathered felt bound by every sense of duty, love, and devotion,...when their mother states withdrew, to rally to their standard.... No more loyal men lived on earth. Let no slanderous tongue or libelous pen impugn their motives. Let not their reputation for purity of purpose, as they saw their duty, be handed down to posterity with any stain, but let their children have perpetuated in their minds and hearts the fact that their fathers were neither knaves, fools, cowards, nor traitors.*[1]

The Confederate Navy, and the country it represented, had ceased to exist, however, these men left a legacy of which all Americans, North and South, can be proud. Born of necessity during the most chaotic period in American history, Confederate forces afloat achieved near miracles during the South's desperate struggle for independence. When the record is studied in depth, one comes away simply awed by their examples of courage against enormous odds, determination to accomplish their missions, and their tremendous devotion to a sense of duty. Contrary to what some historians have attempted to portray, the Confederate Navy constitutes one of the greatest success stories in the South's bitter fight for survival. That the enemy was held at bay for as long as they were, can in a large part be attributable to the gallant men who wore the navy gray.

Appendix A

CHAPTER 1
PRIVATEERS COMMISSIONED BY THE CONFEDERATE STATES

Name	Type	Armament	Tonnage	Men	Commander	Comments
C. *Gunnison*	Screw Tug	2, 6-pounders	52	15	Peter G. Cook	Acquired in 1852 by CSN and converted to a torpedo boat at Mobile, Alabama.
Brauregard	Schooner	1, 24-pounder	101	40	Gilbert Hay	Captured in the Bahama Channel by the USS *William G. Anderson*, 12 Nov. 1861.
Bonita	Screw	8 guns	1,110	150		Very fast. Entered service as blockade runner.
Boston	Screw Tug	5 guns		56		U.S. Navy towboat captured in Passà l'Outre, Louisiana, by Acting Master James Duke, CSN. Reported fitting out at Mobile, 22 Aug. 1863.

Name	Type	Armament	Tonnage	Men	Commander	Comments
Charlotte Clark	Steamer	3 guns	1,100	125	J. H. Edmonston	Commission granted 6 Aug. 1863. Never sailed as a privateer.
Chesapeake	Schooner	4 guns	60	50	Thomas Smith	Commission granted 27 Mar. 1863. Schooner was at Baltimore, but no record of her service as a privateer survives.
Dixie	Schooner	3 guns	110	30	Thomas J. Moore	Sailed from Charleston 19 July 1861. Captured 3 prizes, one of which was recaptured by the U.S. Navy. Returned to Charleston, 27 Aug. 1861.
Dove	Steamer	8 guns	1,170	150	Amos P. Chamberlain	No record of service as a privateer.
S. Bartow	Schooner	1, 24-pounder 1, 6-pounder	74	30	Joseph L. Dunham	Engaged the USS *R. R. Cuyler* in Crooked River, Apalachicola, Florida, 11 Sep. 1861. No record of service as a privateer.
Gallatin	Schooner	2, 12-pounders	150	40	William Hone	Application applied for 18 Apr. 1861. No record of service found.
General Reneau	Steamer	5 guns	600	150	James Barbiere	Captured in the Gulf of Mexico, 3 Dec. 1861 before she could be fitted out. Letters of marque were thrown overboard.
Gibraltar	Schooner	2 guns	60	30	W. G. Ford	Fitted out at Mobile and commissioned 5 Feb. 1864. No record of service.

Name	Type	Armament	Tonnage	Men	Commander	Comments
Gordon	Side-wheel Steamer	3 guns	519	50	Thomas J. Lockwood	Very fast. Captured at least 4 prizes. Later became blockade runner *Theodora*. Carried Mason and and Slidell out of Charleston to West Indies.
Governor A. Mouton	Steamer	1, 9-pounder 1, 6-pounder	125	25	Samuel F. Parker	Captured by the USS *Hatteras* in Berwick Bay, Louisiana, 11 May 1862.
Hallie Jackson	Brig	Not mounted		30	John Byers	Captured by the USS *Union* while running from Montanzas, Cuba, to Savannah, Georgia, 10 June 1861.
Isabella	Screw Steamer	8 guns	801	225	James I. Bard	No record of service found.
J. C. Calhoun	Side-wheel Steamer	1, 18-pounder 2, 12-pounders 2, 6-pounders	508	85	John Wilson	Captured six prizes. Transferred to CSN, and served as Commander Hollins' flagship at the engagement at the Head of the Passes below New Orleans, 12 Oct. 1861. Captured 23 Jan. 1862. Later served as USS *Calhoun*.
J. M. Chapman	Schooner	2, 12-pounders	90	15	William C. Law	Fitted out at San Francisco, California. Taken captive by USS *Cyane* as she was preparing to sail, 15 Mar. 1863.

Name	Type	Armament	Tonnage	Men	Commander	Comments
J. O. Nixon	Schooner	1, 18-pounder 2, 6-pounders	95	40	John Wilson	Sailed from New Orleans on 2 Aug. 1861. Sighted USS *Huntsville* and returned across the bar. Traded shots with the Federal warship for about twenty minutes.
Jefferson Davis	Brig	2, 32-pounders 2, 24-pounders 1, 18-pounder	230	75	Louis M. Coxetter	Sailed from Charleston 28 June 1861. The most successful privateer. Captured 8 prizes before being shipwrecked while trying to enter St. Augustine, Florida, 16 Aug. 1861.
Joseph Landis	Side-wheel Steamer	2 guns	400	100	M. Davis	Very fast. Acquired by CSN in 1862 & used as a tender to CSS *Louisiana*. Surrendered to Federal forces 28 Apr. 1862. Utilized by Union Navy as tugboat for the rest of the war.
Josephine	Schooner	15 shotguns, 15 pistols	75	42	O. Tennyson Weems	Commission returned because of a dispute between Weems and the owners.
Lamar	Schooner	1, 12-pounder pivot	35		E. J. Black	No record of service.
Lorton	Schooner	1 pivot gun	95	25	W. T. Kendall	Fitted out at Baltimore. Commission granted 11 June 1861. No record of service.

Name	Type	Armament	Tonnage	Men	Commander	Comments
Manassas	Steamer Ram	1, 64-pounder Dahlgren	387	36	John A. Stevenson	Seized in September of 1861 by the Confederate Navy. Lost at the Battle of New Orleans, 24 Apr. 1862.
Mariner	Steamer	1, 6-pounder 2, 12-pounders	134	30	B. W. Berry	Fitted out at Wilmington, N.C. Captured one prize, schooner *Nathaniel Chase*, 25 July 1861.
Matilda	Bark	6 guns	400	150	Flavel Belcher	Letter of marque granted 8 June 1861. No record of service.
Mocking Bird	Steamer	8 guns	1,290	150	Samuel Smith	No record of service. Probably became a blockade runner.
Monticello	Ironclad Steamer			460	John Brass	This vessel may not have existed.
Music	Side-wheel Steamer	2, 6-pounders	273	50	Thomas McLellan	Commissioned 15 May 1861 at New Orleans where she took several prizes. Transferred to CSN, and became a tender for Forts Jackson and St. Philip. Later served in Atchafalaya and Red River area.
Onward	Schooner	1, 32-pounder	70	30	J. D. Atkins	Named changed to *Emma*. Loading cotton in Ocklockonee River, Florida, when attacked and burned by small boat crew from USS *Amanda*, 20 Mar. 1863.

Name	Type	Armament	Tonnage	Men	Commander	Comments
Paul Jones	Schooner	2 guns	160	30–40	John T. Gordon	Vessel was in the Bahamas. Commission applied for 26 Jan. 1864. No record of service.
Pelican	Steamer	10 guns	1,479	150	Amos P. Chamberlain	No record of service. Probably became a blockade runner.
Petrel	Schooner	2 guns	82	35	William Perry	Commissioned 10 July 1861 at Charleston. On first trip out was overtaken and sunk by the USS *St. Lawrence*, 28 July 1861. Four crewmen drowned.
Phenix	Steamer	6, rifles 1, 32-pounder pivot	1,643	243	Eugene Delany	Largest privateer commissioned. Fitted out at Wilmington, Delaware, and ready to sail in May of 1861. Nothing more is known.
Pioneer	Submarine	Clockwork Torpedo	4	3	John K. Scott	Commissioned issued 31 Mar. 1862 at New Orleans. Sunk to prevent seizure when city was captured by Union forces.
Pioneer II	Submarine	Clockwork Torpedo		5	(Unknown)	Built at Mobile, Alabama. Towed off Fort Morgan preparatory to attacking Federal fleet, but foul weather and rough seas swamped her.

Name	Type	Armament	Tonnage	Men	Commander	Comments
Rattlesnake	Side-wheel Steamer	6 guns	1,221	130	T. Harrison Baker	Commissioned 5 Nov. 1862. Formally CSS *Nashville*/*Thomas L. Wragg*. Destroyed by Federal forces, 28 Feb. 1863, Ogeechee River, Georgia.
Rescue	Schooner		120	30	W. G. Hartsfield	Commissioned 11 Mar. 1864 at Mobile, Alabama. No record of service.
St. Mary's	Schooner	Unarmed	115		John C. Braine	Captured in the Chesapeake Bay by Braine who was a master in the Confederate Navy. After taking one or two prizes, schooner was abandoned at Kingston, Jamaica, in June of 1865.
Sallie	Schooner	1 gun	170	46	Henry S. Lebby	Commissioned at Charleston, 28 Sep. 1861. Over a three-week period, captured four prizes. Sunk one and remaining three sold at auction.
Santiago	Schooner					Believed to have been fitted out at Brownsville, Texas, in 1863.

Name	Type	Armament	Tonnage	Men	Commander	Comments
Savannah	Schooner	1 pivot gun	53	30	T. Harrison Baker	Commissioned on 13 May 1861. Captured one prize before being overtaken and captured by USS *Perry*. Crew tried and condemned on charges of piracy, but later released.
Sealine	Brig	1 pivot gun	179	35	W. T. Kendall	Fitted out at Baltimore, Maryland. Letter granted 11 June 1861. No record of service.
Stephen R. Mallory	Schooner	1, 20-pounder 2, 6-pounders	74	20	J. Samuel Jones	Letter of marque applied for from the Bahamas, 1864. No record of service.
Stonewall Jackson	Schooner	3 guns	150	60	M. W. de Bolle	Commission applied for 12 Feb. 1864. No record of service.
Texas	Side-wheel Steamer	8 guns	800	125	Charles de Montel	May have operated out of Corpus Christi, Texas during 1863.
Triton	Schooner	1, 6-pounder	30	20	Thomas A. Hillier	Commission granted 10 May 1861. No record of service.
V. H. Ivy	Side-wheel Steamer	1, 15-pounder (as privateer)	454	60	Napoleon B. Baker	Commissioned 16 May 1861. Later purchased by C.S. Navy and became CSS *Ivy* under Lieutenant Joseph Fry. Fought at Head of the Passes, 12 Oct. 1861. Destroyed to prevent capture, Yazoo River, May 1863.

Name	Type	Armament	Tonnage	Men	Commander	Comments
William H. Webb	Side-wheel Steamer	4, 12-pounders	655	100	Joseph Leach	Commissioned 18 May 1861. Later became CSS *Webb*, and figured prominently in the sinking of the USS *Indianola*. Later was run down Mississippi by Charles W. Read and destroyed below New Orleans, 24 Apr. 1865.
York	Schooner	1, 8-pounder	68	30	John Geoffrey	Captured at least one prize, but was run ashore at Cape Hatteras and burned by USS *Union*, 24 July 1861.

Appendix B

CHAPTER 2
OFFICERS ASSIGNED TO THE CSS *NASHVILLE*, 1861–1862

Name	Rank	From
Pegram, Robert B.	Lieutenant, (Commanding)	Virginia
Fauntleroy, Charles M.	Lieutenant, (Exec. Officer)	Virginia
Bennett, John W.	Lieutenant	Maryland
Whittle, William C.	Lieutenant	Virginia
Ingraham, John H.	Master	South Carolina
Taylor, Richard	Assistant Paymaster	Virginia
Auchrim, John L.	Assistant Surgeon	South Carolina
Dalton, William R.	Midshipman	Alabama
Thomas, Francis M.	Midshipman	South Carolina
McClintoc, Haratio G.	Midshipman	Alabama
Pegram, James W.	Midshipman	Virginia
Cary, Clarence	Midshipman	Virginia
Hamilton, William P.	Midshipman	South Carolina
Sinclair, William B.	Midshipman	Virginia
Bulloch, Irving S.	Midshipman	Georgia

Name	Rank	From
Hassell, James F. E.	Captain's Clerk	South Carolina
Sawyer, Francis	Boatswain	
Evans, James	Pilot	South Carolina
Jones, Thomas	Pilot	South Carolina
Macon, John	Pilot	Georgia
Hood, James	Chief Engineer	Canada
Smith, William	Assistant Engineer	South Carolina
Murray, John C.	Assistant Engineer	South Carolina
Spidell, John	Assistant Engineer	Alabama

Appendix C

CHAPTER 3

CONFEDERATE VESSELS THAT SERVED WITH THE "MOSQUITO FLEET"

Name	Type	Armament	Tonnage	Commander	Disposition
Seabird	Side-wheel Steamer	1, 32-pounder SB 1, 30-pounder rifle	202	Patrick McCarrick	Sunk in action at Elizabeth City, 10 Feb. 1862.
Ellis	Side-wheel Steamer	1, 32-pounder rifle	100	James W. Cooke	Captured at Elizabeth City, 10 Feb. 1862. Taken into Federal Navy as USS *Ellis*. Ran aground in New River Inlet during attack on Jacksonville, N.C. and destroyed to prevent recapture, 25 Nov. 1862.
Beaufort	Screw Steamer	1, 32-pounder rifle	85	William H. Parker	Escaped up Dismal Swamp Canal, 10 Feb. 1862. Fought at Battle of Hampton Roads, 8–9 Mar. 1862. Action at Trent's Reach, 21 June 1864. Captured 3 Apr. 1865, upon the fall of Richmond.

Name	Type	Armament	Tonnage	Commander	Disposition
Curlew	Side-wheel Steamer	1, 32-pounder rifle 1, 12 pounder howitzer	260	Thomas T. Hunter	Sunk at the Battle of Roanoke Island, 8 Feb. 1862.
Raleigh	Screw Steamer	1, 32-pounder	65	Joseph W. Alexander	Escaped to Norfolk. Participated in Battle of Hampton Roads, 8–9 Mar. 1862. Renamed *Roanoke*, destroyed when Richmond was evacuated, 4 Apr. 1865.
Fanny	Screw Steamer	1, 32-pounder 1, 8-pounder rifle		James L. Tayloe	Captured from the Federals on 1 Oct. 1861. Run aground and blown up, Elizabeth City, 10 Feb. 1862.
Forrest	Screw Steamer	1, 32-pounder		James L. Hoole	Disabled at Battle of Roanoke Island, 7 Feb. 1862. Burned to prevent capture, Elizabeth City, 10 Feb. 1862.
Junaluska	Screw Steamer	2, 6-pounders	79	William H. Vernon	Assisted in capture of USS *Fanny*, 1 Oct. 1861. Dismantled and sold, Aug. 1862.
Appomattox	Side-wheel Steamer	1, 32-pounder 1 small gun	120	Charles C. Simms	Escaped to the entrance of the Dismal Swamp Canal, but was two inches too wide. Burned by her crew to prevent capture.

Name	Type	Armament	Tonnage	Commander	Disposition
Cotton Plant	Side-wheel Steamer	Probably Unarmed	85		Hauled supplies for Mosquito Fleet. Later became tender to CSS *Albemarle*. Surrendered to Federals near Halifax, N.C., May 1865.
Black Warrior	Schooner	2, 32-pounders		Frank M. Harris	Burned to prevent capture, Elizabeth City, 10 Feb. 1862.

Appendix D

CHAPTER 4
OFFICERS ASSIGNED TO THE CSS *LOUISIANA*, APRIL 24, 1862

Name	Rank	From
Arnold, Thomas	Lieutenant	Arkansas
Baker, James McC.	Acting Master	Florida
Beck, Charles	Acting Master's Mate	Louisiana
Bowen, Robert J.	Lieutenant	Mississippi
Bremond, Dennis	Acting Master	
Brooks, Leslie B.	Assistant Paymaster	Alabama
Cherry, Virginius	Carpenter	
Chew, Francis T.	Midshipman	Tennessee
Clarke, William B.	Captain's Clerk	
Emory, Thomas	Assistant Surgeon	Maryland
Ford, Marcellus	Assistant Surgeon	Virginia
Grafton, Joseph D.	Assistant Surgeon	Missouri
Harris, Frank M.	Acting Master	
Hart, Theodore A.	Third Assistant Engineer	Missouri
Jones, Samuel	Boatswain	
Lee, Sidney Smith, Jr.	Acting Master	Virginia

Name	Rank	From
McDermett, Edward J.	Midshipman	Arkansas
McIntosh, Charles F.	Commander (Commanding)	Virginia
Pawson, Milton T.	Second Assistant Engineer	
Pierce, Joseph	Naval Constructor	
Riley, James H.	Third Assistant Engineer	
Shryock, George S.	First Lieutenant	Kentucky
Tombs, James H.	Third Assistant Engineer	Florida
Walker, Robert P.	Captain's Clerk	Virginia
Ward, William H.	Lieutenant	Virginia
Waterman, George S.	Master's Mate	Louisiana
Waters, James	Third Assistant Engineer	
Whittle, William C., Jr.	Lieutenant	Virginia
Wilcox, A. H.	Second Assistant Engineer	
Wilkinson, John	First Lieutenant (Exec. Officer)	Virginia
Wilkinson, William W.	Midshipman	South Carolina
Williams, George W.	Second Assistant Engineer	
Wilson, James	Acting Gunner	New York
Youngblood, Wilson	Second Assistant Engineer	

Appendix E

CHAPTER 4
OFFICERS ASSIGNED TO THE CSS *MISSISSIPPI*
APRIL 24, 1862

Name	Rank	From
Ratcliffe, James B.	Midshipman	Virginia
Sinclair, Arthur	Commander (Commanding)	Virginia
Sinclair, Arthur, Jr.	Captain's Clerk	Virginia
Tift, Nelson	Assistant Paymaster	Georgia
Waddell, James I.	Lieutenant	North Carolina
Williamson, Charles H.	Surgeon	Virginia

Appendix F

CONFEDERATE NAVAL FORCES
Galveston, Texas - January 1, 1863
Major Leon Smith, Commanding

CSS *BAYOU CITY*
Captain Henry S. Lubbock,
  (Master, CSN) Commanding
Captain Michael McCormick, Pilot
Captain Weir, Gunner
Colonel Thomas Green, 5th Texas
Captain Martin
Captain Sherman
Doctor Holland
Chief Engineer L. C. Hersberger
Captain Seymour, Engineer

CSS *JOHN F. CARR*
(Officers Unknown)

CSS *NEPTUNE*
Captain William H. Sangster,
  Commanding
Colonel Arthur P. Bagby, 7th Texas
Lieutenant L. C. Harby
Chief Engineer David Connor
Captain Swift, Pilot
Captain McGovern, Pilot
Captain William A. Bowen, Pilot
Nelson Henry, Engineer

CSS *LUCY GWIN*
(Officers Unknown)

Appendix F

CONFEDERATE LAND FORCES
Galveston, Texas - January 1, 1863
Major General John B. Magruder, Commanding

20th Texas Infantry
Griffin's Texas Infantry Battalion
26th Texas Cavalry
2nd Texas Cavalry
1st Texas Heavy Artillery

- Brigadier General W. R. Scurry, commanded the 2nd Texas Cavalry, remainder of Sibley's Brigade, and the 20th Texas Infantry.
- Colonel Xavier B. Debray, commanded the 26th Texas Cavalry.
- Colonel Charles L. Pyron, commanded the 2nd Texas Cavalry.
- Colonel Joseph J. Cook, led the storming party of 500 men. These consisted of elements of the 2nd Texas Cavalry, 20th Texas Infantry, and Griffin's Infantry Battalion.
- Captain S. T. Fontaine, of the 1st Texas Heavy Artillery, was in charge of the attack at Fort Point with six companies of dragoons from the 2nd Texas Cavalry in support.
- Lieutenant Colonel Leonard A. Abererombie, was immediate commander of the 20th Texas Infantry.
- Lieutenant Colonel John H. Manly, of the 1st Texas Heavy Artillery, commanded at Virginia Point.
- Captain George R. Wilson commanded the six siege pieces.

CHAPTER 6
OFFICERS ASSIGNED TO THE CSS *TALLAHASSEE*
AUGUST 6, 1864

Name	Rank	From
Wood, John Taylor	Commander (Commanding)	Louisiana
Ward, William H.	First Lieutenant (Exec. Officer)	Virginia
Benton, Mortimer M.	First Lieutenant	Kentucky
Gardner, Joseph M.	First Lieutenant	Virginia
Craig, William J.	Passed Midshipman	Kentucky
Curtis, John A.	Acting Master	Virginia
Tynan, John W.	Acting Chief Engineer	Virginia
Levy, Charles H.	Chief Engineer	Virginia
Hall, Elias G.	First Assistant Engineer	
Greene, James F.	Second Assistant Engineer	North Carolina
Lyell, John J.	Second Assistant Engineer	Virginia
Roberts, Henry H.	Third Assistant Engineer	North Carolina
Ross, R. M.	Second Assistant Engineer	
Jones, C. Lucian	Assistant Paymaster	Georgia
Shepperdson, William	Assistant Surgeon	Alabama

Name	Rank	From
Cassidy, John	Boatswain	
Stewart, David	Gunner	
Russell, Charles	Acting Master's Mate	
Crenshaw, Edward	Second Lieutenant, CSMC	Alabama
*Doak, Henry M.	Second Lieutenant, CSMC	Tennessee
Aldert, Benjamin S.	Pilot	
Aldert, Joseph E.	Pilot	
Burriss, E. T.	Pilot	

* Second Cruise

*A*ppendix *H*

CHAPTER 7
OFFICERS ASSIGNED TO THE CSS *CHICKAMAUGA*
OCTOBER 28, 1864

Name	Rank	From
Wilkinson, John	First Lieutenant, (Commanding)	Virginia
Dozier, William G.	First Lieutenant, (Exec. Officer)	South Carolina
Roby, Francis M.	First Lieutenant	Alabama
Stanton, Clarence L.	First Lieutenant	Kentucky
Sevier, Charles P.	Passed Midshipman	Tennessee
Cary, Clarence	Passed Midshipman	Virginia
Lee, Daniel M.	Passed Midshipman	Virginia
Berrien, Thomas M.	Passed Midshipman	Georgia
Gibson, Beverly T.	Acting Midshipman	Kentucky
Ingraham, J. J.	Boatswain	Virginia
Durand, Julius	Gunner	
Wallace, ———	Pilot	
Garrison, Thomas	Pilot/Gunner's Mate	North Carolina
Schroeder, Charles	Chief Engineer	Virginia
Tennent, George W.	First Assistant Engineer	Georgia

Name	Rank	From
Tucker, John T.	First Assistant Engineer	Virginia
Peck, Charles S.	Third Assistant Engineer	Virginia
Tomlinson, J. W.	Third Assistant Engineer	Virginia
Barry, Thomas P.	Assistant Paymaster	Alabama
Bradford, David	First Lieutenant, CSMC	Louisiana
Smith, William H.	Pilot	South Carolina
Jenkins, ——	Captain's Clerk	
Bain, A. W.	Paymaster's Clerk	
Paschall, J. A.	Acting Master's Mate	

*A*ppendix *I*

CHAPTER 9
OFFICERS ASSIGNED TO THE CSS *SHENANDOAH*
OCTOBER 20, 1864–NOVEMBER 6, 1865

Name	Rank	From
Waddell, James I.	First Lieutenant (Commanding)	North Carolina
Whittle, William C.	First Lieutenant (Exec. Officer)	Virginia
Grimball, John	First Lieutenant	South Carolina
Lee, Sidney Smith, Jr.	First Lieutenant	Virginia
Chew, Francis T.	First Lieutenant	Missouri
Scales, Dabney M.	Second Lieutenant	Virginia
Bulloch, Irvine S.	Acting Master	Georgia
Lining, Charles E.	Passed Assistant Surgeon	South Carolina
Smith, William B.	Acting Assistant Paymaster	Louisiana
O'Brian, Matthew	Acting Chief Engineer	Louisiana
McNulty, Fred J.	Acting Assistant Surgeon	Maryland
Browne, Orris A.	Passed Midshipman	Virginia
Mason, John T.	Passed Midshipman	Virginia
Codd, William H.	First Assistant Engineer	Maryland
Hutchinson, John	Second Assistant Engineer	Scotland

Name	Rank	From
Mugguffeney, Ernest	Acting Third Assistant Engineer	Ireland
Minor, Joshua F.	Master's Mate	Virginia
Hunt, Cornelius E.	Acting Master's Mate	Virginia
Colton, Lodge	Acting Master's Mate	Maryland
Harwood, George	Acting Boatswain	England
Guy, John L.	Acting Gunner	England
Alcott, Henry	Acting Sailmaker	England
O'Shea, John	Acting Carpenter	Ireland
Lynch, John C.	Carpenter	New York
Manning, Thomas S.	Acting Master's Mate	Maryland
Blacker, James C.	Captain's Clerk	

CHAPTER 1

THE PRIVATEERS STRIKE THE FIRST BLOW

1. ———, *Official Records of the Union and Confederate Navies in the War of the Rebellion* (Washington: Government Printing Office, 1894–1927), ser. 1, vol. 5, p. 796.
2. J. Thomas Scharf, *History of the Confederate States Navy* (New York: Crown Publishers, Inc., 1877), p. 54.
3. Ibid., p. 91.
4. *Official Records Navy*, ser. 2, vol. 1, p. 336.
5. William Morrison Robinson, Jr., *The Confederate Privateers* (Columbia: Yale University Press, 1928), pp. 37–38.
6. Ibid., p. 37.
7. Robinson, p. 38.
8. Ibid., p. 40.
9. Ibid.
10. Ibid., p. 106.
11. *Official Records Navy*, ser. 1, vol. 1, p. 50.
12. Ibid.
13. Robinson, p. 110.
14. Ibid., pp. 112–113.
15. Ibid., pp. 59–60.
16. Stephen R. Wise, *Lifeline of the Confederacy* (Columbia: The University of South Carolina Press, 1988), p. 115.
17. Robinson, p. 67.
18. Ibid., pp. 67–68.
19. Ibid., pp. 68–69.
20. Ibid., pp. 82–84.

21. Ibid., pp. 148–151.
22. Scharf, pp. 79–80.
23. Robinson, pp. 70–71.
24. *Official Records Navy*, ser. 1, vol. 6, pp. 56–59.
25. Robinson, pp. 74–75.
26. Ibid., p. 76.
27. Scharf, p. 82.

CHAPTER 2

THE STARS AND BARS IN THE ENGLISH CHANNEL

1. Chester G. Hearn, *Gray Raiders of the Sea* (Camden: International Marine Publishing, 1992), p. 45.
2. ———, *Official Records of the Union and Confederate Navies in the War of the Rebellion* (Washington: Government Printing Office, 1894–1927), ser. 2, vol. 1, pp. 334–335.
3. Hearn, p. 43.
4. Ibid.
5. Thomas T. Moebs, *Confederate States Navy Research Guide* (Williamsburg: Moebs Publishing Company 1991), p. 248.
6. Hearn, p. 44.
7. *Official Records Navy*, ser. 1, vol. 1, p. 745.
8. Ibid., pp. 745–746.
9. Hearn, pp. 44–45.
10. *Official Records Navy*, ser. 1, vol. 1, p. 746.
11. Ibid.
12. Richard N. Current, *Encyclopedia of the Confederacy* (New York: Simon & Schuster, 1993), vol. 4, pp. 1619–1621.
13. *Official Records Navy*, ser. 1, vol. 1, p. 746.
14. Ibid.
15. Ibid., ser. 2, vol. 2, p. 118.
16. Ibid., ser. 1, vol. 1, p. 277.
17. William R. Dalton, "The Cruise of the Nashville," *Confederate Veteran*, June 1918, p. 249.
18. William F. Spencer, *The Confederate Navy in Europe* (Birmingham: The University of Alabama Press, 1983), p. 30.
19. *Official Records Navy*, ser. 1, vol. 1, pp. 750–751.
20. Hearn, pp. 48–49.
21. Ibid., p. 50.
22. *Official Records Navy*, ser. 1, vol. 1, p. 747.
23. H. Jerry Morris, "Nashville," *Civil War Times Illustrated*, March 1986, p. 43.
24. *Official Records Navy*, ser. 1, vol. 1, p. 748.
25. William C. Whittle, "Cruise of the C. S. Steamer Nashville," *Southern Historical Society Papers*, vol. 29, p. 209.
26. Philip Van Doren Stern, *The Confederate Navy, a Pictorial History* (New York: Bonanza Books, 1962), p. 70.
27. Whittle, p. 209.
28. Ibid., p. 210.
29. Morris, p. 43.
30. Ibid.
31. Ethel S. Nepveux, *George Alfred Trenholm and the Company That Went to War* (Charleston: Electric City Printing Co., 1994), p. 63.
32. *Official Records Navy*, ser. 1, vol. 13, p. 134.
33. Morris, p. 44.

CHAPTER 3

THE "MOSQUITO FLEET"

1. J. Thomas Scharf, *History of the Confederate States Navy* (New York: Crown Publishers, Inc., 1877), pp. 377–378.
2. Ibid., p. 378.
3. Walter Clark, *North Carolina Regiments* (Goldsboro: Nash Brothers Book and Job Printers, 1901), vol. 5, p. 680.
4. Scharf, p. 377.
5. John G. Berrett, *The Civil War in North Carolina* (Chapel Hill: The University of North Carolina Press, 1963), pp. 48–49.
6. Barrett, pp. 50–51.
7. Scharf, p. 380.
8. Barrett, p. 52.
9. Ibid.
10. Scharf, p. 381.
11. Ibid.
12. Ibid.
13. Barrett, pp. 54–55.
14. Ibid.
15. Ibid., p. 61.
16. ———, *Official Records of the Union and Confederate Navies in the War of the Rebellion* (Washington: Government Printing Office, 1894–1927), ser. 1, vol. 6, p. 729.
17. Ibid., p. 739.
18. Ibid., p. 761.
19. William R. Trotter, *Ironclads and Columbiads* (Winston–Salem: John F. Blair, Publisher, 1989), pp. 70–71.
20. Barrett, pp. 73–74.
21. *Official Records Navy*, ser. 1, vol. 6, p. 765.
22. William H. Parker, *Recollections of a Naval Officer* (New York: Charles Scribner's Sons, 1883), pp. 246–247.
23. Parker, pp. 247–248.
24. Ibid., p. 248.
25. Ibid., pp. 248–249.
26. *Official Records Navy*, ser. 1, vol. 6, p. 599.
27. Parker, pp. 249–250.
28. Ibid., p. 250.
29. *Official Records Navy*, ser. 1, vol. 6, p. 595.
30. Barrett, pp. 80–82.
31. Ibid, p. 85.
32. *Official Records Navy*, ser. 1, vol. 6, p. 595.
33. Ibid., pp. 595–596.
34. Parker, pp. 256–257.
35. Parker, pp. 257–258.

CHAPTER 4

THE BEHEMOTHS OF NEW ORLEANS

1. Maurice Melton, *The Confederate Ironclads* (New York: Thomas Yoseloff, Publisher, 1968), pp. 61–62.
2. ———, *Official Records of the Union and Confederate Navies in the War of the Rebellion* (Washington: Government Printing Office, 1894–1927), ser. 2, vol. 2, p. 571.
3. Melton, pp. 62–63.
4. Charles L. Defour, *The Night the War was Lost* (Lincoln: University of Nebraska Press, 1960), p. 101.
5. *Official Records Navy*, ser. 2, vol. 1, p. 532.

6. Melton, p. 63.
7. William N. Still, "Confederate Behemoth, The CSS *Louisiana,*" *Civil War Times Illustrated,* Nov. 1977, p. 20.
8. Melton, p. 73.
9. *Official Records Navy,* ser. 2, vol. 1, p. 535.
10. Ibid., pp. 760–761.
11. William N. Still, *Iron Afloat* (Columbia: University of South Carolina Press, 1965), pp. 45–46.
12. *Official Records Navy,* ser. 2, vol. 1, pp. 756–757.
13. Melton, p. 78.
14. Still, "Confederate Behemoth," p. 24.
15. Ibid., p. 21.
16. Raimondo Luraghi, *A History of the Confederate Navy* (Annapolis: Naval Institute Press, 1996), p. 128.
17. *Official Records Navy,* ser. 2, vol. 1, pp. 605–606.
18. Luraghi, pp. 130–131.
19. *Official Records Navy,* ser. 2, vol. 1, p. 512.
20. *Official Records Navy,* ser. 1, vol. 18, pp. 836–837.
21. Dufour, p. 244.
22. Still, "Confederate Behemoth," p. 22.
23. John Wilkinson, *The Narrative of a Blockade Runner* (New York: Sheldon and Company, 1877), pp. 32–33.
24. Luraghi, p. 157.
25. Ibid., p. 159.
26. William B. Robertson, "The Water Battery at Fort Jackson," *Battles and Leaders of the Civil War,* vol. 1 (New York: The Century Company, 1884–1888), p. 100.
27. *Official Records Navy,* ser. 1, vol. 18, pp. 294–296.
28. Scharf, p. 297.
29. Luraghi, p. 162.
30. *Official Records Navy,* ser. 1, vol. 18, p. 351.
31. Ibid., pp. 351–352.
32. *Official Records Navy,* ser. 1, vol. 18, p. 158.
33. Ibid., p. 298.
34. Ibid.
33. Ibid., pp. 298–299.

CHAPTER 5

VICTORY AT GALVESTON

1. J. Thomas Scharf, *History of the Confederate States Navy* (New York: Crown Publishers, Inc., 1877), p. 497.
2. Ibid., p. 498.
3. O. M. Roberts, *Confederate Military History* (Atlanta: Confederate Publishing Company, 1899), vol. 11, pp. 73–79.
4. ———, *Official Records of the Union and Confederate Navies in the War of the Rebellion* (Washington: Government Printing Office, 1894–1927), ser. 1, vol. 19, p. 262.
5. Ibid., p. 263.
6. Clemant A. Evans, "Texas," *Confederate Military History* (Atlanta: Confederate Publishing Company, 1899), vol. 11, p. ix.
7. *Official Records Navy,* ser. 1, vol. 19, p. 471.
8. Scharf, p. 505.
9. *Official Records Navy,* ser. 1, vol. 19, p. 471.
10. Ibid., p. 472.
11. Ibid., p. 473.
12. Scharf, p. 506.
13. Donald A. Frazier, "Cotton-clads in a Storm of Iron," *Naval History* (Annapolis: United States Naval Institute, May/June, 1994), pp. 28–29.

14. Ibid.
15. *Official Records Navy,* ser. 1, vol. 19, p. 469.
16. Ibid.
17. Frazier, pp. 29–30.
18. Ibid., p. 30.
19. Ibid., p. 31.
20. Scharf, p. 511.
21. *Official Records Navy,* ser. 1, vol. 19, p. 460.
22. Ibid., p. 470.
23. Frazier, p. 31.

CHAPTER 6

HAVOC OFF THE EAST COAST - PART I

1. Chester G. Hearn, *Gray Raiders of the Sea* (Camden: International Marine Publishing, 1992), p. 129.
2. Royce Gordon Shingleton, *John Taylor Wood, Sea Ghost of the Confederacy* (Athens: University of Georgia Press, 1979), p. 120.
3. Stephen R. Wise, *Lifeline of the Confederacy* (Columbia: University of South Carolina Press, 1988), pp. 268–269.
4. Hearn, pp. 129–130.
5. Richard N. Current, *Encyclopedia of the Confederacy* (New York: Simon & Schuster, Inc., 1972), vol. 4, p. 1743.
6. Shingleton, pp. 123–124.
7. Ibid.
8. John Taylor Wood, "The Tallahassee's Dash into New York Waters," *The Century Magazine,* 56, 1898, pp. 409–410.
9. Shingleton, p. 124.
10. Wood, p. 409.
11. Shingleton, p. 125.
12. Wood, p. 410.
13. Shingleton, pp. 126–127.
14. Ibid., pp. 127–128.
15. Ibid., pp. 128–129.
16. Wood, p. 411.
17. Shingleton, p. 130.
18. Wood, p. 413.
19. Ibid.
20. ———, *Official Records of the Union and Confederate Navies in the War of the Rebellion* (Washington: Government Printing Office, 1894–1927), ser. 1, vol. 3, p. 141.
21. Shingleton, pp. 130–131.
22. *Official Records Navy,* ser. 1, vol. 3, p. 705.
23. Hearn, p. 136.
24. Ibid.
25. Wood, p. 415.
26. Hearn, p. 137.
27. Wood, p. 415.
28. Ibid., p. 416.
29. Ibid., p. 137.
30. Hearn, p. 138.
31. Shingleton, p. 138.
32. *Official Records Navy,* ser. 1, vol. 10, pp. 793–794.
33. Ibid., p. 836.
34. Ibid., p. 328.
35. Ibid., pp. 328–329.

36. John Wilkinson, *The Narrative of a Blockade Runner* (New York: Sheldon & Company, 1877), pp. 231–233.
37. Ibid., p. 243.

CHAPTER 7

HAVOC OFF THE EAST COAST - PART II

1. Stephen R. Wise, *Lifeline of the Confederacy* (Columbia: University of South Carolina Press, 1988), pp. 238–248.
2. J. Thomas Scharf, *History of the Confederate States Navy* (New York: Crown Publishers, Inc., 1877), pp. 462–463.
3. John Wilkinson, *Narrative of a Blockade Runner* (New York: Sheldon & Company, 1877), pp. 209–210.
4. ———, *Official Records of the Union and Confederate Navies in the War of the Rebellion* (Washington: Government Printing Office, 1894–1927), ser. 1, vol. 3, pp. 710–714.
5. *Official Records Navy*, ser. 1, vol. 11, p. 375.
6. Rod Gragg, *Confederate Goliath* (New York: Harper Collins Publishers, 1991), pp. 66–98.
7. Ibid., p. 130.
8. *Official Records Navy*, ser. 1, vol. 11, p. 560.
9. Gragg, p. 245.
10. ———, *Civil War Naval Chronology* (Washington: Naval History Division, 1971), p. v–49.

CHAPTER 8

THE LAST BLOCKADE RUNNERS

1. Stephen R. Wise, *Lifeline of the Confederacy* (Columbia: University of South Carolina Press, 1988), pp. 233–275.
2. Thomas E. Taylor, *Running the Blockade* (London: John Murray Publishing, 1896), p. xxvi.
3. Ibid., p. 124.
4. Ibid., p. 148.
5. Wise, p. 250.
6. Taylor, p. 149.
7. Wise, p. 133.
8. Taylor, pp. 149–157.
9. ———, *Civil War Naval Chronology* (Washington: U.S. Government Printing Office, 1971), p. vi–339.
10. Wise, p. 315.
11. ———, *Official Records of the Union and Confederate Navies in the War of the Rebellion* (Washington: Government Printing Office, 1894–1927), ser. 1, vol. 10, p. 410.
12. Ibid., p. 739.
13. *Naval Chronology*, p. iv–278.
14. *Official Records Navy*, ser. 1, vol. 10, pp. 741–742.
15. Ibid., p. 744.
16. Ibid., ser. 1, vol. 11, pp. 769–770.
17. John Newland Maffitt, "Blockade Running," *United Service 7*, July 1882, p. 30.
18. Royce Shingleton, *High Seas Confederate* (Columbia: University of South Carolina Press, 1994), p. 94.
19. John Wilkinson, *The Narrative of a Blockade Runner* (New York: Sheldon & Company, 1877), p. 234.
20. Maffitt, pp. 30–31.
21. Ibid., p. 32.
22. Shingleton, p. 95.
23. Maffitt, p. 33.
24. Shingleton, p. 96.
25. Ibid.

26. *Official Records Navy,* ser. 1, vol. 27, p. 195.
27. J. Thomas Scharf, *History of the Confederate States Navy* (New York: Crown Publishers, Inc., 1877), p. 490.
28. Shingleton, p. 97.
29. ———, *Civil War Naval Chronology* (Washington: Naval History Division, 1971), p. v–118.

CHAPTER 9

THE RENDEZVOUS

1. James D. Bulloch, *Secret Service of the Confederate States in Europe* (New York: Lanox Hill Pub. & Dist. Co., 1883), vol. 2, p. 112.
2. Ibid., p. 125.
3. Chester G. Hearn, *Gray Raiders of the Sea* (Camden: International Marine Publishing, 1992), pp. 251–251.
4. Bulloch, vol. 2, pp. 126–127.
5. J. Thomas Scharf, *History of the Confederate States Navy* (New York: Crown Publishers, Inc., 1877), p. 810.
6. James D. Horan, *CSS Shenandoah, The Memoirs of Lieutenant Commanding James I. Waddell* (New York: Crown Publishers, Inc., 1960), pp. 75–76.
7. William C. Whittle, "The Cruise of the Shenandoah," *Southern Historical Society Papers,* 1907, vol. 35, pp. 235–236.
8. Ibid., p. 236.
9. Hearn, p. 253.
10. Bulloch, vol. 2, pp. 131–132.
11. Ibid., p. 134.
12. Stanley F. Horn, *Gallant Rebel, The Fabulous Cruise of the CSS Shenandoah* (New Brunswick: Rutgers University Press, 1947), p. 31.
13. Whittle, p. 242.
14. Murray Morgan, *Dixie Raider* (New York: E. F. Dutton & Co., Inc., 1948), pp. 33–34.
15. Horan, pp. 92–93.
16. Murray, pp. 35–36.
17. Hearn, p. 259.
18. Whittle, p. 244.
19. Ibid.
20. Horn, p. 50.
21. Murray, p. 42.

CHAPTER 10

AN ARDUOUS BEGINNING

1. James D. Horan, *CSS Shenandoah, The Memoirs of Lieutenant Commanding James I. Waddell* (New York: Crown Publishers, Inc., 1960), p. 95.
2. William C. Whittle, "The Cruise of the Shenandoah," *Southern Historical Society Papers,* 1907, vol. 35, p. 245.
3. Horan, pp. 95–96.
4. Chester G. Hearn, *Gray Raiders of the Sea* (Camden: International Marine Publishing, 1992), p. 262.
5. Horan, p. 96.
6. Murray Morgan, *Dixie Raider* (New York: E. F. Dutton & Co., Inc., 1948), pp. 44–45.
7. Horan, pp. 103–104.
8. Morgan, pp. 46–48.
9. Ibid., p. 52.
10. Horan, p. 105.
11. Hearn, p. 264.
12. Cornelius E. Hunt, *The Shenandoah, the Last Confederate Cruiser* (New York: C. W. Carleton & Co., 1868), pp. 38–39.

13. Morgan, p. 64.
14. Horan, p. 110.
15. Morgan, pp. 67–68.
16. Ibid., pp. 68–69.
17. Hearn, p. 267.
18. Whittle, pp. 246–247.
19. Ibid., pp. 258–269.
20. Morgan, p. 82.
21. Horan, p. 113.
22. Hearn, p. 271.
23. Morgan, pp. 78–79.
24. Hearn, pp. 270–271.
25. Morgan, p. 100.
26. Ibid., p. 104.
27. Ibid., pp. 106–107.
28. Hearn, p. 272.
29. Horan, p. 120.
30. Morgan, p. 117.
31. Ibid., pp. 121–123.

CHAPTER 11

AUSTRALIAN INTERLUDE

1. Chester G. Hearn, *Gray Raiders of the Sea* (Camden: International Marine Publishing, 1992), p. 274.
2. Murray Morgan, *Dixie Raider* (New York: E. F. Dutton & Co., Inc., 1948), pp. 124–125.
3. ———, *Official Records of the Union and Confederate Navies in the War of the Rebellion* (Washington: Government Printing Office, 1894–1927), ser. 1, vol. 3, p. 760.
4. Morgan, p. 128.
5. Ibid., p. 130.
6. Hearn, pp. 274–275.
7. Ibid., p. 276.
8. Morgan, p. 137.
9. Ibid., p. 138.
10. *Official Records Navy*, ser. 1, vol. 3, p. 770.
11. Morgan, pp. 140–141.
12. *Official Records Navy*, ser. 1, vol. 3.
13. Morgan, p. 147.
14. Ibid., p. 150.
15. Horan, pp. 139–140.
16. Morgan, pp. 150–151.
17. Horan, p. 137.
18. *Official Records Navy*, ser. 1, vol. 3, p. 814.
19. Ibid.
20. Ibid.
21. Morgan, pp. 162–163.
22. Ibid., pp. 168–169.
23. *Official Records Navy*, ser. 1, vol. 3, p. 816.
24. Morgan, pp. 172–173.
25. *Official Records Navy*, ser. 1, vol. 3, p. 817.
26. Hearn, p. 283.

CHAPTER 12

THE LONG VOYAGE HOME

1. ———, *Official Records of the Union and Confederate Navies in the War of the Rebellion* (Washington: Government Printing Office, 1894–1927), ser. 1, vol. 3, p. 822.

2. Murray Morgan, *Dixie Raider* (New York: E. F. Dutton & Co., Inc., 1948), p. 93.
3. Ibid., p. 195.
4. Ibid., pp. 197–198.
5. *Official Records Navy*, ser. 1, vol. 3, p. 775.
6. Ibid., p. 824.
7. Morgan, p. 202.
8. *Official Records Navy*, ser. 1, vol. 3, p. 824.
9. Morgan, p. 203.
10. Ibid., p. 204.
11. Ibid., p. 214.
12. Ibid.
13. Ibid., p. 216.
14. Ibid., p. 218.
15. *Official Records Navy*, ser. 1, vol. 3, p. 826.
16. James D. Horan, *CSS Shenandoah, The Memoirs of Lieutenant Commanding James I. Waddell* (New York: Crown Publishers, Inc., 1960), p. 166.
17. Cornelius E. Hunt, *The Shenandoah, or the Last Confederate Cruiser* (New York: C. W. Carleton & Co., 1868), p. 182.
18. *Official Records Navy*, ser. 1, vol. 3, p. 827.
19. Hunt, p. 183.
20. Morgan, p. 226.
21. Ibid., p. 232.
22. Hunt, pp. 191–193.
23. *Official Records Navy*, ser. 1, vol. 3, p. 828.
24. Ibid., p. 791.
25. Ibid., p. 828.
26. Ibid.
27. Horan, pp. 169–170.
28. Hunt, pp. 202–203.
29. *Official Records Navy*, ser. 1, vol. 3, p. 828.
30. Hunt, pp. 203–206.
31. *Official Records Navy*, ser. 1, vol. 3, p. 830.
32. Hunt, pp. 208–210.
33. Morgan, p. 263.
34. Hunt, p. 218.
35. Morgan, p. 263.
36. *Official Records Navy*, ser. 1, vol. 3, p. 832.
37. Ibid.
38. Hunt, pp. 222–223.
39. *Official Records Navy*, ser. 1, vol. 3, p. 832.
40. Hunt, p. 224.
41. Morgan , pp. 277–282.
42. *Official Records Navy*, ser. 1, vol. 3, pp. 782–783.
43. Morgan, p. 284.
44. *Official Records Navy*, ser. 1, vol. 3, pp. 833–834.
45. Ibid., p. 834.
46. Ibid.
47. Hunt, p. 223.
48. Ibid., p. 225.
49. Morgan, p. 298.

EPILOGUE

1. Murray Morgan, *Dixie Raider* (New York: E. F. Dutton & Co. Inc., 1948), p. 328.

*B*ibliography

_____   *Civil War Naval Chronology, 1861–1865.* Washington: Naval History Division, Navy Department, 1971.

_____   *Official Records of the Union and Confederate Navies in the War of the Rebellion.* 31 volumes. Washington, D.C.: Government Printing Office, 1894–1927.

_____   *The War of the Rebellion: A Compilation of the Official Records of the Union and Confederate Armies.* 130 volumes. Washington, D.C.: Government Printing Office, 1880–1901.

Barrett, John G.   *The Civil War in North Carolina.* Chapel Hill: The University of North Carolina Press, 1963.

Bulloch, James D.   *The Secret Service of the Confederate States in Europe, or How the Confederate Cruisers Were Equipped.* 2 volumes. New York: Putnam Publishers, 1883.

Clark, Walter — *North Carolina Regiments.* Goldsboro: Nash Brothers Book and Job Printers, 1901.

Cochran, Hamilton — *Blockade Runners of the Confederacy.* New York: The Bobbs-Merrill Company, Inc., 1958.

Current, Richard N. — *Encyclopedia of the Confederacy.* 4 volumes. New York: Simon & Schuster, 1993.

Dalton, William R. — "The Cruise of the Nashville." *Confederate Veteran Official Records* (June 1918).

Davis, William C. — *Jefferson Davis, The Man and His Hour.* New York: Harper Collins Publishers, 1991.

Donnelly, Ralph W. — *The Confederate States Marine Corps.* Shippensburg: White Mane Publishing Company, Inc., 1989.

Dowdey, Clifford (Editor) — *The Wartime Papers of R. E. Lee.* New York: Bramhall House, 1961.

Dufour, Charles L. — *Nine Men In Gray.* Garden City: Doubleday & Company, Inc., 1963.

Durkin, Joseph T. — *Confederate Navy Chief: Stephen R. Mallory.* Chapel Hill: The University of North Carolina Press, 1954.

Evans, Clement A. — "North Carolina," *Confederate Military History.* Atlanta: Confederate Publishing Company, 1899.

Frazier, Donald A. — "Cotton-clads in a Storm of Iron," *Naval History.* Annapolis: United States Naval Institute, 1994.

Gragg, Rod — *Confederate Goliath.* New York: Harper Collins Publishers, 1991.

Hearn, Chester G. — *Gray Raiders of the Sea.* Camden: International Marine Publishing, 1992.

Horan, James D. — *CSS Shenandoah, The Memoirs of Lieutenant Commanding James I. Waddell.* New York: Crown Publishers, 1960.

Horn, Stanley F. — *The Gallant Rebel, The Fabulous Cruise of the CSS Shenandoah.* New Brunswick: Rutgers University Press, 1947.

Horner, Dave — *The Blockade Runners.* Port Salerno: Florida Classics Library, 1992.

Hunt, Cornelius E. — *The Shenandoah, the Last Confederate Cruiser.* New York: C. W. Carleton & Co., 1868.

Jones, Virgil C. — *The Civil War at Sea.* 3 volumes. New York: Holt, Rinehart, and Winston, 1960–1962.

Luraghi, Raimondo — *A History of the Confederate Navy.* Annapolis: Naval Institute Press, 1996.

Maffitt, John Newland — "Blockade Running." *United Service 7* (July 1882).

Melton, Maurice — *The Confederate Ironclads.* New York: A. S. Barnes and Co., Inc., 1968.

Merli, Frank J. — *Great Britain and the Confederate Navy.* Bloomington: Indiana University Press, 1970.

Moebs, Thomas Truxtun (Compiler) — *Confederate States Navy Research Guide.* Williamsburg: Moebs Publishing Co., 1991.

Morgan, Murray — *Dixie Raider.* New York: E. F. Dutton & Co. Inc., 1948.

Morris, H. Jerry — "Nashville." *Civil War Times Illustrated* (March 1986).

Nepveux, Ethel S. — *George Alfred Trenholm and the Company that Went to War.* Charleston: Ethel S. Nepveux, 1994.

Parker, William H. — *Recollections of a Naval Officer.* New York: Charles Scribner's Sons, 1883.

Read, Charles W. — "Reminiscences of the Confederate States Navy." *Southern Historical Society Papers,* vol. 1 (May 1876).

Roberts, O. M. — *Confederate Military History.* Atlanta: Confederate Publishing Company, 1899.

Robertson, William B. — "The Water Battery at Fort Jackson." *Battles and Leaders of the Civil War.* New York: The Century Company, 1884–1888.

Robinson, William Morrison, Jr. *The Confederate Privateers.* New Haven: Yale University Press, 1928.

Scharf, J. Thomas — *History of the Confederate States Navy.* New York: Rogers & Sherwood, 1887.

Shingleton, Royce G. — *High Seas Confederate, The Life and Times of John Newland Maffitt.* Columbia: University of South Carolina Press, 1994.

Shingleton, Royce G. — *John Taylor Wood, Sea Ghost of the Confederacy.* Athens: University of Georgia Press, 1979.

Silverstone, Paul H. — *Warships of the Civil War Navies.* Annapolis: Naval Institute Press, 1989.

Spencer, William F. — *The Confederate Navy in Europe.* Tuscaloosa: The University of Alabama Press, 1983.

Sprunt, James — "Blockade Running," *Histories of the Several Regiments and Battalions From North Carolina in the Great War 1861–1865.* Goldsboro: Nash Brothers, Book and Job Printers, vol. 5, 1901.

Stern, Philip Van Doren — *The Confederate Navy, A Pictorial History.* New York: Bonanza Books, 1962.

Still, William N., Jr. — "Confederate Behemoth, the CSS *Louisiana.*" *Civil War Times Illustrated* (November 1977).

Still, William N., Jr. — *Confederate Shipbuilding.* Columbia: University of South Carolina Press, 1987.

Still, William N., Jr. — *Iron Afloat.* Nashville: Vanderbilt University Press, 1971.

Strode, Hudson — *Jefferson Davis, Confederate President.* New York: Harcourt, Brace & World, Inc., 1959.

Taylor, Thomas E. — *Running the Blockade.* London: John Murray Publishers, 1912.

Trotter, William R. — *Ironclads and Columbiads.* Winston-Salem: John F. Blair, Publisher, 1989.

Wells, Tom Henderson — *The Confederate Navy, A Study in Organization.* Tuscaloosa: The University of Alabama Press, 1971.

Whittle, William C. "Cruise of the C. S. Steamer *Nashville.*" *Southern Historical Society Papers*, vol. 39.

Whittle, William C. "The Cruise of the *Shenandoah.*" *Southern Historical Society Papers*, vol. 35 (1907).

Wilkinson, John *Narrative of a Blockade Runner.* New York: Sheldon & Company, 1877.

Wise, Stephen R. "Blockade Runners." *Encyclopedia of the Confederacy.* Vol. 1. New York: Simon & Schuster, 1993.

Wise, Stephen R. *Lifeline of the Confederacy.* Columbia: University of South Carolina Press, 1988.

Wood, John Taylor "The Tallahassee's Dash into New York Waters." *The Century Magazine* (1898).

*I*ndex

A

A. J. Bird, 130
Abigail, 216, 217
Adelaide, 190, 191
Adriatic, 120, 124
Advance, 7, 128
Alabama, CSS, 18, 156, 167, 168, 216, 227
Albany, Georgia, 68
Albatross, USS, 14
Albemarle and Chesapeake Canal, 45
Albemarle Sound, 52
Albion Lincoln, 138
Alcot, Sailmaker Henry, 173
Alexander, Lieutenant Joseph W., 45, 55
Algiers, Louisiana, 68
Alina, 185, 186, 187
Alverado, 16, 17
Amelia Island, 16
Amiel, Master Montague, 15
Amphrite Strait, 216, 221
Amukta Pass, 233
Anglo-Confederate Trading Co., 149, 151
Anna Jane, 188
Annie, 137
Appomattox, CSS, 49, 61; Battle of Roanoke Island, 55–60; Battle of Elizabeth City, 62–64
Archer, First Assistant Engineer E. R., 163

Arcole, 130
Arctic Ocean, 213, 221, 227, 231, 241
Arkansas, CSS, 74, 173
Armstrong, James F., 34
Ashby's Landing, 59
Atlanta, 110, 111, 133
Atlanta Rolling Mill, 69
Atlantic Ocean, 115, 192
Attu Island, 221
Austin, T. S., 12

B

B. Wier and Company, 124, 125
Babcock, Surgeon W. H., 12, 18
Bachman, Boatswain's Mate Andrew, 173
Bagby, Colonel Arthur, 95
Bahia, Brazil, 170, 192, 211
Baker, T. Harrison, 39
Ballarat, Australia, 204
Ballast Point, North Carolina, 56
Banshee II, 136, 149, 163; runs into Galveston, 152–155
Barracouta, 233, 235
Barron, Captain Samuel, 45, 170, 198
Bass Strait, 210
Bat, 155
Battery Buchanan, 140, 141, 143

Bayley, Colonel, 96
Bayou City, CSS, 95; Battle of Galveston, 98–106
Beam, Inspector, 207
Beaufort, NCS, 7, 55; Battle of Roanoke Island, 55–60; Battle of Elizabeth City, 62–64
Beaufort, North Carolina, 9, 31
Bering Sea, 213, 221, 222, 233
Bering Strait, 227
Beveridge, Pilot J., 31
Black Warrior, CSS; Battle of Roanoke Island, 55–60; Battle of Elizabeth City, 62–64
Blacker, James, 238
Blanchard, Consul William, 204, 209
Bragg, General Braxton, 137
Britannia, USS, 128
Brooke, Commander John M., 68, 169
Brooklyn, USS, 6
Brown, Colonel W. L., 46
Brown, W. C., 166, 167
Browne, Midshipman Orris, 221, 222, 237
Brownsville, Texas, 92, 95
Brunswick, 228, 230
Buffalo Bayou, 95
Bulloch, Acting Master Irvine S., 185, 191, 227, 235, 241
Bulloch, Commander James D., 24, 27, 132, 156, 166, 175, 184, 241; purchases *Sea King*, 169–170; assigns officers, 173
Burnside Expedition, 51, 56
Burnside, Brigadier General Ambrose E., 34, 51, 56
Burrell, Colonel Isaac S., 96, 105
Burroughs, Pilot Tom, 157
Butcher, Matthew J., 156
Butler, Major General Benjamin, 141

C

Calhoun, C. S. Privateer, 4; first captures, 5, 6
Callahan, James, 119
Camm, Midshipman Robert A., 58
Cape Fear River, 11, 113, 128, 143, 146, 149, 151, 156, 159
Cape Hatteras, North Carolina, 6, 14
Cape Horn, 237
Cape of Good Hope, 193
Cape Town, South Africa, 193, 195, 197, 237, 238
Cardenas, Cuba, 23
Carlisle, Hiram, 8
Carolina, 132
Carrol, 118, 120
Carter, Lieutenant Robert R., 169
Cary, Midshipman Clarence, 135, 141; log of *Chickamauga*, 136–140
Catherine, 227

Chameleon, 131, 132
Charleston, South Carolina, 7, 11, 12, 21, 23, 38, 132, 160
Charlie the Cook, 206, 207, 208
Charter Oak, 187
Chattahoochee, CSS, 172
Chew, Lieutenant Francis T., 173, 192, 212, 229, 238
Chicamacomico, North Carolina, 44, 46, 47, 49
Chicamacomico Races, 50, 51
Chickamauga, CSS, 133, 143, 145; cruise of, 136–140; destroyed, 146
Chicora, 132
Clark, Captain James, 227
Clark, Governor Henry T., 51
Clifton, USS, 92, 105, 107
Clyde River, 169
Cobb's Point, 62, 63
Colbert, Captain Peter, 169, 173, 176, 178, 183, 185, 192
Collie and Company, 133
Columbus, Kentucky, 76
Confederate Army forces
    8th North Carolina, 54, 61
    31st North Carolina, 54
    2nd Texas Cavalry, 96, 105
    5th Texas Cavalry, 95
    7th Texas Cavalry, 95, 96, 101
    26th Texas Cavalry, 96
    20th Texas Infantry, 96, 99
    21st Texas Infantry Battalion, 96
    1st Texas Heavy Artillery, 97
Confederate Point, 128, 140, 143
Congress, 231
Conolly, Thomas, 162
Cook, Colonel Joseph J., 93, 97, 99
Cooke, Lieutenant James W., 55, 63
Corfield, William, 190
Corpus Christi, Texas, 94
Corypheus, 107
Cotton Plant, CSS, 49
Covington, 231
Coxetter, Louis M., commands *Jeff Davis*, 11–18
Craig's Landing, 143
Craven, Commander T. Augustus, 29, 30
Crawford, Gunner's Mate William, 173
Crenshaw, Second Lieutenant Edward, 113
Crescent Artillery, 79
Croatan Sound, 42, 49, 56, 58
Crossan, Lieutenant Commander Thomas M., 7
Cunningham, First Mate, 229
Curlew, CSS, 45, 46, 54; attack on USS *Fanny*, 47; Battle of Roanoke Island, 55–60

D

Daily Crescent, 5
Dalton, William R., 29
Darling, Governor Sir Charles H., 200, 206, 207
David Brown, 198
Davidson, James, 208
Davis, President Jefferson, 1, 3, 4, 14, 112, 128, 163, 218, 235
De Godfrey, 187
Deer, 155
Delphine, 196, 197
Department of Texas, 94
Diana, CSS, 164
Dismal Swamp Canal, 42, 61, 64
Donegal, H.M.S., 243
Downard, Gunner's Mate John, 60
Dozier, First Lieutenant William G., 135
Dream, 132
Drummond Island, 211
Duke of Somerset, 30
Duncan, Brigadier General Johnson J., 78, 81, 87
Duncan, H.M.S., 123
Dunnington, First Lieutenant John W., 156

E

E. F. Lewis, 130
Echo, 11
Edith, 110, 133
Edward, 193
Edward Carey, 212
Elias, 55, 107
Elizabeth City, North Carolina, 60; battle of, 62–64
Ella, 5
Ellis, CSS, Battle of Roanoke Island, 55–60; Battle of Elizabeth City, 62–64
Emily L. Hall, 138
Empire, CSS, 49
Empress, 111
Empress Theresa, 130
Enchantress, 14
Euphrates, 221, 222
Excellent, H.M.S., 50

F

Falcon, 136
Fanny, USS, 46; captured, 47; Battle of Roanoke Island, 55–60; Battle of Elizabeth City, 62–64
Farragut, Admiral David G., 66, 76, 81, 82, 171
Faucon, Lieutenant E. H., 130

Favorite, 229, 230, 231
Fernandina, Florida, 7, 16
Fingal, 24
Fitfield, Captain, 13
Five Fathom Hole, 136
Fleming, Pilot Jock, 125, 126
Florida, CSS, 18, 167, 168, 170, 211
Fontaine, Captain S. T., 97, 98, 99
Foreign Enlistment Act, 208
Forrest, CSS, Battle of Roanoke Island, 55–60; destroyed, 64
Fort Bartow, North Carolina, 45, 56, 57, 58, 59
Fort Blanchard, North Carolina, 56
Fort Caswell, North Carolina, 113, 115, 159, 160
Fort Clark, North Carolina, 44, 47, 49
Fort Fisher, North Carolina, 113, 114, 127, 128, 130, 131, 137, 140, 141, 144, 145, 151, 159
Fort Forrest, North Carolina, 56, 59
Fort Hatteras, North Carolina, 44, 45, 46, 47, 49, 51
Fort Huger, North Carolina, 42, 56, 59
Fort Jackson, Louisiana, 76, 77, 78; Battle of New Orleans, 81–89
Fort Macon, North Carolina, 34, 36, 53
Fort McAllister, Georgia, 39, 40
Fort Point, Texas, 92, 93, 97, 98, 99
Fort St. Philip, Louisiana, 76, 79; Battle of New Orleans, 81–89
Fort Sumter, South Carolina, 21
Fortress Monroe, Virginia, 218
Foster, Seaman P. A., 143
Francis, Commissioner James G., 208
Fraser, Trenholm and Company, 34, 38, 39, 164
Frying Pan Shoals, 117
Funchal, Maderia, 176

G

Galveston Bay, 92, 96, 154, 164
Galveston Island, 92, 95
Galveston, Texas, 91, 92, 151, 152, 154, 162, 163, 164; captured by Federals, 93–94; captured by Confederates, 98–108
Gardner, Midshipman James M., 46
General Armstrong, 137, 138
General Beauregard, 12
General Pike, 228
General Williams, 227
Georgetown, South Carolina, 37, 172
Georgia, CSS, 18
Giraffe, 134

Glasgow, Scotland, 149, 169
Glen Cove, 70
Glenarvon, 120, 122
Goldsborough, Rear Admiral Louis M., 51, 56
Gooding, Captain, 36, 38, 39
Goodspeed, 138
Gordon, C. S. Privateer, 7, 22; cruise of, 8–11
Gosport Navy Yard, 45, 68
Governor Moore, 84
Grace Worthington, 12
Gray, Captain S. L., 229
Green, Colonel Thomas, 95
Grimball, Lieutenant John, 173, 191, 192, 200, 206, 207, 212, 227, 230, 238
Guy, Gunner's Mate John, 173
Gypsey, 228

H

Halifax, Nova Scotia, 123, 124, 126, 156
Hannum, Master J. A., 105
Hardrocke, Thomas, 212, 213, 214
Harriet Lane, USS, 92, 93, 97, 98; captured by Confederates, 99–105
Harris, Master Frank M., 55, 63
Harrisburg, Texas, 95
Hartford, USS, 84
Harvest, 212
Harvey Birch, 25
Harwood, Boatswain George, 173
Hatteras Inlet, 7, 11, 56
Hatteras Island, 46
Hatteras lighthouse, 9, 44, 49, 50
Hattie, 136
Havana, Cuba, 23, 151, 162
Hawkins, Colonel Rush C., 46
Hay, Gilbert, 16
Hébert, Brigadier General Paul O., 93
Hector, 212
Helen, 136, 137
Henry James, USS, 92
Henry Nutt, 9
Herald, 12
Heylinger, Louis, 38
Higgins, Seaman J. F., 143
Hill, Brigadier General Daniel H., 52
Hillman, 231
Hobson's Bay, Australia, 198, 207, 209
Hollins, Captain George N., 67, 73, 74, 76
Hood, Engineer James, 36
Hoole, Acting Master James L., 55, 58
Hope, Rear Admiral Sir James, 124, 125
Houston, Texas, 95, 155
Huger, Brigadier General Benjamin, 52
Hunt, Acting Master Cornelius E., 187, 198, 202, 204, 209, 213, 217, 219, 222, 225, 230, 231, 233, 235, 237, 239, 243

Hunter, Commander Thomas T., 45, 55, 59, 61
Hunter, Commander William W., 91, 92, 95
Hurst, Frank, 151
Hutton, Captain T. H., 78

I

Indian Ocean, 192, 195, 211
Indian Wells, North Carolina, 146
Ingraham, Master John H., 33
Iroquois, USS, 211
Isaac Howland, 231
Isaac Wells, 143, 145
Isabella, 228

J

Jackson and Company, 69
Jackson, Midshipman William C., 63
Jackson, Mortimer M., 124, 156
James Funk, 118
James Littlefield, 123
James Maury, 229, 230
Jamestown, USS, 16, 211
Jeff Davis, C. S. Privateer, 11; cruise of, 12–18
Jefferson City, Louisiana, 68
Jireh Swift, 224
John Adams, 6
John and William Dudgeon Co., 107
John Carver, 17
John F. Carr, CSS, 95, 96, 102, 107
John Welsh, 13
Johnson, Pilot Edward, 209
Johnson's Island, 146
Jonas Island, 219
Jones, Paymaster Charles L., 124
Junaluska, CSS, 45; attack on USS *Fanny*, 47

K

Kamchatka Peninsula, 216
Kate Prince, 190, 192
Kearsarge, USS, 167
Keystone State, USS, 33, 38, 39
King Louis XV, 2
King's Ferry, 30
Kinnakeet, North Carolina, 50
Komandorskies Islands, 221
Kuhn's Wharf, 96, 97, 99, 105
Kuriles Islands, 216

L

Lady Sterling, 136
Lamb, Colonel William, 143
Langlands Brothers & Company, 204
Laurel, 173, 175, 176, 177, 178, 179, 180, 182
Law, Captain, 105, 107
Lea, Lieutenant Commander Edward, 102, 105

Lea, Major A. M., 105
Lee, Lieutenant Sidney Smith, Jr., 173, 190, 212, 219, 221, 237, 238
Leeds & Company, 69, 70
Libby, Captain Henry, 190, 192
Liddy, Second Mate Malcom, 15
Lincoln, President Abraham, 1, 5
Lining, Surgeon Charles E., 185, 188, 193, 211, 216, 227, 235
Liverpool, England, 132, 149, 156, 164, 236, 237, 239, 241
Lizzie M. Stacey, 191
Lockwood, Captain Thomas J., 8, 22, 23; commands the *Gordon*, 9–11
Loggerhead Inlet, 46, 49
London, England, 110, 133, 166
Lord Howe Island, 210
Louisiana, CSS, 66, 172; construction of, 69–73; launched, 74; moved down river, 79; Battle of New Orleans, 81–87; destroyed, 87–88
Louisville, Kentucky, 72
Lovell, Major General Mansfield, 78
Low, Lieutenant John, 160
Loyall, Lieutenant Benjamin P., 57, 58, 59, 61
Lubbock, Captain Henry S., 95, 101, 105, 107, 109
Lucy, 137
Lucy Gwin, CSS, 95, 96
Lynch, Captain William F., 44, 45, 156; commands Mosquito Fleet, 46–64
Lynch, Carpenter John C., 183, 217
Lynx, 136
Lyons, Foreign Minister Lord John, 27
Lyttleton, Superintendent, 206, 207

M

MacDonnell, Lieut. Governor Richard G., 124, 125
Maffitt, Commander John N., 11, 156, 157, 171; commands the *Owl*, 158–164
Magruder, Major General Bankhead, 94, 95; commands at Battle of Galveston, 96–109
Mallory, Secretary Stephen R., 21, 38, 45, 53, 67, 69, 73, 76, 111, 118, 123, 128, 134, 156, 167, 169, 170, 200
Mantinicuss Island, 123
Mariner, 9
Mark L. Potter, 138
Martha, 231
Mary Boardman, 107
Mary E. Thompson, 16
Mary Goodell, 15, 16
Mason, James M., 22, 23, 24, 25, 29, 163, 217
Masonboro Inlet, 140

Maury, Commander Matthew F., 156
McCarrick, First Lieutenant Patrick, 54
McCormick, Captain Michael, 101
McDougal, David, 233
McGarvey, Captain James H., 164
McIntosh, Commander Charles F., 73, 74; commands *Louisiana*, 78–84; mortally wounded, 84
McNulty, Assistant Surgeon Fred J., 192, 217
McRae, CSS, 79
Melbourne, Australia, 193, 198, 200, 204, 208, 210
Memminger, Christopher G., 21
Mermaid, 6
Mersey River, 164, 175, 176, 241
Middletown Island, 210
Milan, 5
Millaudon, Laurent, 68
Milo, 222, 224, 225, 233
Minor, Lieutenant Robert D., 74
Minto, Constable Alexander, 208, 209
Mississippi River, 5, 66
Mississippi, CSS, 66, 67, 171; construction of, 69–76; launched, 77; attempt to tow up river, 85; destroyed, 86
Mitchell, Captain John K., 75, 78, 81, 86, 87
Mongul, 185
Montauk, USS, 39
Montgomery, Alabama, 4, 69
Montgomery, USS, 130
Monticello, USS, 51, 127, 145
Morehead City, North Carolina, 34, 36
Morrison, J. H., 46
Mosquito Fleet, 42, 44; attack on USS *Fanny*, 47; defense of Roanoke Island, 49–60; destroyed at Elizabeth City, 61–64
Mound Battery, 141
Murray, E. C., 69, 70

N

Nashville, CSS, 21, 172; purchased by C. S. Navy, 22; sails for England, 24; captures *Harvey Birch*, 25; at Southampton, 26–30; sails from Southampton, 30; arrives Morehead City, 34; escapes from Morehead City, 36; arrives Georgetown, 38; name changed, 38; destroyed, 40
Nassau, 231
Nassau, Bahamas, 38, 132, 133, 162
Neptune, CSS, 95; Battle of Galveston, 98–102
New Bern, North Carolina, 7, 34, 53
New Inlet, 113, 114, 127, 130, 137, 140
New Orleans, Louisiana, 4, 5, 6, 66, 68, 70, 72, 171
New Zealand, 210, 211

Nichols, Captain William G., 195
Nichols, Lillias, 195, 196, 198, 200, 202
Night Hawk, 149, 151
Nile, 231
Nimrod, 198, 227
Norfolk Island, 210
Norfolk, Virginia, 42, 61, 68
North, Commander James B., 27
Nye, Captain Ebenezer, 216, 217

O

O'Brien, Chief Engineer Matthew, 193
O'Shea, Carpenter John, 173, 187
Ocean Eagle, 5
Ogeechee River, 39
Okhotsk Sea, 213, 216, 219, 221
Old Inlet, 113, 114, 115, 136
Olustee, CSS, 128, 129
Onward, USS, 192
Ossabaw Sound, 39
Otter Rock, 138
Outer Banks, North Carolina, 9, 44
Owasco, USS, 92, 101, 102, 107
Owl, 132, 136, 149, 155, 156, 157, 159, 160, 162, 163, 164

P

Pamlico Sound, 7, 9, 11, 44, 49, 52, 56
Panama, 6
Parker, First Lieutenant William H., 55, 57, 58, 62, 63, 64
Pasquotank River, 62
Pass a L'Outre, 5
Pass Cavailo, Texas, 92
Patey, Captain Charles G., 29, 30
Patterson Iron Works, 69, 70
Pea Island, 46
Pearl, 31, 212
Pegram, Lieutenant Robert B., 172; takes command of *Nashville*, 22; sails for England, 24; captures *Harvey Birch*, 25; at Southampton, 27–30; sails from Southampton, 30; arrives Morehead City, 34
Pelican Island, 98, 107
Pennsylvania, USS, 170
Penobscot Bay, 123
Peytona, 85
Pierce, Constructor Joseph, 86
Ponape Island, 212, 216, 229
Ponchatoula, Louisiana, 70
Pontoosuc, USS, 126
Port Phillip, Australia, 198, 209
Porter, Commander David, 77, 87, 141, 143

Porter, Constructor John L., 67, 82
Postell, First Lieutenant W. Ross, 13
Potter, Captain A. T., 228, 229
Priscilla, 8
Protector, 9

R

Raleigh, NCS, 7, 9, 45, 55, 61; attack on USS *Fanny*, 47; Battle of Roanoke Island, 55–60
Ramsay, Lieutenant John F., 173, 175, 176, 178, 179
Randolph, Secretary George W., 74
Rattlesnake, C. S. Privateer, 39, 40
Reliance, 138
Renshaw, Commander William B., 92, 93, 105, 107
Richmond, Virginia, 67, 70, 163
Rio Grande River, 91, 94
Roach & Long, 72
Roan, 127
Roanoke Island, North Carolina, 42, 44, 47, 51; battle of, 52–60; surrender of, 61
Robert Gilfillan, 33
Robert Kirk Co., 72
Robert L. Townes, 221
Robinson, Gun Captain Jack, 60
Rowan, Captain Stephen, 62
Russell, Lord John, 31, 243

S

S. J. Waring, 15
Sabine Pass, Texas, 92
Sachem, 107
Sailor's (Saylor's) Creek, Virginia, 146
San Antonio, Texas, 95
San Francisco, California, 233
San Jacinto, USS, 24, 25
San Juan, Puerto Rico, 16
Sandridge, Australia, 202
Sandvrie, Surgeon Frederick, 12
Sandy Hook, New Jersey, 15, 118
Sangster, Captain William H., 95, 101, 109
Santa Clara, 16, 17
Sarah A. Boyce, 118
Savannah River, 17
Savannah, Georgia, 13, 17
Saxon, 107
Scales, Lieutenant Dabney M., 173, 212, 216, 224, 235, 237, 238
Scharf, Midshipman J. Thomas, 2, 92, 163
Schofield & Markham Iron Works, 69
Scurry, Brigadier General William R., 105
Sea King, 167, 169, 170, 174, 177

Sea Witch, 9
Seabird, CSS, 54, 61; Battle of Roanoke Island, 55–60; Battle of Elizabeth City, 62–64
Seabrook, Second Lieutenant Edward M., 12
Semmes, Captain Raphael, 171
Seven Years War, 1
Seward, Secretary of State William, 4
Shallotte Inlet, 163
Shannon, H.M.S., 30
Shantaska Island, 216
Shaw, Colonel H. M., 47, 49, 57, 61
Shenandoah, CSS, 18, 167, 172; sails from England, 175; rendezvous with the *Laurel*, 177; departs on cruise, 180; first half of cruise, 182–198; arrives Australia, 199; in Australia, 200–208; departs Australia, 209; last half of cruise, 210–243
Siberia, 221, 222
Sibley Brigade, 95, 96
Sidney, Australia, 221, 236
Simms, First Lieutenant Charles C., 49, 55, 64
Sinclair, Commander Arthur, 76, 85, 86
Slidell, John, 22, 23, 24, 25, 29
Smith, Captain, 33
Smith, Captain Francis, 222
Smith, Major Leon, 96; commands naval forces at the Battle of Galveston, 97–108
Smith, Paymaster Breedlove, 185, 200, 241
Smith, William W., 14
Smith's Island, 113, 117
Smithville, North Carolina, 114, 136, 138
Snead, Lieutenant Colonel Claiborne, 47, 49
Sophia Thornton, 224
Southampton, England, 20, 25, 28, 29
Southward, 38
Speedwell, 139
St. Augustine, Florida, 17
St. Charles, 85
St. George, Bermuda, 24, 31, 111, 131, 139, 156, 159
St. George's Channel, 241
St. Lawrence Island, 227, 233
St. Marks, Florida, 163
St. Mary's River, 16
St. Paul Island, 197
Stag, 155
Staples, Captain Edward, 185
State of Georgia, USS, 34
Steele, Captain Jonathon, 149
Stevens, C. H., 21
Stevens, First Mate George, 15
Stevens, J. W., 13
Stone, A., 17

Stuart, R. H., 12
Summit, Mississippi, 70
Sumter, CSS, 18, 30
Susan, 188, 189
Susan Abigail, 225

T

T. D. Wagner, 130
Tallahassee, CSS, 111, 133, 136, 137, 138, 139, 140; cruise of, 113–123
Talisman, 136, 137
Tayloe, Midshipman James L., 49, 55
Taylor, Tom, 149, 151, 163; runs *Banshee II* into Galveston, 152–155
Teaser, 9
Tennessee, CSS, 74
Terry, Brigadier General Alfred H., 143
Texas Marine Department, 95
Thames River, 111, 166
Theodora, 23
Thomas Collyer Shipyard, 21
Thomas L. Wagg, 38, 39
Tift, Asa, 66, 67, 68, 78
Tift, Nelson, 66, 67, 68, 72, 78
Tillman, William, 15
Treaty of Paris, 4
Tredegar Iron Works, 70, 73, 74, 75
Trent, 23, 31
Trinity River, Texas, 92, 95
Tristan da Cunha, 193
Tucker, Captain Moses, 224
Tuscarora, USS, 29, 30
Tynan, Chief Engineer John W., 113, 114, 115, 117, 123, 126, 127

U

U.S. Army forces
  20th Indiana, 50
  42nd Massachusetts Infantry, 96, 99, 105
Usina, Lieutenant Michael P., 111

V

Van Dorn, General Earl, 91, 92
Vance, Governor Zebulon, 128, 140
Vanderbilt, USS, 139
Vapor, 130
Varuna USS, 84
Velocity, 107
Vernon, Midshipman William H., 46
Vicksburg and Shreveport Railroad, 70
Virginia, 137, 138
Virginia, CSS, 67, 112
Virginia Point, Texas, 92, 95, 96

W

Wachusett, USS, 211

Waddell, First Lieutenant James I., 86, 172; assigned to command *Shenandoah*, 170; takes command, 177–179; first half of cruise, 182–198; arrives Australia, 199; in Australia, 200–208; departs Australia, 209; last half of cruise, 210–243

Wainwright, Lieutenant Jonathan M., 92, 93, 102, 105

Walker, Major Norman S., 160

Wando, 137

War of 1812, 2

Ward, First Lieutenant William H., 113, 115, 119, 126; commands cruise of *Olustee*, 128–130; commands *Chickamauga*, 140–147

Washington, North Carolina, 53

Watson, Assistant Surgeon D. S., 163

Waverly, 228

Weldon Railroad, 52

Welles, Secretary Gideon, 122

Westfield, USS, 92, 93, 105, 107

White, Lieutenant Colonel Moses J., 36

Whiting, General W. H. C., 128, 140

Whittle, Captain William C., 76, 78

Whittle, First Lieutenant William C., Jr., 34, 36, 38, 177, 178; assigned as first officer of *Shenandoah*, 172; first half of cruise, 182–198; arrives Australia, 199; in Australia, 200–208; departs Australia, 209; last half of cruise, 210–243

Wier, Captain John, 99, 101

Wild Rover, 136

Wilkes, Captain Charles, 25

Wilkinson, Lieutenant John, 78, 110, 160; assumes command of the *Louisiana*, 84; destroys *Louisiana*, 88–89; given command of *Chameleon*, 131–132; takes command of *Chickamauga*, 134; cruise of *Chickamauga*, 136–140

Will-o'-the-Wisp, 152

William Bell, 119

William C. Nye, 227

William McGilvery, 8

William Thompson, 221, 222

Williams, Thomas, 224

Williamstown, Australia, 202

Wilmington, North Carolina, 11, 38, 111, 127, 128, 130, 131, 133, 137, 140, 143, 145, 149, 156, 157

Wilson, Captain George R., 97

Wilson, Captain John, 5, 6

Winder, Brigadier General John H., 14

Windward, 16, 17

Winslow, NCS, 7, 9

Wise, Brigadier General Henry A., 54

Wise's Legion, 54, 61

Wood, Commander John Taylor, 111, 112; commands *Tallahassee*, 113–123

Wood's Hotel, 166, 173

Worden, Commander John L., 39

Worth, Captain Charles P., 193

Wright, Colonel A. R., 44, 50

Wright, Richard, 167, 169

Y

Yancey, William L., 25

York, 9

Young, Captain, 229, 230

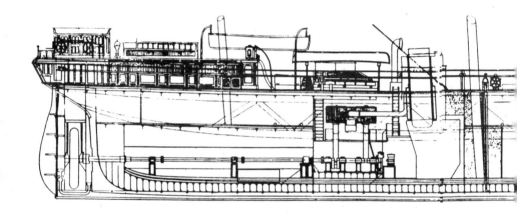